Last Moments of a World

Last Moments of a World

ᕙᕗᕙᕗᕙᕗᕙᕗ

Margaret Gaan

W·W·*Norton & Company·Inc*
New York

Library of Congress Cataloging in Publication Data

Gaan, Margaret.
Last moments of a world.

1. China—Social life and customs. 2. Gaan,
Margaret. I. Title.
DS721.G2 1978   951.05   77-20700
ISBN 0-393-05657-0

1 2 3 4 5 6 7 8 9 0

Contents

Contents

Photographs appear following page 136.

Last Moments of a World

I

The Ancestors

My sister Jane was the first of us to go to a western country. She married a Frenchman and went to France with him to meet his family. The family was provincial bourgeois, the kind to whom Bordeaux or Nantes or Lyon is the hub of the world, to whom places like Shanghai are no more than a dot on the map.

"It was strange," Jane wrote me. "At first they seemed to think that I was just out of the jungle and might take my clothes off any minute. But I didn't eat with my fingers, and the answers I gave to their questions seemed to be right. I was educated at the Sacred Heart Convent—that really pleased them. Father was an accountant, which was very respectable, it appeared, and by the end of dinner they were approving of me. I was glad to be a success, of course, but at the same time I felt frightened—the old 'kidnapped feeling' you know—and when somebody asked me 'and what was your grandfather?' it just popped out of my mouth, I said, 'He was a pirate.'"

When we were children we always talked of him among ourselves as a pirate. We knew that as a young man he had left his native land and had sailed all the way to China in a ship with great white sails, like Ralph Morgan. He must have been a pirate, we thought. We told each other stories about him: how he had captured enemy ships in furious battle, taken plunder, keel-hauled vanquished captains, rescued damsels in distress whom the captains had kept prisoner in the poop. When one day our mother heard us and firmly disillusioned us, we felt cheated, as though Grandfather had betrayed us by being just an ordinary businessman.

But his reputation was retrieved in our eyes when we learned from a cousin that, if he had not been a pirate, he had at least been a bigamist. How our cousin learned this carefully kept secret we never knew, but one rainy day he whispered the whole story to us while we clustered around him, agog.

Grandfather was born in a town on Portugal's Atlantic coast with the wonderful name Figuera da Foz. Many years later I visited his birthplace and did not wonder that he had left it. In his day that coastline, now breakwatered and bordered with esplanades and hotels, must have been still as rugged as nature made it. Those ruined stone walls must have been battlements standing strong against an invader, brooding over the heaving green sea to a far horizon. Something beyond that horizon must have called to Grandfather, urged him to board a clipper ship that carried him to Macao, Portugal's tiny island off the south coast of China.

In Macao he set up in business, married, and fathered two sons. But Macao must have been even smaller and more self-consciously proper in his day than it was in ours, or else something must still have been calling to him from beyond the horizon, because in 1850 he decided to extend his business and went alone to Shanghai when that city was still a sprawl of low buildings and warehouses along the banks of the muddy Whangpoo River. In Shanghai he prospered and became very rich. He met and married our grandmother. Nobody seemed to have known or cared that he already had a wife in Macao, whom he never saw again, although he supported her until she died.

Grandmother came from Ningpo, a city famous for its lively people. She died when I was two years old, and all I know of what she looked like is from a yellowed photograph of a heavy old woman sitting straight up in a great, carved blackwood chair, looking directly at the photographer. Her face is square, jowled but hardly lined, the skin over the high cheekbones smooth as ivory. Her eyes are bold and humorous, her mouth willful. Her sparse hair is pulled back tightly, almost hidden by a wide, flat satin band which dips over the ears. Although it does not show in the photograph, I know that in the style of Chinese matrons of her day the ends of the headband are tucked into the bun of hair at the back of her head, secured by tall golden pins from which ornaments dangle. Perhaps also a fragrant white jasmine flower is tucked into the bun.

In her photograph, Grandmother is dressed in a long satin overblouse with a high, stiff collar and frog buttons of knotted cord across the right shoulder and down the side. Under the blouse she wears loose silk trousers, and from these peep her tiny lily feet. In Grandmother's time, normal feet were the prerogative of peasant women. Girl children of the better classes had their feet bound tightly to prevent them from growing. In adulthood, their feet were stumps like horses' hooves but pointed where the big toe should be. The other toes were atrophied appendages, folded limply back against the sole. Lily feet were shod in gorgeously embroidered and beaded cloth shoes made to fit the stumps exactly. Women with lily feet, while still young, hobbled about with a mincing gait which was considered gracefully elegant, and which also prevented them from running away when they were sold as concubines to rich old men. When they grew old and heavy, women with lily feet had to be helped to walk or remain sitting. Grandfather bought Grandmother two slave girls to help her walk, and in her photograph they are standing stiffly one on each side of her, dressed like her but in coarse cotton, their feet big and normal, their faces wooden, their hair in pigtails. Standing, they are taller than grandmother sitting, but they are shadows. She dominates the photograph, erect, heavy, strong.

She was the great love of Grandfather's life, this blunt, tough-fibered, willful woman, whose every trait of character belied her puny lily feet. He bought her a huge, rambling house in a compound that later constituted four square blocks of the most expensive land in the city of Shanghai, and lived with her there for the rest of his life, fathering by her six sons and six daughters, all, in our delighted view, distinguished by the bigamy.

How we reveled in the secret. We never let our parents know we knew it. Father might have laughed and told us more details, but Mother would have been horrified at our knowledge. In fact, we never told anybody we knew the secret, although our family consisted of seventy-two relatives, counting only aunts, uncles, and first and second cousins.

For Mother too had a large family, three full and nine step brothers and sisters, all strictly legitimate. Mother's father was Swedish, a tall, thin, frail, holy man who could never have been either pirate or bigamist. He was the manager of a mill. He and his second wife, our step-grandmother, and all our step-aunts and uncles, lived in a house on the mill site to which we hated to be taken.

That house and our Mother's step-family were the origin of the "kidnapped feeling." In it, and with them, we felt strange and desperately uncomfortable, as we would feel, we imagined, had we been kidnapped. The house on the mill site was big, dark, wooden, and badly built. It shuddered constantly with the thunder of the mill's machinery. It was a kind of shadowy, shaking nest in which a lot of bird-aunts lived, who fluttered about on our arrival and insisted on hugging and kissing us. Father's family never wanted to kiss us. They spanked our bottoms, and one of Father's brothers gave us what he called "chocolate beans," a painful form of pinching which we stoically endured because he had no wife nor children of his own and we knew he loved us.

Kissing we hated, especially when accompanied by a burrowing of the kisser's nose into our necks and a loud sniff-sniff. I remember exactly how I felt one day when, after I had endured the kiss-and-sniff from each of the bird-aunts, a cousin as small as I was wanted to kiss me too. I backed away, glaring, but she did not take the hint. She followed me, her mouth puckered for the kiss, as I retired under the dining table which had been pushed against the wall to make room for the party. Finally, with my back to the wall, I turned at bay and could see nothing for it but to bite her. I can still hear her screams and Mother's mortified apologies, and I can still feel the flood of relief in my heart when Father picked me up and took me out onto the terrace. He sat me on the railing and leaned over me, making strange noises. It was a while before I realized he was trying not to laugh out loud. How I loved him.

What we hated most about the mill house was the presence of our step-grandmother. My grandfather had married her less than a year after his first wife had died, and we knew she had been a real storybook stepmother. Mother's two older sisters had been sent at once to boarding school, and Mother and her brother had been relegated to the servants' quarters, where they lived for years in a tiny room with the amah—nurse—who had helped bring them up. The amah now wept over them and tried her best to care for them as their own mother would have. But when Mother, only four years old, acquired lice in her hair, the beautiful hair that her mother had loved to brush, amah knew no other way to get rid of the vermin than to cut off all her hair and wash her head with kerosene. When Mother or her brother fell ill in the freezing cold of the tiny north room, no doctor was sent for. Amah dosed them with herb teas that she bought with her own money from the medicine shop and wrapped their throats with old stockings soaked in lard. Amah bought them oranges on Chinese New Year and Moon Cakes on the Moon Festival, because they were always either too young or too old to participate in family feasting at Christmas and birthdays. Amah taught Mother how to embroider, with the result that she was not allowed to play after school but had to sit and embroider initials on her stepsisters' stockings and handkerchiefs.

Mother assured us that these things had not been the result of deliberate cruelty, but of ignorance on the part of her stepmother and lack of time on the part of her father. We didn't believe her because we knew that Father hated Mother's family with a deep hatred. We knew that while he was being polite to them he was bursting inside. These cross-currents were the basis of the deep confusion and resentment that we called the "kidnapped feeling," which we suffered on being forcibly taken to the mill house.

Our real maternal grandmother was a shadowy figure to us, because Mother remembered very little about her. She had died of the black pox. She had been so vivacious and attractive that she had been the center of every gathering. We wondered how she had ever married our colorless, sanctimonious grandfather and how, after her, he had been able to marry our coy, smug, stepgrandmother.

We discussed these mysteries when we were not telling stories about our pirate grandfather, sitting in the dark box-room of our house on Dixwell Road, to which we retired when it was too wet to play outdoors. The box-room was windowless, filled with pig-skin trunks in which our winter clothes were kept smothered in mothballs. The smell of the mothballs seeped out of the trunks and lingered in the stale air. We breathed it as we whispered to each other, perched on the trunks, hugging our knees, our small-est sister sitting close and wide-eyed. That was when I was eight years old, Luke six, Jane five, and Veronica four. The smell of mothballs always brings back to me their dim shapes, their whis-pering voices, and Veronica's eyes shining solemnly in the dark.

My brother and sisters were born in the house on Dixwell Road, brought, we were told, by the Japanese midwife Mrs. Yoko whom we all knew and respected for her mysterious abilities. But I was born in the big old rambling house where Father and all his eleven brothers and sisters had come into the world. Grandfather had died some years before I was born, but Grandmother was still controlling and commanding the family from her great carved blackwood chair. When Grandfather died, what money remained had gone to her and she held the pursestrings with an iron fist, especially because what was left in the purse was mostly what she herself had squirreled away. Grandfather would have spent prodi-gally all the money he made in that rough-and-tumble young city, which just suited his nature and abilities. He lived on a grand scale. He had twenty-five suits and dozens of shirts, with the days of the week marked on the tails so that grandmother could see that they were arranged in seven neat piles when they came back from the wash. He traveled around the city in a shiny black private rickshaw, pulled by Ah-Ching, who could run faster than any other rickshaw puller. As his children went to school, he bought six more shiny black private rickshaws, one for every pair of children. He demanded the best of food and wine, enough not only for the enormous family but also for the guests he brought home nearly every night. He gave his friends money so that they could play poker with him at his preferred high stakes. He kept a flat-bottomed houseboat and a permanent crew of rowers so that he could go up-country whenever he wished to hunt wild boar and game birds. He enjoyed life enormously until he got Bright's Disease. When he knew that he was to die, he sent for the padre and confessed to bigamy. The padre gave him a severe penance: he was to rise and walk to church barefoot through the market place, stand at the church door, and ask prayers of all who entered. He did it, and our father walked beside him carrying his shoes. He died shriven but nearly penniless.

But Grandmother had put away a goodly pile in land and jewels, and she became the typical Chinese matriarch of her time. All unmarried daughters were obliged to live at home, and each son as he married was obliged to bring his wife home to live under her mother-in-law's eye and bear her children into the family. My mother remembers how bitterly cold the big old house was—fires were not allowed until Christmas day. She remembers breaking the ice in the water jar to brush her teeth in the mornings. She remembers especially the yearly ceremony when Grandmother's coffin was lacquered. Grandmother bought her coffin ten years before her death and kept it on trestles in a small room next to her bedroom. Once every year it received a fresh coat of lacquer to keep it shining and to preserve the wood. All sons and daughters and daughters-in-law had to be present for the lacquering. My mother, pregnant with me, fainted because of the smell, to Grandmother's great displeasure.

All six sons had inherited their father's love of hunting, and the compound of the big house was always full of hunting dogs of the best breeds, highly trained, kept in the pink of condition. My father used to ride me on the dogs' backs before I could walk. Hunting was a central theme of that old house. I remember the boars' heads, mounted on oval plaques of wood, with beady brown glass eyes and fierce tusks, that were hung in the hallways of our own and our uncles' homes. They had all come from the old house, together with silver-backed brushes made of boars' bristles, mouldering decorations of pheasants' tails, and the double-barreled twelve-gauge shotguns shining with oil that were kept lovingly in the long, flat, felt-lined leather gun cases.

When Grandmother died and was at last buried in her splendid coffin, the family broke up. Before her death she had made over gifts of land to her favorite son, our father, and of jewelry to her favorite daughter. Upon her death, her will was found to leave the remainder of the money and property to be divided among the six sons, with nothing to the daughters: daughters marry and share in their husbands' families' properties—if they were to inherit from their parents, they would take the money out to their husbands' families.

The will created a furor. Three of the six daughters were not married and were left with nothing to live on. One of the sons, our father, had much more than the other five because of the property Grandmother had given him before she died. One daughter had jewelry, the others none. There were loud, long, and bitter complaints.

Finally our father decided that everything should be sold, including the old home property, the land his mother had given him, and the jewelry she had given one daughter. The proceeds were divided equally among all the brothers and sisters. Each took his share and went his way, and the family so vigorously given birth, nourished, and controlled by the domineering woman from Ningpo was dissolved.

2

⊗⊇⊗⊇⊗⊇

The World

OUR BRANCH of the family went to live in the house on Dixwell
Road where, when she and I were both nine years old, my beloved
Ah-May came to join us, and from where, later in the same twelve
months, we were to flee in haste and fear from the big guns.

When we moved into the house on Dixwell Road I was not yet
two years old and Luke was about to be born. It was a nice house,
one of a long row, semidetached, three-storied, red-roofed, like
millions to be seen in suburban London, for at that time the
English were the most influential foreigners in Shanghai. The
house had a garden in which Father made a wire enclosure for the
dogs that inevitably came with us. They were let out twice a day
to run in the garden, barking and leaping with excitement, and
they accompanied us on all our walks, except when we went to
Big Park, for there was a sign on the park gate which said "Dogs
and Chinese not allowed—By Order."

I was terrified to go to Big Park with my baby-amah, even
without the dogs, because she was Chinese and I was part Chinese
and the park superintendent, a red-faced, tight-collared, puffing
Englishman, naturally called Red Face by all Chinese, would one

day, I was sure, wreak a terrible vengeance on us for daring to step into his park against the Order. I had heard him shouting violently at two small Chinese boys who had sneaked into the park to play on the swings.

"Get out of here, you yellow barstuds! Get out! Get out!"

He chased them, his red face shining with perspiration, swinging the small stick he usually carried under his arm, and caught one of them a thwack on the back that made the child scream in pain and terror.

When we met Red Face in the park I trembled and clung to Baby-amah's hand, my ears already thrumming with the loud rough shout that I expected him to utter at any moment. Useless for Mother to explain that, as far as Red Face was concerned, I was a foreigner and although Baby-amah was Chinese she was exempted from the Order because she was in charge of me in the park. I hated Red Face, and so did Baby-amah. Whenever we saw him she glared at him, a look full of defiance, anger, and hatred. It was the first time I was impressed by the look cast more and more often as time went on by Chinese at foreigners who swaggered on Chinese soil and put up Orders contemptuous of the Chinese.

For Shanghai was the largest and most affluent of the Treaty Ports conceded to foreigners by the Manchu Emperors as part of the price of defeat in the Opium Wars. For a hundred years, from 1842 until the end of World War II, foreigners in the Treaty Ports enjoyed extraterritoriality, which meant that they were not subject to Chinese law but to their own national laws, applied by courts which were conducted by their own ambassadors and consuls, guarded by their own warships anchored in the rivers and their own soldiers quartered in the cities. Extraterritoriality, casually called "extrality" by those who enjoyed it, operated as a kind of self-righteous colonialism sanctified by the consent of the colonialized.

Shanghai was a city of three parts: the contiguous International Settlement and French Concession, surrounded by the peripheral areas which had different names but were generally called the Chinese City. The Settlement and the Concession had their own municipal councils, their own city services, and their own police forces. The British dominated the International Settlement. People like Superintendent Red Face of Big Park, almost all of them British, enforced the bylaws and orders promulgated by the municipal council. Under this echelon of superintendents and inspectors, the rank and file of city functionaries were Chinese, but the police force included, as a cautious British security factor to dilute the concentration of Chinese in the potentially armed custodial forces, a large group of Sikhs imported from colonial India.

We were too young in those days to feel the yoke of British colonialism which pervaded the city. The only two aspects of which we were conscious, and both aspects frightened us, were Superintendent Red Face and the Sikh policemen. The Sikhs stood out from our familiar background, an alien group. They were distinguished from the smooth-faced friendly Chinese to whom we spoke at will by their big black beards, oiled and carefully curled up into rolls around their chins, and by their guttural speech which no one but they could understand. They reeked unpleasantly, a rancid smell that Baby-amah said came from eating a kind of rotten butter. They were darker-skinned and taller than the Chinese, and very thin, their legs long and lanky with bony knees protruding from their khaki shorts in summer. On duty, they wore bright red turbans into which the ends of their rolled-up beards disappeared. They were called Red-headed Number Threes, Number Three being the familiar term of address for a male person.

We heard frightening stories about the Red-headed Number Threes. They were moneylenders and extorted exorbitant interest from those foolish enough to fall into their clutches. If a debtor could not repay, they sometimes demanded that he hand over his daughter in marriage to one of them. Veronica begged Father never to borrow money from a Red-headed Number Three.

"If you need money, I'll give it to you. When I grow up I'm going to be Mata Hari (from pirates and bigamists, we had switched to spies) or maybe a bus driver, and I'll make lots of money and give it all to you."

Father laughed and promised. Mother tried to reassure us by pooh-poohing the stories, but I was more reassured by Father's promise to Veronica because Baby-amah believed the stories, and she was my most steadfast point of reference.

Baby-amah always knew what I would like and not like. When Mother gave us stewed rhubarb for dessert she said we would like it, but Baby-amah said in her dour way "Doo-bebe won't like that," and I did not—in fact, I hated it. But if she said "You'll like that" I swallowed it happily and was sure I liked it. I could not understand why Mother often got exasperated with Baby-amah when she was clearly so wise and trustworthy.

Baby-amah came to take care of me when I was born. She also cared for my brother and sisters, but in my mind she was always *my* Baby-amah, and to her I was always Doo-bebe, the Eldest Child, her special charge. She was tall, so thin as to be emaciated, gaunt-faced, unsmiling, but to me solid and stable as the earth itself. When I was sleepless at night, as I often was, she would be there, silhouetted in the dim night-light, sitting on the red velvet prie-dieu in front of Mother's altar, upright and still. She would ignore my tossing and turning until I called to her.

"Baby-amah, I can't sleep!"

"Then lie still. I am here."

And I would lie still and sleep would come.

Baby-amah had no children of her own, but she had a husband who was very bad. He came to see her only when he wanted money, which was always on or about payday. He would sneak into the house at night, although Mother had strictly forbidden it, and take Baby-amah's salary away from her.

"Why do you give it to him?" Mother asked.

"To get rid of him," she answered shortly.

"But he'll come back again and again if you give him money every time he comes. Next time, call me or the master, and we'll call the police."

"Huh," said Baby-amah, brief and dry.

"But he's nothing but a burden to you!" Mother insisted.

Baby-amah did not answer. Chinese women of her day were born to bear burdens.

The doyen of our household in Dixwell Road was Ah-Ching, Grandfather's former rickshaw puller. After Grandfather's death he had been promoted to the position of Father's valet, and in Dixwell Road he became our houseboy, generally in charge of the house and the other servants. Mother had made for him long white cotton gowns which he wore over his everyday cotton trousers and short frog-buttoned jacket. With the gowns, the dignity that he had always had deepened and his gruff temper grew sardonic. He was always silent and reserved. He had a wife to whom he went home at night, but we never saw her. We supposed he had children, but he never told us. Behind his back we, like the servants, called him Old Tiger, but to his face we were respectful. He could quell our most exuberant moments with a glare. When he had to communicate, he spoke to Father. Mother he tolerated, but she could never make him do what he did not want to do. When he was old and tired she bought him a vacuum cleaner, but he refused even to try it, saying brusquely that he had always used a broom and feather duster and would do so until he died. One day we found him asleep in the best armchair in the parlor, his feather duster clasped upright in his hands. We tiptoed out—he would have been embarrassed if we had wakened him, and we did not want that.

He had cancer, the doctor told us when Father at last prevailed on him to be examined, but to him it was a knot in his tube.

"You don't understand," he told Mother impatiently. "I am weak and have pain because I can't eat. And I can't eat because I can't swallow. And I can't swallow because the tube that leads from my mouth to my stomach has become knotted, so the food can't pass."

When Father told him he would have to go to the hospital for treatment, he shook his head decidedly.

"I'll go to my country. I can't stand the city anymore. It's too dirty and noisy. It makes me nervous, which has caused the knot in my tube."

"Your country might be different now," Father told him. "It might no longer even be there. It might have been destroyed in the fighting."

"There will be something there, and it will be better than the city."

He turned away, and then turned back to Father. To our astonishment, there were tears in his eyes.

"Tung-kah." He bowed to Father. "I have known you all your life, and your father before you." It was acknowledgment, benediction, and farewell.

And so he went to his "country," to the village where he was born, saying to each of us a gruff "Take care," and leaving behind on the kitchen table his long white gowns. We said, "Take care, Ah-Ching," and watched him go, and never knew whether he reached his country or whether, if he reached it, it was still there.

Our cook, Dahsoo, could not have been more different from Ah-Ching. He was sociable and garrulous, with three wives who came to the house each payday to quarrel in the back yard over his salary. When they made their appearance he sighed resignedly, shrugged his shoulders, and got out the pastry board. He loved to make pastry and he made it best under pressure. Every few months Mother discharged him for some new peccadillo, and after a few days took him back because he was such a marvelous cook and because she never could help laughing at his sly humor.

Once, when she fired him, he sent his Number One wife to do the cooking because (he sent a message by her) it would be such a nuisance for Mother to have to cook herself. Another time, Mother fired him on the spot because there was a worm in the soup. She was sure it had got in because he had been talking to his friends in the kitchen and had paid no attention to the soup. Dahsoo came into the dining room, sad-faced, shuffling, a clown without a circus. We began to laugh. Mother glared at us and spoke shortly to Dahsoo:

"Go away. I've fired you and I don't want to see you anymore."

Dahsoo addressed her reproachfully:

"Tah-tah, did you notice the cabbage in the soup? Was it not all chopped up very finely?"

"Yes," grudgingly.

"Ah!" portentuously.

From his pocket Dahsoo produced a dirty piece of wadded-up paper which he carefully smoothed out to expose the worm.

"And look at this worm, Tah-tah." He extended it toward Mother, who turned her face away. "Is it chopped up, as it must have been if it had been in the cabbage when I chopped that? No. It is whole and entire. It is a big, fat worm and could not have escaped my chopping knife."

He paused solemnly, the three long hairs which grew from the wart on his cheek trembling with portent. Then he knelt and banged his forehead on the floor, at the same time pointing to heaven with the hand that held the worm.

"I have an enemy," he intoned. "I have an enemy who put the worm into the soup *after* I had made it!"

We burst out laughing and Mother's lips trembled.

"If you have an enemy, he must be among your ragtag friends who are always inhabiting my kitchen!"

Dahsoo got to his feet triumphantly.

"Yes, it must be so. I will watch carefully and when I find out who he is I will expel him from your kitchen. But in the meantime, of course, you cannot let him get away with this dirty trick, so I will stay."

After a time Mother stopped firing him because she realized that he enjoyed it. Each time it meant two or three days holiday for him. Instead, she found another and more effective way of punishing him. She would tell him to go to one of her friends to learn how to make a certain dish, which she said the friend made better than he did. That touched his pride, and for days after one of these incidents we would eat superbly.

Our household was completed by Small Amah, whom Mother employed after Luke's birth to help Baby-amah. She came from Baby-amah's village and they called each other "big sister" and "small sister," as was the custom, whence came our name for her.

Small Amah's main duty was to empty the chamber pots. We

were in the days before flush toilets, and we used small enamel
pots with handles. Small Amah cleaned them each time they were
used, emptying them into the bucket in the back yard and washing them with the bundle of stiff twigs traditionally used for the
purpose. Early each morning the night-soil man came, with his
closed cart like a large iron coffin creaking along on its two wheels.
If one woke before dawn, it was to hear the eerie creak-creak of
the cart and the thrash-thrash of the twig brush as the buckets
up and down the street were emptied into the cart and cleaned
out.

We supposed that the night-soil man eventually wheeled his
cart out to the village and emptied it into one of the farmers' pits.
The pits were dug where they would be convenient to the fields,
and the farmers emptied their chamber pots into them or used
them directly. At the proper seasons, the farmers dipped out the
contents in wooden pails fixed to long poles and spread it over the
fields where vegetables were to grow. The vegetables grew beautifully, and I cannot recall that any of us ever got sick from eating
them. But we were careful about the pits, nevertheless, because
they were unmarked and quite big enough to fall into. Some were
big enough for a horse and rider to fall into, which was what
happened to one of our uncles, to the enormous amusement of
the villagers.

Dixwell Road was on the outskirts of the city and there were
villages not far from home to which we went on our Sunday walks
with Father. In the summer, the villages lay in the hot bright
sunlight, humped roofs barely visible from a distance over the
myriad golden stalks of rice, tall and heavy, waving gently in the
teeming fields which stretched as far as the eye could see. From
nearby, the low houses, dun-colored, with mud-and-bamboo walls
and straw-thatched roofs, clustered on the hard-beaten reddish

earth of the village square. Their doorways stood hospitably open
—they were closed only at night, not by doors but by planks
which were slid upright into the high, grooved thresholds. Chickens ran about busily pecking, babies played in and out of the black
shadows cast sharply in the dazzling sunlight by the sheltering
trees. Women cooked outdoors, squatting over the small round
clay stoves, stirring the bubbling pots, pushing the faggots as they
slowly burned further into the stove openings. There was an
intricately mingled smell of wood smoke, of earth, straw, dung
baked dry and clean by the sun. There was chatter and crowing
laughter from the children, the cluck of the chickens, an occasional grunt from a fat sow sprawling with her piglets in a shady
corner. The water buffalo soaked themselves peacefully in the
pond, only their horns, their nostrils, and their sleepy long-lashed
eyes above water. For them summer was an easy time. At other
times they lumbered over the fields pulling the heavy plows or,
blindfolded and hitched to the waterwheels, trudged endlessly
around and around working the chain of paddles that clacked
down into the stream and up again full of water to flood the fields
where the rice was to be planted.

We went, too, in the winter, when the villages lay huddled
under the bare trees and the icy wind whistled around the houses,
lifting the straw from the roofs, when the hard-trodden summer
earth turned into soggy clogged mud that sucked at one's shoes
or froze in swirling ridges, when the smell was sharp and seemed
to freeze in one's nostrils, and the sounds were of dripping from
the leafless branches and of crackling ice. Then the villagers
dressed in their cotton-padded garments which they put on in the
first cold spell and did not cast off again until the spring sun
shone.

When we first went to the villages we were objects of delighted amusement to the villagers. Both men and women wore loose trousers, cut straight, with a wide band around the waist which was folded to fit the wearer and tied or belted. The bare legs of my sisters and myself were astonishing and amusing to the village girls and women. They followed us about to tweak up our skirts when we were not looking, to see if we wore panties underneath. But soon we were well known. We talked with everyone we met, inquired about the crops, played with the children, carried the babies, and lifted up the toddlers who, in winter, were so fat in their padded garments that they could not get up without help when they fell down. We knew better than to say that any child was good or beautiful. The spirits might hear and decide to take that child for themselves, and the mother would have to say loudly that the child was ugly and naughty. We said only that the children were "nice to play with."

All the village children and some of the women used to accompany us on our Sunday excursions. We made a procession, walking single file along the narrow banks that separated the rice fields. Father walked in front, Luke next with his B.B. gun that shot tiny pellets. He practiced his aim on sparrows and doves. The dogs ranged around and we walked some way behind in order not to be in the path of Luke's pellets. Behind us walked the line of villagers, chattering and calling out, the mothers or older sisters carrying the babies who were tied to their backs in long strips of cloth, only their heads free and bouncing. The babies were nearly always peacefully asleep. "They feel our heartbeats" the mothers said, "and they are calm, so they sleep."

In spring we would stop to catch tadpoles in the water along the edges of the flooded rice fields. In summer we watched the villagers catching frogs for the evening meal. They used a short stick to which was tied a length of string with a ball of meat fixed to the end of it. The meat was dangled in the water, a frog gulped it down whole and was lifted out on the end of the string to be plopped into a long narrow bag, the mouth kept open by a hoop of split bamboo. A deft flick and the meat popped out of the frog's belly. He flopped down into the bottom of the bag on top of his brothers who were already there, and the meat went back into the water to entice another frog.

Autumn was the season for seeing the leaves turn red and brown. We trod on them, crunch-crunch, and breathed the pellucid air, watching the fluffy clouds chase each other across the deep blue sky. Autumn was a lovely season in China. Winter was the time for sliding down the roofs of ice-houses. After the rice harvest, the farmers flooded their fields again and when the bitter winter came the water froze. The farmers cut the ice into blocks and stored it in big, low bamboo houses insulated with double straw roofs. The upper roof was high and sloped steeply, which made a wonderful slide. The ice stayed frozen in those straw houses and in the summer the farmers sold it. Housewives bought it to set in their wood-and-zinc ice boxes, where it melted slowly and dripped into the tin pans set underneath.

Winter, too, was the time for birds. Even so close to the city, the dogs raised pheasants which father would shoot, or Luke after he graduated to a shotgun. Luke is now a citizen of the United States of America, and on strictly regulated days he takes his son to shoot a strictly regulated number of pheasants, many of which have been bred on farms and do not know enough to flee man. Luke's son does not really believe that there was a time in China when his grandfather and granduncles, and his own father, shot so many pheasants that we were sick of eating them. In the season they hung in our pantry, row on row. Dahsoo roasted them, stewed them, boiled them with bitter cabbage, barbecued them, sautéed them with bread crumbs, curried them, and roasted them again, and still more arrived, carried back by runner from father, the uncles, and later Luke too, up-country in the houseboats or in the lean-tos they paid farmers to build for them against the farmhouses. One of our uncles even had a headquarters in the mountain stronghold of a bandit.

It was Uncle Bill whom the bandit befriended. The countryside in those days was overrun by bandits, men from the private armies of the warlords who, since the overthrow of the Manchu Emperors in 1911, had divided China among themselves, carving out their own empires, fiercely fighting each other, preying on the peasantry. It was inevitable that men from those armies, knowing nothing but war, should become bandits and in their smaller way maintain their armies of thieves and cutthroats and define their own territories in which they plundered.

Uncle Bill was hunting wild boar and, intent on following the trail, failed to notice that he had climbed halfway up the mountain on the top of which a notorious bandit had his stronghold. Suddenly three ragged men armed with rifles pounced on him and at gunpoint forced him the rest of the way up the mountain into the presence of their chief. The bandits' camp was in a clearing shaded by ancient trees. It consisted of tattered tents and a few bamboo-walled, straw-thatched huts standing in the midst of litter, clothes flapping from strings tied to trees, clay cooking stoves smoking, pigs and chickens foraging. The chief bandit was a large, rough man clad in the remnants of a uniform; his skin was like leather tanned to the color of tree bark. Uncle Bill, who spoke all the major Chinese dialects, addressed him haughtily in Mandarin, hoping that offense would be the best defense. Uncle Bill stood no higher than the bandit's shoulder and had to peer up at him through his thick-lensed glasses. The bandit stared in astonishment, then burst into a roar of laughter.

"You—a hunter! With those glasses! Its no wonder you can't see the boar, nor even the mountain!" Then, suspiciously: "How do I know you're not a spy?"

"With these glasses?"

The bandit roared again and clapped Bill on the back, nearly knocking him down.

"We'll eat and drink before we discuss the matter further."

The wine was Mao Tai, the strongest of Chinese wines, and in a short time both the bandit and Bill were drunk, but Bill far more than the bandit. Ordinarily, a glass of beer made him red in the face. When they could eat and drink no more, the bandit decided it was time to put Bill to the test. He ordered two empty cigarette tins set up in the crotch of a tree.

"Now we'll see if you're really a hunter. The tin on the left is mine, the one on the right is yours. We'll shoot together. If you hit I'll believe you. But if you miss . . . " He grinned and drew his finger across his throat.

Bill could barely stand. The gun shook in his hands. He peered at his tin and saw it waver into three or four tins which shifted unsteadily to and fro. He shut his eyes—so he told us—and fired as the bandit gave the word. Miraculously, both tins flew into the air.

By the time Bill left the next morning, the bandit was his fast friend. He gave Bill a standing invitation to use the camp as his hunting headquarters whenever he wished, and in addition assigned two of his men to be his beaters to flush the boar out of the undergrowth. While Bill was peering right and left through his glasses, they spotted sign across the valley and raced off, shouting to Bill to follow. The bandit held his sides laughing.

3

Baby-amah

SOON AFTER MY ninth birthday, Baby-amah died. She did it as she
did everything else, quickly and without fuss. One morning, she
did not come to get us children out of bed. Mother went to her
room and found her in a high fever. The doctor said she had a
severe case of bronchitis which could turn into pneumonia. She
did not have a strong constitution. She should be sent to the
hospital. But Baby-amah absolutely refused to go. In those days
few Chinese willingly went to a hospital or sent their relatives to
one. Hospitals, with their strange customs, their closed doors
behind which unknown rituals were performed, their glittering
instruments, their odors, their mysterious white-gowned inhabitants, were fearsome places to be avoided.

Nobody knew where to find Baby-amah's husband, and Small
Amah, her "small sister" from the village, was not really her sister.
There was no alternative but to keep Baby-amah at home. The
doctor left medicine, and between them Mother and Small Amah
cared for her.

I was forbidden to see her, but on the third day of her illness
I felt so uncomfortable without her that I crept quietly to her

room and softly opened the door. The room was almost dark, only a little light seeping through the closed shutters. There was a heavy smell and the sound of labored breathing, and suddenly I was afraid.

"Baby-amah?"

She turned over slowly. Her face, more gaunt than ever, glimmered with sweat. I tiptoed to her bedside and, for the last time, took the familiar bony hand. It was hot and dry. After a while she whispered:

"Doo-bebe, I am going to die."

The effort of speaking made her pant.

"Don't be frightened. Death can be a good thing."

A little later:

"You're a big girl now. You don't need me any more. Don't cry."

And finally, on a sighing breath:

"Go away now."

I went. When, next morning, Mother found her dead, I didn't cry.

4

The Coming of Ah-May

SMALL AMAH proposed to Mother that she should not employ a new amah to take Baby-amah's place. Small Amah would bring her daughter from the country to help her, and between them they would be able to handle the work now that the children were big enough to do most things for themselves. Mother agreed, and so Ah-May came.

Ah-May was my age when she arrived, a small, thin, ugly girl, hair in a skimpy pigtail, button eyes, large pockmarks all over her broad face. She sat in the kitchen, dumb with fright, stubbornly keeping her head turned away from us, refusing to answer our greetings.

"Leave her alone," Small Amah said angrily. "She's stupid."

She went over and shook Ah-May roughly, repeating "stupid, stupid" in a loud voice. Ah-May's head snapped back and forth with the shaking, but she didn't react. We stared at Small Amah in astonishment—she had always been quiet and gentle with us.

Someone turned on the faucet over the sink, and suddenly Ah-May came to life. With a loud scream she leaped off her stool and rushed outside into the sleety rain. She pressed herself against the wall of the back yard, her face white as a sheet, trembling. We went to persuade her to come in again, but she shook her head.

"There's a devil in the house! Water came out of the wall!"

"Stupid!"

Small Amah came rushing out, grabbed Ah-May by the ear, and dragged the sobbing child up the outside stairs into the room that they would share.

We went back in, wondering.

For another week Ah-May remained quiet and afraid, eating little, climbing upstairs with a tight hold on the bannister, coming down by sliding from step to step on her bottom. She had never seen stairs before, as she had never seen water coming from a faucet.

But at last she began to lose her fear, and she began to eat enormously, ravenously. In a little while she became chubby, her pigtail grew thick and sleek, her black button eyes took on a sparkling intelligence, and speech came bubbling from her smiling mouth. She was good-natured, cheerful, always ready to giggle, and full of earthy wisdom.

Mother had finally threatened Dahsoo: if he did not get rid of two of his three wives, she would discharge him and this time she really meant it. She could no longer stand the monthly quarrels in the back yard over his salary, and anyway it was immoral to have three wives. Dahsoo himself must have been feeling that polygamy was more trouble than it was worth because, after a few half-hearted protests, he agreed and went back to the kitchen, only pretending to be outraged.

We had been interested spectators of this scene and we all followed Dahsoo to the kitchen to help him make the big decision as to which of the three to keep.

Veronica thought he should keep Number Three, who was youngest, plump and roly-poly. She laughed a lot, played with Veronica, and allowed her to carry her equally plump and roly-poly baby. Dahsoo said, however, that one of his friends was eager to have her as his fourth concubine, and she was therefore easiest to place—there was no question of his keeping her.

Number Two was not particularly nice, but she was pretty and, we thought, preferable to Number One, who was old and bad-tempered. Dahsoo hesitated between them, extolling the virtues and deploring the vices of each.

"Well," said Ah-May, "Number One has much to be bad-tempered about."

Dahsoo looked sheepish and admitted she was right.

"When Number Two and Number Three have gone, I think her temper will improve. And besides, she's the only one who'll look after the children of the other two in addition to her own."

Again, she was right. We looked at her with enthusiasm. Dahsoo said he could send Number Two back to her parents—they were farmers and would be glad of her help in the fields—and there was nowhere for Number One to go. So it was decided, and before the end of the next month Dahsoo's two younger wives had gone. Their daughters went with them, but their sons stayed with their father under the care of Number One. For the first time since we had known her, Number One smiled at us when she came next payday and amicably shared his salary with Dahsoo.

We stood in awe of Ah-May's wisdom, which had been much greater than our own. She herself saw nothing extraordinary in it. She ran about the house all day, helping her mother, and soon, with the same practicality with which she had spoken to Dahsoo, she was doing much of the work herself.

Mother's conscience hurt. Small Amah had spoken of her

daughter without mentioning that she was only nine years old. Mother had imagined a grown-up girl. Now she tried to back out of the arrangement with Small Amah.

"Ah-May should be in school."

"She has no need of learning. She's only a female person." Small Amah spoke shortly.

"But she's too young to be doing the work of an adult."

"Is she not capable? Are you not pleased with her?"

"She's extremely capable and intelligent. But she's a child."

"If you won't let her work here, I'll put her out to work elsewhere, where she may have to work much harder and where they may even beat her."

That was quite possible. We knew of several instances. One of our aunts played mahjong in a house where a slave girl no older than Ah-May was kept awake all night to serve tea to the mahjong players. Mother knew a rich Chinese lady who had two slave girls. She took them to church with her, not to pray, but to stand on each side of her with paper fans to fan her while she prayed loudly and endlessly. If they grew drowsy with the heat while they kept her cool, if the rhythm of the fanning slowed down, she would turn and give each of them a hearty slap to wake them up, and then turn back to her prayers.

Small Amah's argument silenced Mother. She insisted, however, on one change in her arrangement with Small Amah, which had been to increase Small Amah's salary by half as a family salary for the work of herself and daughter. Now, at the end of each month, Mother gave Ah-May two silver dollars for herself. She always gave her clean, shiny dollars and she always put them into her hands, saying, "This is for you, Ah-May."

"Two dollars!" We were impressed. Our own allowances were fifty cents a month each. Ah-May shrugged.

"They're pretty," I said to Ah-May. "They shine!"
She looked at me, saying nothing.
"You can buy lots of things!"
Again she shrugged.

It was puzzling. She did not seem to care for two silver dollars
every month, and she never reacted when Small Amah shouted
at her and called her "stupid," and even slapped her for no reason
we could see, although she never did so in front of Mother.
Ah-May was always the same toward her mother, silent and ex-
pressionless.

Although she was said to be nine years old, in fact Ah-May was
younger, because Chinese babies are a year old when they are
born. But she seemed to me older than I was in many ways, more
experienced, calmly accepting things that made me stamp my
feet with temper, knowing depths that were unknown to me. I
was fascinated. I wanted to tell her things—all the things that I
knew Mother would dismiss with an admonition. She was always
prepared to consider what I told her, and to discuss it at length.

One night we discussed Lulu, a girl from school who was always
asking for rides home in the rickshaw in which Jane and I rode
to and from school. Runny was our rickshaw puller. He ran very
fast and was always grinning, his square face kind under the
cropped black hair. In winter he kept our rickshaw rug in the
space under the seat. He would take it out, usher me into the
rickshaw, lift Jane up beside me, tuck the rug around us carefully.
When it was raining, the folding hood of the rickshaw would be
up, and he would fasten the waterproof sheet that extended from
the hood to the shafts, closing us up darkly, while out in the rain
he picked up the shafts and ran swiftly off, the rickshaw on its two
big wheels moving smoothly behind him. We enjoyed those rickshaw rides, except when Lulu rode with us.

"Of course there's no place for her on the seat," I told Ah-May petulantly. "She sits on the footboard. Its so squashy! We can't move our legs, and she keeps squirming about. And Mother says we have to give her a ride if she asks. It's such a nuisance! Why can't her mother get a rickshaw for her?"

Ah-May considered.

"Well, I suppose she would if she could. And anyway, it's Runny who has to pull the extra weight, for no extra money."

I was silenced.

"And perhaps she'll do something for you one day."

Twenty-five years later, in another country, I remembered those words when Lulu, remet by accident, did indeed do something for me far more important than those rickshaw rides that Runny gave her.

Ah-May too was fascinated by the things I knew that she did not. I was not afraid of the big city, I dared to get onto trams, I went to school, I could read and write. Ah-May never understood what she called "foreign writing." Although she knew not a single Chinese character, she understood that each character conveyed a meaning, and she knew there were many thousands of characters and thus many thousands of meanings. To her, the twenty-six characters of the foreign alphabet meant twenty-six meanings. How was it possible to use only twenty-six meanings to write anything one wished?

"Each character has a *sound*," I tried to explain to her. "If I write d-o-g, the sounds make 'dog.' If I write g-o-d, the sounds make 'god.'"

But she could not conceive of that. Until the day of her death she stood in awe of the written word.

The best time for Ah-May and me to talk was in the evenings when I took my bath. Every day she came to help me. I luxuriated in the hot water, sticking out an arm or a leg which she vigorously soaped while we talked of many things.

"Who is Luke's wife?" she asked me one night.

"Luke! He's much too young to be married."

"But isn't he betrothed?"

"Of course not! If he wants to get married when he grows up, he'll get betrothed then."

"You mean he'll choose his own wife?"

"Yes, of course."

"But how will your parents know that she'll be a good wife?"

"Well, I suppose they won't know. Nobody'll know till after."

"But why do your parents leave it to chance?"

"What can they do?" I asked impatiently.

She was silent, soaping my back. Then:

"I am betrothed to Small Amah's son. She isn't my real mother. She made arrangements with my parents for me to be betrothed to her son, and then she adopted me, to train me, so that I'll be a good wife for her son."

"What!" I swallowed soapy water in my astonishment.

She nodded.

"But do you like him?"

"No."

"How can you marry somebody you don't like?"

"He's my betrothed husband. I have to marry him."

"But didn't your parents ask you before they betrothed you?"

"I was two years old. I didn't even know it till much later."

"Two years old! How can you be betrothed when you're two years old!"

"I was."

We stared at each other.

"You're not betrothed?" she asked me slowly.

"No. Nor are Jane and Veronica, any more than Luke."

"When you grow up, you'll choose your own husband?"

"Yes, of course."

"And if you don't want to marry, you won't have to?"

"No, of course not."

We were silent, contemplating the enormity of the gap between us. Slowly, she resumed soaping my legs.

"If I could choose, I wouldn't get married. Then I could keep the dollars for myself."

"But the dollars are yours! Mother gives them to *you*, they're *your* salary!"

"They're my salary, but they're not my dollars. Small Amah takes them for her son."

I splashed water all over her as I jumped up in the bath.

"Small Amah takes your dollars! I'm going to tell Mother!" Furiously I jumped out of the water and seized the towel.

"No, no. Don't tell your mother! Don't tell anybody! Please don't! She'll beat me!"

"If she beats you, I'll beat her!" I was boiling.

Ah-May began to cry.

"I wish I hadn't told you! She'll beat me! Once in the village she beat me with a piece of firewood until I couldn't walk! Don't tell! Don't tell!"

She threw herself on me, sobbing. I was shocked into immobility. Ah-May, the self-possessed, abandoning herself to wild grief!

"But she can't take your money, Ah-May. It's stealing! In fact, she's not only stealing from you, she's stealing from Mother because Mother gives the money to *you*, for *your* work—not because you're Small Amah's daughter!"

"I know, but I'm betrothed to her son!"

"That doesn't make you her possession!"

"It does."

"That's *wrong!*"

Ah-May rubbed her hands over her eyes and blew her nose with her fingers. I handed her a piece of toilet paper.

"Doo-bebe, why do you speak of right and wrong? There's no right and wrong in this. It is as it is. I am betrothed to her son and she is my mother-in-law as well as my mother. Its not my money. Nothing is mine. My stomach is hers. My blood is hers. And his."

"Then you have to break your betrothal."

Ah-May gaped. Then she laughed, a high, tittering giggle.

"Don't laugh!" I stamped my foot. "If there's nothing else to be done, then your betrothal has to be broken. Mother's friend was betrothed, but she decided she wanted to marry somebody else, so she broke her betrothal and gave back the ring."

"But I have no ring!" She giggled again at the idea. "And I didn't decide anything. My betrothal was between Small Amah and my parents."

"Then you have to ask your parents to break the betrothal."

"I don't even know who they are! I was two years old when they gave me to Small Amah!"

"Then you'll have to do it yourself."

She stared at me, her bright black eyes blank and still. She had stopped giggling.

"Break my own betrothal?"

"Yes."

In the silence that followed, our hard breathing was audible. Then there was a rushing, whistling noise above our heads, over the roof, and an instant later an ear-cracking explosion. With one accord, hands to our ears, hearts pounding, we rushed out of the bathroom and down the stairs.

5

⊗⊗⊗

Kitchen Politician

In addition to being a polygamist and a humorist, Dahsoo was a kitchen politician. He was the only servant in our neighborhood who could read and write, and this gave an ideal outlet to his sociable inclinations because it attracted the servants of our neighbors into our kitchen to hear him read the newspapers, expound on the news of the day, give his views on the policies of the government, speculate on the strategies of this or that warlord.

It was from Dahsoo that we absorbed our first consciousness of current events in the city outside our home and in the vast country of which our city was a part. In school we were taught English history exclusively, to an extent which might suggest that no other nation had a history. In our living room our parents read the English language *North China Daily News,* and discussed the news, often with grave faces, but if we asked questions we were asked in turn if we had done our lessons and sent away to do them or to play. In our kitchen, however, Dahsoo never objected when we listened to him read the Chinese newspapers, and he never tired of answering our questions. So, to us, news came from Chinese newspapers and politics was a subject that Dahsoo knew about.

Dahsoo's literacy was limited to a few hundred characters, and when he read the newspapers he must have made a free interpretation of the characters he did not know. Nevertheless, his audience listened fascinated and carried away what they remembered, sometimes even more distorted than the version they had heard from him. In spite of these inadequacies, we had from Dahsoo a fairly accurate if simplified idea of events then occurring in China.

We knew well the name of Dr. Sun Yat-sen and his San Min Chu I, his Three Principles of the People: nationalism meant fighting the warlords and chasing out of China people like Barstud Red Face; democracy meant that rich people as well as poor people had to pay taxes; people's livelihood meant that the man who grew the rice should own the land that he grew it on. Sun Yat-sen, we knew, was a saint, the Father of the People, the leader of the great Nationalist Party, the Kuomintang, and the Savior of China, especially of the Chinese peasant and his myriad woes.

He had woes? The people in our villages were always laughing and happy.

Because, when we went to the villages, we amused the people and broke the monotony a little. Peasants led deadly dull and unbelievably hard lives, and took advantage of every slightest opportunity to laugh, to forget. Peasants paid the major part of the taxes. They could not evade, as could the rich, because the tax collectors came to them, and the source of their income, the rice, was plain to see. Rice was plentiful in the fields, but not in the clay storage jars in the homes. Everything the farmers had to pay, they paid in rice or in money from the sale of rice. And the farmers paid many people—the tax collectors, the warlord who was kingpin in their territory, his soldiers who demanded tribute under threat, most of all their "wangtung," their landlord. Hardly any of the farmers owned the land they worked, and they had to pay rice for rental of the land. Some years when crops were bad, the land-rent and all the taxes took three-quarters of the rice harvest. The rest might last the farmers till the next harvest, but if they needed cash to buy seed, padded clothes for the bitter winter, illness, wedding feasts, funerals, they had to borrow it. And they had no one to borrow from but the landlord, who charged them high interest. If they could not pay, they might be beaten and thrown into jail, for he was magistrate as well as landlord and money-lender, and he had his own police force.

At first we listened to Dahsoo's harangues as we listened to the stories Mother read to us in the evenings, but their reality was shockingly brought home to me one day when Ah-May and I went to the village for a walk. We saw a crowd of people, silent, huddled, in front of one of the meanest houses. It was very cold and their exhalations made a mist around their heads. From inside the house came a harsh voice shouting orders. Suddenly, in a startling crescendo which drowned out the voice, came the cries of women and the wailing of children. The crowd stirred uneasily. From the house strode an officer in a thickly padded gray cotton uniform and a tall fur hat with ear pieces. The crowd gave way, the people in front backing hurriedly into those behind. The officer strutted up and down in front of them showing off his strength and magnificence. He thrust out his chest and arched his neck, made his mouth into a snarl, glared out of his eyes. Pointing his finger at the crowd and then back at the house, he shouted a speech in which the words "be careful" and "learn this lesson" were repeated several times.

Two soldiers erupted from the doorway pushing before them a peasant we had often seen in the village. He was stripped to the waist. In spite of the cold, sweat poured down his face, plastering the coarse black hair in jagged peaks on his forehead. Streams of bright blood slithered down his body. The officer grabbed something that protruded from his shoulder and dragged him forward. He screamed, a sound that stopped my breath, and fell to the ground. His wife rushed out of the house and threw herself on her knees before the officer. Her raised hands were clasped into fists, pressed together knuckles to knuckles. She shook them violently, frantically, in the ancient gesture of supplication. The officer turned away contemptuously. Two soldiers grabbed her by the hair and flung her aside. They jerked the man to his feet, and forced him forward, pushing him from behind and pulling him by the thing that stuck out of his shoulder.

The villagers watched in total silence until the procession disappeared from sight. Then women ran forward and lifted the wife who lay where she had fallen, tumbled in a heap, and shook her until her head snapped one way and her feet the other, calling out loudly to her spirit, which had fled her body in grief and terror, to return. An old woman, the mother, bent almost double, hobbled out of the house to tell the story.

Her son owed the landlord money. He had gone to the town the previous day with fifty coppers, all he could scrape up, to pay interest on his debt. In the courtyard of the landlord's house he had seen servants filling the pigs' trough with swill. Hearing the pigs grunt and snuffle happily, he thought of his family with no rice in their bowls, only soup made from hot water and stewed leaves. So he had picked up the bottom of a broken clay bowl and filled it from the pigs' trough to bring home to his children. But the soldiers had seen him and chased him from the courtyard. Today they had come for him. They had heated a piece of thick wire until it was red hot and had tried to force it through the fleshy part in his shoulder. When it stuck, the officer had made a hole in his shoulder with a knife and had pulled it through. They had twisted the ends to make a handle with which to drag him away to prison.

"Ai-yah! Ai-yah!" the old woman lamented. The wife was still unconscious. The children, terrified, bewildered, clung to the old woman's clothes.

Ah-May and I went home, silent. By tacit consent we never told what we had seen. Mother wondered why, that night, I vomited my dinner and cried for hours. I could not have said why even if I had wanted to.

When Sun Yat-sen died, Dahsoo and his friends were much depressed, but their spirits revived when Chiang Kai-shek assumed his mantle. Chiang Kai-shek would implement the Three Principles! We were glad too. We expected them to be implemented very soon, in the assured future, just as we expected Santa Claus at Christmas and firecrackers at Chinese New Year. The Northern March had begun in July 1926. The army of the Kuomintang, the glorious army of the revolution, commanded by Chiang Kai-shek himself, was sweeping from Canton toward Shanghai, conquering warlords all along the way. The army was almost bloodlessly victorious. Much blood was shed, but it was not the blood of soldiers. From south to north along the route of march, peasants were revolting, arming themselves with picks and hoes, killing landlords and their officials, disarming police. The soldiers of the warlords assumed battle stance but at sight of the enemy turned coat and joined him. The Kuomintang army was victorious before it arrived.

Every night the company in our kitchen rejoiced. All of them were servants in well-to-do households, living the comparatively easy life of the city, well paid and well fed. But in each of them lived the eternal peasant, who was himself, or his father, or his grandfather. To each of them, every warlord put to flight was his own warlord, his devil, the one who had made a misery of his life, or his father's, or his grandfather's. Every landlord killed was his landlord, his oppressor, or his father's, or his grandfather's, back to the beginning of memory. They were jubilant in our kitchen, identifying with the glory of the revolution, with the victorious Kuomintang, with the savior Chiang Kai-shek, believing that the good days would start tomorrow.

Sometimes Dahsoo mentioned the Communists, the Reds, but so vaguely that Veronica thought they were a football team—Luke played football for the Blues. It was a long time before we knew that the Chinese Communist Party had been founded in Shanghai in July 1921 by twelve men, among them a man from Hunan province, a student, a scholar, who was working in a laundry at the time, whose name was Mao Tse-tung. That the Shanghai party had been joined by another formed the same year in Paris by Chinese students in France, among them a man called Chou En-lai. Their principles had coincided with Sun Yat-sen's, and in 1924, for the sake of unity, they had joined the Kuomintang. When the Northern March began, the Communists were part of it. The revolt of the peasants along the route of march was organized by them. In Shanghai, preparing for the arrival of the army of the revolution, organizing labor, was Chou En-lai.

A new word had entered our vocabulary: Strike. Workers were laying down their tools, shutting down factories, congregating in the streets, shouting slogans. For months revolts had thundered in the countryside, but now they were thundering on the doorstep of the city, the chopper was hanging over the heads of its bankers, merchants, industrialists. They were trembling. Tremendous investments were at stake, both of Chinese and of foreigners under extraterritoriality. These were the events that brought gravity to the faces of the grown-ups in our parlor, while in the kitchen we rejoiced because the warlords were fleeing, the landlords dying, the villagers would always have rice to eat—never again stewed-leaves soup—and Barstud Red Face would be chased away.

And so the army of the revolution marched, ten times its original size by the time it reached Shanghai, hailed with fierce joy by tens of millions of people drunk with what they thought was liberation. And so it was on the night when, over the roofs of the twilit city, over the heads of two children arguing in that attic bathroom, the big guns spoke.

But they were not the guns of the revolution. They were not the guns that would free the peasants from their burdens and bring to the whole land justice, peace, prosperity, as Dahsoo foretold.

They were the guns of racketeers and thugs, turned against the city's workers and the Communists. They sealed Chiang Kai-shek's breach of faith with his Communist allies, and confirmed his new alliance with Big Business. They aborted the Three Principles, for they launched the Kuomintang as the new super-bandit government of China with Chiang Kai-shek as its supreme warlord, and although Chiang was to present to the community of nations the semblance of a unified China, and was to accomplish the abolition of extraterritoriality and the "unequal treaties," for another twenty years the Chinese peasant was to seek in vain for justice and humanity.

6

Big Guns

SHELL AFTER SHELL whizzed over the house and exploded somewhere to the north. We huddled in the living room around Father and Mother, terrified, clamoring.

"What is it? What is it?"

"It's big guns."

"What's big guns?"

"I don't want big guns!" Veronica shrieked. "Make them stop! I don't want them! Make them stop!"

Her piercing cries, our sobs, the high-pitched whine of the shells, the splintering crashes, made pandemonium. With each crash my teeth felt as though they were cracking into jagged pieces. Everything was confusion, heart-stopping, stomach-sickening. Every safe and familiar thing had vanished. We were buffeted in a black and depthless void of shattering sound.

Father dragged the big sofa across the corner of the room farthest from the windows and pushed us down to the floor behind it. He got mattresses from the beds and stood them up against the windows. The electricity went off and the room was plunged into darkness, relieved only by the glow of the dying coals in the fireplace and the blinding light that flashed intermittently around the edges of the mattresses. We crouched behind the sofa, quiet now except for Small Amah, who whimpered unceasingly "Ai-yah! Ai-yah!" Ah-May sat beside me, her hands over Veronica's ears, comforting her even as she herself sobbed.

At last the barrage moved away. The ear-cracking explosions became dull thuds. Father got up to light candles and Mother to go to the kitchen for cocoa. She called to Small Amah for help, but Small Amah seemed unable to hear or to move. She had pulled her hair out of its usually tidy bun and it hung in straggly wisps about her face. In the flickering candlelight she looked horrible, staring-eyed, open-mouthed, drooling. Uneasily, we shifted as far as we could from her. Mother put a cup of cocoa into her hand and she jerked away violently, shrieking, the shriek turning into hiccups. We began to giggle hysterically. Mother told Ah-May to crawl over and rub Small Amah's back. Ah-May put her face down over Veronica's hair and shook her head silently. I could feel her pigtail flick against my cheek.

"Ah-May, did you hear me?"

A low whisper: "Yes."

"Then why don't you do as I told you?"

Silence. Another headshake.

"Ah-May's holding Veronica," I said. "I'll rub Small Amah's back."

I crawled over and started to rub her back as hard as I could, digging my fingernails into her padded jacket, wishing I could reach her flesh and draw blood. I hated her. I hated her. Everything was her fault—jagged teeth, hollow stomach, pounding heart. The flashes of light that still showed from behind the mattresses began to seem like the shine of silver dollars as Mother put them into Ah-May's hand, and as Small Amah took them away again into her own greedy, thieving fists. Wetness of tears was on my cheeks. I rubbed and rubbed that back, still jerking with hiccups.

It was morning. Jane and Luke still slept on the floor, entangled in each others' knees. Ah-May leaned against the back of the sofa, Veronica sprawled half off her lap, both fast asleep. With a sickening lurch in my stomach I remembered the big guns. But now all was so quiet that the close air behind the sofa seemed to hum. I crept out. The mattresses had been removed from the windows and the gray March dawn lit the cold, tumbled room. I peeped out of a window. To either side Dixwell Road stretched, silent, empty of people. A pile of broken bricks and tiles lay helter-skelter across it. The house in front of ours had a gaping hole smashed out of the angle of its roof and back wall. As I stared, the people who lived in it came out. All of them carried bags and bundles. The father drove his motorcar out of the garage. They piled the bags and bundles into it and went back for more. Soon the car was bulging. The mother and children squeezed in. The father carefully locked the house door and got behind the steering wheel. They drove off, engine clattering, wheels bumping over the broken bricks.

Ah-May joined me at the window.

"They've gone! They've left their house and gone away!"

She nodded calmly. "They're running away."

Running away? Cats fled dogs, robbers fled police, Chinese children fled Barstud Red Face. But families? Families leave their house and run away? We?

I rushed to find Mother. She was upstairs, surrounded by bags and suitcases into which she was packing clothes and bedding.

"What are you doing?" My voice came hoarsely from my painful throat.

"I'm packing as much as I can. We're going to live with Aunt

Inez for a while. Father's gone to get a carriage. Go down and wake the other children and help them get dressed."

"Why are we going away?"

"Because it's dangerous here. We're going south of the Creek where its safer."

Suddenly I was very angry.

"I won't go! I don't want to go! This is our house. Why can't we stay here!"

"I told you—because it's dangerous. Don't argue. We must go."

"You go. You go and take the others. Ah-May and I will stay here."

"Will you do as I tell you!" Anxiety made Mother's voice shrill. "I don't know what's the matter with you, and Ah-May too. Disobedient and argumentative! And don't you dare glare at me like that!"

Ah-May took my hand and drew me toward the staircase.

"There's no help for it, Doo-bebe. It's no use to erupt with anger. When it's time to flee, one must flee."

And so we left our house in Dixwell Road—refugees, Mother said, packed like sardines into a carriage. Father sat outside with the driver on his perch. The rest of us sat inside the square boxlike body of the carriage which was lined with rubbed and ragged red felt and smelled of thousands of previous occupants. We squeezed ourselves in, elbows in each other's ribs, flanks rubbing against flanks, bags and bundles all over us. The horse stank as usual, the poor little mangy horse who seemed not big enough to draw the lot of us and our baggage. The driver jerked the reins, the horse raised his drooping head and strained against the traces, the wheels began to turn, and we clippety-clopped for the last time down Dixwell Road.

The road was no longer empty. From almost every house people were coming out with their own bags and bundles, piling into carriages or rickshaws or an occasional automobile. We joined the exodus and proceeded slowly toward North Szechuen Road, where our horse turned south. Immediately he slowed to a snail's pace, hesitating before the wild crush of vehicles, the bedlam of movement, noise, smells.

"The East is running to the West and the West is running to the East!" Ah-May said, giggling. It was true. Vehicles and people were everywhere, heading in all directions, thousands of people hurrying to the urgent destinations of those caught in calamity, to fathers, mothers, husbands, wives, children, homes, businesses, shops, pushing and shoving, slapping reins on the backs of horses, pulling rickshaws, straining at carts, honking horns. Wheel to wheel with other vehicles we moved along a yard at a time. The shops lining both sides of the road were all closed with iron grills or door planks. Here and there a single plank had been removed, leaving a narrow opening through which faces peered. The shop owners would probably stay, Mother said, fearful behind their planks, to guard their merchandise against looters.

At last we reached Soochow Creek, which bisected the city into its southern and northern sections. But we could not cross Szechuen Road bridge. It was barricaded with big wooden trestles wreathed in barbed wire and guarded by soldiers. Harassed policemen waved and shouted at the crowds to go to Garden Bridge. With all the other vehicles, our carriage inched its way to the left, along the Creek. The muddy brown waters were almost hidden under hundreds of boats. High-sterned junks maneuvered ponderously, the round painted eyes glaring uselessly from their prows. Motorboats chugged. Bobbing sampans darted in and out of the spaces that opened and closed. Near us, a woman stood at the huge sweep-oar of a junk, the baby tied to her back jouncing about as she struggled frantically to keep the oar steady while her husband scampered on the boat's side planks, splashing in the water, fending off other boats with his pole while other boatmen fended off his. The flexible bamboo poles flashed in and out, criss-crossing, arching as they were pushed against the side of a boat, springing straight again as they were released. The boatmen worked silently, their breath misting in the freezing air while they panted and sweat poured down their foreheads.

Garden Bridge spanned the Creek at the point where it ran into the Whangpoo River. It was the widest of the bridges, and the tramway ran over it. We loved to be taken for tram rides, to cross Garden Bridge, the tram driver clanging his bell by pressing with his foot on a pedal, the breeze from the river blowing our hair, the small boats from the Creek emerging under us to round the bend of Garden Park and dodge between the big boats steaming slowly on the river. The Whangpoo was a treacherous river, heavily silted, which had to be regularly dredged if bars were not to form and if the water were not to back up into the drains of the city, forcing dirt and refuse into the streets to float about like black scum.

Today Garden Bridge was an ant mass of people. A tram was stranded on its peak, unable to move. Barbed wire barricades were drawn halfway across the bridge leaving a narrow passage through which people and vehicles moved slowly. There was a trickle moving north but a heavy stream going south, into the part of the city guarded by foreign soldiers, where law and order would be secure, where a great deal of rice was known to be stored.

"The rice in the villages and in the Chinese city will be all eaten up by the revolution army," Ah-May remarked; "there'll be none for the people."

"But its Chiang Kai-shek's army!" We had the impression that neither Chiang nor his army could do wrong.

"It doesn't matter whose army. The soldiers always take all the rice."

Police and soldiers from the Shanghai Volunteer Corps guarded the barricade on the bridge and watched carefully as the stream of traffic moved by. Sometimes they stopped and searched a loaded rickshaw, or one of the two-wheeled flat-bedded carts used to move heavy loads, which were pushed and pulled by teams of men, some at the shafts and some hitched in front with ropes, like draft animals. Many of these carts were struggling up the bridge, loaded with furniture and household goods, women in front pulling on the ropes, children leaning their small weight on the wheel spokes to help make them turn, men straining at the shafts, the sinews in their necks popping with effort.

At last we passed the barricade and were on the other side of the bridge, descending toward the Bund where it was less crowded. Everyone felt better, even the horse who picked up his feet and clacked down onto the wide avenue. On the river's edge there were strips of garden, green with grass in summertime and decorative with flowers, dotted with iron benches where people could sit to enjoy the breeze and watch the ships go by. On the opposite side, facing the river, were the city's most imposing buildings, the banks, the great hotels, the insurance companies, the Shanghai Club, which had the longest bar in the world and to which only British and selected friends of theirs were admitted. Now the buildings were all closed, their windows blankly shuttered or criss-crossed with gummed strips of paper. The doors were barred off with barbed wire trestles and sandbag walls.

In front of the Hongkong and Shanghai Bank the pair of bronze lions, sitting proudly on their pedestals, faced each other across the broad flight of steps that led to three sculptured bronze doors. They were disdainful, guarding the treasure, uncaring of the tired people who sometimes shared their pedestals. Today they stared blankly across the body of a small girl lying on the steps, head down, pigtail hanging.

"Is she dead?" Jane whispered in a tiny voice.

No one answered. Suddenly the interior of the carriage was unbearable, breathlessly hot, excruciatingly uncomfortable. We had been sitting still, our cramped limbs numb, but now we began to fidget and push each other. Petulant quarrels began to flare. Ah-May stretched her legs and toppled a bundle onto Small Amah, who glared and told her sharply not to move. Mother told me to lift the leather strap that controlled the carriage window and let it down a little to give us some fresh air. It was heavy and slipped from my hand. The window thudded all the way down and a blast of freezing wind rushed in, causing us all to gasp. Coughing and spluttering, Ah-May began to giggle. Small Amah reached across and slapped her face.

"Stop that!" Mother shouted. "Why do you ill-treat your daughter?"

"She no longer behaves as a daughter!" Small Amah's voice was furious. She was beginning once again to look as she had the night before. Her eyes were glassy and a little froth appeared at the corners of her mouth. "She speaks freely like a big person. She laughs. She thinks she can do as she likes!" She turned to glare at me viciously. "Doo-bebe is teaching her bad things!"

"I am not!" I burst out. "It's *you* who're *doing* bad things to her!"

"Be quiet," Mother told me sharply. To Small Amah: "In any case, whatever happens, you will not slap your daughter again. I will not have it."

Small Amah subsided, glowering. Glowering equally, I turned

my back on her as much as I could and stared out of the window. Ah-May sat like an image, her face pale around the red mark on her cheek.

We had come to the end of the garden strips along the river's edge and were approaching the piers where the smaller ships docked. There were stretches of concrete, machinery, sheds, capstans, ropes, dirty and oily. Between the sheds, in sheltered spots, we began to see people camping out. Each group had spread a mat on the concrete, piled belongings around the edges to make an enclosure, and erected an awning overhead. Some had already made fires in the clay cooking stoves and were going down the steps to the river to fetch water. Others were moving about, sitting, lying, hushing babies, scolding children, arranging belongings, settling down.

"They're going to live *outside?*" We were astonished.

"They've nowhere to go."

We stared at them, our first refugees. Mother had said that we were refugees, but we were in a carriage going to a house with a real roof, bedrooms, bathrooms. These were real refugees. Years later, millions of refugees later, I was to reflect that these had been elite refugees, with belongings, food, and fuel with which to cook it, temporary refugees with hope for the future—not forever refugees, with no hope and no future.

A black automobile overtook us, honking its superior way through the traffic. For a few minutes the window through which Ah-May and I were looking became a mirror in which Ah-May and I looked at each other. At once I knew that her mind was not on the refugees. It was on the breaking of betrothals—an act no longer an impossibility to be giggled at, an act which had come into the realm of the possible.

I glanced at Small Amah over my shoulder. Slap her again, I thought, slap her again.

7

French Town Crook

WE STAYED NEARLY a month at Aunt Inez's. With the utmost courtesy and forbearance, that maiden lady saw her gracious, spotless, meticulously cared-for home turned into a rough-and-ready camp. Mother and Father admonished us all the time to be tidy, clean, careful, quiet, gentle, polite, but we couldn't help making a noisy mess. There was only one bedroom in addition to Aunt Inez's, and Mother and Father had that. We four children slept on mattresses on the floor in the parlor, with furniture pushed together all around us that we couldn't help kicking and nicking. Our clothes were kept in suitcases and bundles piled in corners and in corridors, where we inevitably stumbled over them. There was only one bathroom, which always seemed to be occupied when we couldn't wait to go. We were always banging on its door, squirming with legs squeezed together, shouting desperately "Hurry up! Will you PLEASE HURRY UP!" There was not enough hot water for all of us, so we were bathed two together every other night, which made for tidal waves slopping over onto the floor while we grabbed and shoved for soap, sponge, and towels. Where Aunt Inez's toothbrush and immaculate towels had hung, there were six more toothbrushes and towels, of which four were always damp and grubby. Schools were closed and we were strictly forbidden to leave the house and garden, so we were always rubbing elbows, getting in each other's and the grown-ups' way, quarreling, fractious. Our dogs lived in the tiny garden, crowded with monotonous dark-leaved shrubs which they evidently hated because they were forever trying to dig them up. The only time Aunt Inez displayed the faintest emotion at the disruption of her life and home was when she looked out of a window and saw the dogs digging. Then she would give a half-laugh, flutter her beautiful hands, and say to one of us, her dignified voice a little breathless: "Would you please go out and STOP those animals!"

Aunt Inez had two servants, both women, a cook who also served table, and an amah who cleaned house and did the washing. The two had each had a room in the back quarters but were now sharing a room so that Small Amah and Ah-May could be accommodated. Aunt Inez's cook was not accustomed to buying food and cooking for so many, and she was not nearly as good a cook as Dahsoo. Our meals varied from a lot of something we did not like at all to a little of something that tasted good to us. Mother's eagle eye was on us throughout every meal, glaring equally when we helped ourselves to half a spoonful from a piled dish and pushed it around our plates pretending to eat, or when we gobbled our food, each trying to finish first, and then quarreled over scraping the dish. Only cook-amah smiled approvingly when we did that.

There were three servants to share the housecleaning and clothes washing, and the only problem about that was where to hang the clothes to dry, especially on those dark grey days when a cold drizzle made everything and everyone miserable. Small Amah would come into the parlor and ostentatiously drape our washing around the fireplace, where it dripped onto the carpet and steamed up against the wallpaper, leaving large damp spots. Mother asked her not to do that, but she replied sharply: how did Mother expect her to provide clean dry clothes for the children otherwise? Aunt Inez said it didn't matter and spread a thick towel on the floor to catch the drips, but we grumbled because the wet clothes made a shield which kept the warmth of the fire away from us while we crouched on our mattresses doing the lessons that Mother made us do every day.

We had started doing lessons on the dining room table, but after the first few days that had had to stop. Aunt Inez was a piano teacher, and when her pupils began coming back for their lessons we had to move our lessons to our mattresses.

Aunt Inez had two pianos, a small upright on which she gave lessons, which had been moved into the dining room, and a baby grand which remained in the parlor and which we had been instructed not to touch. Aunt Inez looked strange whenever she saw us go near it: she was holding her breath.

Each night we were sent to bed immediately after dinner. Some days I thought Aunt Inez could hardly wait for dinner to be over, but she never allowed herself more than a slight lift of the eyebrows when we were especially noisy, and she would even intervene when Mother, in nervous exasperation, scolded us with particular bitterness.

One night I lay sleepless on my mattress in the dark parlor. The sliding door leading to the dining room was closed, but light shone around it and through it came clearly the sound of five-finger exercises and of the rhythmic tick of the metronome. My thoughts ticked along with it. How had I known that it would be no fun to be a refugee? I had known it. I had wanted and wanted to stay home in Dixwell Road. Squirming on my thin, hard mattress, I thought about my bed in Dixwell Road, with its white-painted iron scrolls reaching halfway down the sides, making a cozy secret place into which my pillow just fitted, into which I could scrunch up, pulling the quilt over my head, warm and safe and comfortable, and tell myself stories until I fell asleep. I thought of Baby-amah sitting on the red velvet prie-dieu, silhouetted against the dimness of the night-light. My eyes, staring into the lighted crack of the sliding door, ached to see her. In my stomach an empty place ached for lost loved things.

The piano pupil was leaving. Aunt Inez spoke to her quietly and led her to the front door. Mother and Father came down and went into the dining room for the evening chat with Aunt Inez. Their low voices were soothing. My ache began to go away. I was almost asleep when the front door bell rang shrilly, making my eyes jump open again. Father went to the front door. It was Uncle Bill.

There were greetings and the shifting of chairs in the dining room, and the clink of china as tea was poured for Uncle Bill. They began to talk again, but I couldn't hear what they were saying. Earlier their voices had lulled me, but now I was trying to make out their words. After a few minutes I got up quietly and slipped into the dining room, blinking in the light. I went to Father, who was more likely to be lenient than Mother.

"I can't sleep," I said as pathetically as I could. Then, hypocritically, with a big smile: "Oh hello, Uncle Bill! I didn't know you were here." Uncle Bill was likely to be the most lenient of all.

Bill said: "Let her stay! She's a big girl now" and I went quickly and squeezed into the armchair beside him. He patted me and went on with what he had been saying.

"It was Doo Yue-sung."

"Him!" Mother, Father, and Aunt Inez spoke together. Father added: "That crook!"

"Depends which side you're on," Uncle Bill said. "It's true he was the big vice chief of French Town. Most of his money comes from opium, and he's incredibly rich. But he's made himself very useful to the police both in French Town and the Settlement because he's got control of the secret societies. And he's become very respectable lately, with bank chairmanships and seats on the boards of all sorts of companies."

"But what happened?"

"I don't think anybody will ever know exactly what happened, but what I heard, and it sounds true to me, is that a couple of Chiang Kai-shek's generals got in touch with the French Town people—the chief of police, they say—and he got hold of Doo. Of course, he knows Doo, and Doo's so smart he must have smelled what was coming and he must have been hanging around waiting to be got hold of. Anyway, I'm told that the arrangement they made was for Doo to supply a small army of gangsters, and for the foreigners to supply the arms and ammunition for the operation in Shanghai."

"By Joj!" said Father. Mother didn't like him to take the name of God in vain, so he had switched to saying "By George," which somehow always came out "By Joj."

"You see how it was? Outside the city, Chiang fought the Communists. But of course the city fathers couldn't let Chiang's troops into the city because that would have been the opening wedge to the death of extrality. Chiang would never have moved his troops out of the city once the foreigners had let them in. But at the same time, they wanted to get rid of the strikers and the Communists inside the city. They've been disrupting business— and more strikes to come, lots more. The Communists have been busy as beavers around here lately. And they also couldn't use foreign troops against the strikers. The troops are here to protect extrality, and the strikers weren't doing anything against that.

They were just striking, they didn't even have arms. So Chiang and the city fathers were stuck as to how to put down the Communists in the city—until somebody thought of Doo. They gave Doo the arms and ammunition, and he got his gangsters together and did it for them. God knows how much he made out of it! But it was logical—Doo was just the man they needed."

"It was immoral!" Mother's voice trembled with indignation. "Thousands were killed!"

"More than fifteen thousand," Bill said. "Mostly factory workers. I'm told that some of the poor devils thought Doo's gangsters were the liberation army. They welcomed them with open arms and got shot for it."

Everyone began to talk loudly at once, and the conversation became very difficult to understand. It appeared there was some kind of stick with a dirty end which the factory workers always got. Gradually, Mother won the floor because she was angrier than anyone else. When I could understand clearly again, she was shouting at Uncle Bill about the children working in factories.

"Kids of nine or ten working twelve, fifteen hours a day! In those silk factories especially. The cocoons are dipped into boiling water, and that's done by small children! They burn themselves, of course, and sometimes they even fall into the vats and get scalded to death!"

Bill held up his hands. "It's not my fault, you know! I've nothing whatever to do with it!"

Aunt Inez murmured placatingly and Father laughed.

"The child labor law! That interferes with money-making, doesn't it! You won't find that law enforced very hard!"

I spoke up. "The Kuomintang will make good laws when Chiang Kai-shek has conquered all the war lords. Yes, he will. Dahsoo told us." I nodded vigorously when the grown-ups laughed, more to assure myself than them. I didn't really think anybody would make me go to work in a factory, but I was ten years old and that seemed to be a dangerous age.

I thought about factories. Some were red brick and had tall chimneys, like the one of which Mother's father was manager. But some were shacks that looked as though they might fall down any minute. They stood in courtyards that oozed slime and sent up a bad smell. Did children work in those too? Small Amah had threatened to send Ah-May to work elsewhere—to such a factory? My hate of Small Amah jerked me awake. Father was saying:

"But that night when we ran away from Dixwell Road, those weren't small arms. Those were big guns."

"Oh, not so big," said Uncle Bill deprecatingly.

"They *were* big!"

I felt surprised at myself, shouting like that at Uncle Bill and punching him in the chest. Normally I liked him very much, but suddenly I was furious with him. Did we run away from our own house on Dixwell Road for not-so-big guns? Of course not! Of course they were big—very, very big. I glared at him. He sat me on his lap, facing him, and squeezed up his eyes behind his thick glasses.

"You're right," he said, nodding. "They were big."

He pulled my head against his chest and resumed his talk quickly to keep Mother quiet.

My cheek, pillowed on the front of his jacket, was pressed against something hard and the hand with which I had punched his chest was sore. He must have something in the inside pocket of his jacket, something harder than a wallet. I squirmed around and at an opportune moment, when he leaned forward and his jacket gaped, slipped my hand inside it. There was something. Gently I took hold of it and drew it out. It was a gun, a very small one, so small that it almost fitted my own hand. Father had taught us that there were only two things to remember about guns: never touch the trigger unless the gun is aimed, and never aim the gun unless you intend to pull the trigger. So I pointed this gun at the floor, kept my finger off the trigger, and said to Uncle Bill maliciously:

"*Your* gun is not so big. In fact, it's tiny!"

The ceiling might have fallen in. Everyone jumped up and shouted, Aunt Inez loudest of all. It was the only time I ever heard her make a loud noise. Uncle Bill grabbed my wrist so hard he hurt me, carefully took the gun from my hand and slipped it back inside his jacket. I was forgotten in the flurry and in Bill's apologetic attempts to explain.

He had had dinner with Doo Yue-sung the night before the big guns. He had some Japanese customers who wanted Doo's cooperation in a business deal, so they had all had Chinese dinner together and then visited several cabarets. Many people had seen them together. If there were any Communists left in Shanghai, they might be out gunning for Doo and, if they were suspicious, for Bill too. It wasn't only Doo—it was also the fact that several Japanese had been present. People were becoming very doubtful of Japanese motives in China. People were beginning to hate the Japanese.

Mother proceeded to give Bill a scolding. It wasn't enough for him to be best friends with an up-country bandit, he had also to be friends with a big city crook like Doo Yue-sung! Never mind how respectable Doo had become. The whole of Shanghai knew that he owned most of the brothels and opium dens in French Town. Never mind if Bill were not actually his friend—if doing business with him meant being seen with him in restaurants and cabarets, Bill had better stop doing such business!

"And," Aunt Inez added, "please do not again bring a loaded revolver into my house!"

Bill apologized humbly.

"What's a brothel?" I asked.

But that was pushing my luck. In a minute I was back in bed in the dark parlor.

8

Swear Word

WE WERE NOT going back to Dixwell Road, Father decided, because the northern part of the city was expected to become less and less secure. When a house a few doors from Aunt Inez's became vacant, we moved into it. Our furniture and belongings came from Dixwell Road on flat-bedded carts and were carried into the house, some through the door and some through the windows, by the cart coolies. Father had an enormous teak-wood wardrobe, bought by his father for his mother, which had not been too big in the huge rambling old house where father and I had been born but was very difficult to fit into smaller houses. It was divided into three sections, the side sections with heavily carved doors and the middle section with a great beveled-edge mirror. Underneath was a drawer stretching the width of all three sections and about two feet deep which could not be budged by one person—it took two people to wrestle it open and shut. On top, like a ponderous crown, was a fitted edging carved and decorated, about eight inches deep and wider at the upper edge than at the base. This edging was supposed to hide trunks and boxes that might be stored on top of the wardrobe.

Fortunately, it was removable. When the coolies moved this monstrosity into our new house they took it off, removed the drawer, and unscrewed the three doors and the shelves. And still it took six coolies, four hauling on ropes from the windows above, and two maneuvering ropes from below, to keep the wardrobe from banging against the walls and the windowsills, to get it into the house.

"Ang-hor-air-hor" the coolies chanted as they hauled, over and over. "Ang-hor-air-hor," the chant that gave rhythm to the efforts of many, uniting them in a single combined effort of accomplishment. The chant, the lament, of all Chinese coolies, whose name means "bitter strength." For a prolonged operation, like pile driving, the coolie gangs had a boss—not the most senior nor the strongest, but the wittiest. The piledriver was a huge log of wood attached to pulleys on a high frame which had to be hauled up to its topmost point and then dropped with an earth-shaking thud onto the pile, which was driven into the ground a few inches at a time. The boss stood on the top of the frame handling the guide ropes and looking out on the passers-by. As the coolies hauled on the ropes which lifted the piledriver, the boss chanted verses, ad lib, in the tempo of the "ang-hor-air-hor" chant. The verses were rude and bawdy, commenting on the passers-by, their appearance, their presumed ancestry, their probable destination, and made everybody laugh, not only the coolies but also the maligned passers-by themselves.

But the coolies who moved us into our new house did not laugh. When finally the monstrous wardrobe had been installed without its accessories, they refused to give them up unless Father paid them double the price that had been agreed to. They sat down on the front steps, obstructing the door, arguing, shouting, mopping their sweat, clearing their throats—aaaaark—and—tttooo—

spitting onto our garden path, large oysters of greenish mucous. All Chinese did that, and we were accustomed to avoiding the oysters when we were walking on the streets, but we had never before had them on our own garden path. Veronica was horrified.

"That's *dirty!* Look, Mother! Its *dirty!*"

One of the coolies, the most skeletal, viciously spat a word at Veronica.

"Tsor-lor."

A swear-word. A big, big swear-word. We didn't know what it meant, but we knew it was awful to say it or have it said to one. Nobody had ever said it to us before. Veronica burst into tears and Mother began to shout, not at the coolies, but at Father. "Get them out of here" was the substance of what she said. The coolies shouted louder, Veronica howled, and for a moment disaster threatened. Then Dahsoo stepped forward, extending his arms and slowly, with the flat of his hands, pushing back one sleeve and then the other, the time-honored gesture of the arbitrator. He held his palms toward the coolies and they quieted, prepared to submit to arbitration. He turned to Father, smiled in his most placating way, and said:

"Tung-kah. Mama-foofoo."

Mama-foofoo. That wonderful word that means "not good" but also "not bad"—"careless" but also "it doesn't matter." Overlook this, Dahsoo was asking Father, let it pass, be careless about it. You are being exploited, but never mind, be generous. So Father paid them double. An extra tip would have been enough, they had demanded double as a first bargaining point, but— mama-foofoo, Father paid them double, and they were shamefaced at their victory. Brusquely they stood up, restored the bits and pieces of our wardrobe, and crowded through the gate. At the last moment the one who had said the swear-word to Veronica

looked back and said to her, "Teh nung vachee—I'm sorry."
Suddenly everybody started smiling. The coolies said "zia-zia,
zia-zia—thank you, thank you" and went gaily down the street.

Dahsoo shut the gate, grinning broadly at the success of his
arbitration. We laughed too, glad to have Dahsoo back with us.
We had been extremely worried that he would never find us again
because we had left Dixwell Road when he and Ah-Ching were
not there. We had left messages to tell them where we were
going, with neighbors' servants, with the driver of our carriage,
and with the electrician who served the inhabitants of Dixwell
Road. He was a minor capitalist. He had a small wooden box on
wheels, the top part covered with glass like a showcase in which
a few plugs and wires were displayed. His screwdrivers and tools
were kept in the bottom part. Every morning he wheeled his cart
onto the street and stood behind it, waiting to be called. When
a call came he rushed to the house, wheeling his frantically
squeaking cart with him, to perform the service and receive his
minute pay. At night he wheeled his cart into an archway which
led into a narrow lane, covered it with a bit of oil cloth, chained
it to his wrist, lay down on the sheltered step, and slept all night,
motionless, perfectly balanced on the narrow strip of hard cold
stone.

But Dahsoo and Ah-ching turned up at our new house, as
Mother had said they would. Somebody had passed them the
message. Even Runny turned up.

"You see," Mother said to me, "you were so angry when we
left Dixwell Road, but it's just the same now, isn't it?"

"Yes," I said—but it wasn't just exactly the same. That coolie
had said "Tsor-lor" to Veronica.

9

Beggar Girl

ON ONE SIDE our new house had a blank wall in common with
the one next door. On the other, it looked out from a window on
the staircase across a few feet of space into an identical window
on the staircase of our neighbor. If our neighbor's front bedroom
door were not closed, we could look straight into it through the
staircase window, as they could look into ours. Our neighbors were
a husband and wife, with no children. He was European—German, we thought. She was Russian, a very pretty White Russian
lady called Tanya who wore shoes with stiletto heels, walked in
a dancing way that made her heels twinkle, snuggled cozily in
winter into a leopard skin coat and a leopard skin cossack hat
cocked over one eye, and in summer breezed about in sleeveless
dresses with low necklines. She talked to us when she saw us,
laughed a lot, gave us slabs of a delicious Russian sweet called
halvah, and hugged Veronica. "Darrrlink, you getting beeg beeg
gairl now, every day more beeg." We thought her charming and
liked her very much.

"She's a countess," we said at dinner.

Father laughed. "Not a princess or a duchess? Only a countess?"

"And she used to dance, before she got married. She's a famous dancer."

"Where did she dance?"

"She said a place called Venus Cafe."

"Venus is a cabaret," Luke said. "If she danced at Venus she's a taxi dancer. All the Russian ladies are countesses or duchesses and taxi dancers in cabarets. And they're all pretty and have rich boyfriends."

"Where did you learn that?" Mother asked.

"I learned it in school."

"Time to change schools!" said Father.

Veronica started school the year after we moved into the new house. She rode with Jane and me in Runny's rickshaw, sitting on my lap. Luke had a bicycle and was allowed to ride it to his school, which was nearer home than ours. We had to go a long way each day, through streets which were much busier than those around Dixwell Road and which seemed to become busier and noisier all the time. Especially Peking Road, which was a kind of thieves' market. It was said that if you had something stolen, you could always eventually buy it back on Peking Road. It was a dirty, narrow road, lined on both sides with shop-houses. Their street floors consisted of open shops without show windows, like garages, floored in grey cement, from which steep staircases led to upper floors where the shop owners lived or rented out premises, even the boxlike spaces under the stairs, airless, windowless, just large enough for a narrow plank bed, but sheltered from the elements. Several people might live under a staircase, a family perhaps with two or three children, all sleeping together on the planks, sweating in summer under a mosquito net, huddled in winter under a ragged quilt, but warm with each other's body heat, sharing lice and fleas, intimately passing to each other diseases—scabies, tuberculosis, leprosy.

In our rickshaw we passed the shops crowded with goods—chains, rolls of wire, implements, used clothes, old luggage, furniture, thousands of things spilling out of the shops, piled helter-skelter into baskets on the pavements or dangled from nails over the shop fronts, competing with the forest of shop signs suspended overhead, obscured by washing which flap-flapped from wires strung outside upper windows.

We saw the passers-by, crowds of them, a few well dressed, many shabby, many ragged, threading their way along the pavements, dodging the boxes and baskets, some with destinations, some loitering, stopping to gape vacantly at anything that attracted their wandering attention, nowhere to go, nothing to do, unemployed, unemployable. Even if they had been literate, even if they had been trained, jobs were at a premium. Number One Office Boys, foremen of factories, bosses of construction gangs, all who had power to hire and fire underlings, charged a fee to those they hired and collected a percentage of their salaries every month. The loiterers on Peking Road were qualified for nothing but rickshaw-pulling, cart-pushing, cooliedom. They might earn by the bitter strength of their bone-thin sinewed bodies, but even rickshaws and carts were licensed and their number was limited. Nothing to do for most of them but slide into beggary.

And, from our rickshaw, we saw the beggars. Had there been so many beggars before, when we lived in Dixwell Road? There had been the baby-shoe amah, who came to our gate every few weeks and stood there silently until someone noticed her. She had not been a real beggar, for she had for sale hand-made baby shoes, exquisitely sewn, embroidered in the finest stitches. Mother always bought a pair—she kept them to give away as presents. The baby-shoe amah was an opium smoker, Baby-amah said. "See how thin she is?" What bones we could see protruded sharply under the frailest, most papery of skins. Her forehead seemed to bulge because her eyes were so sunken. Her eyes were not blank. They held an expression of patient, enduring sadness. "She sells the baby shoes and buys opium with the money. When it's finished, she brings your mother another pair. Nobody else buys them, but she knows your mother will." She never spoke, never argued, never bargained. Just waited at the gate until Mother came out with the money, took it quietly, handed over the baby shoes, and went away. "She'll die soon," said Baby-amah. And she must have, because at last she didn't come back any more.

And there had been the church-door beggars, lazy ones, sure of their patronage: penitents temporarily suffused with virtue, the superstitious who gave because charity is said to cover a multitude of sins, the ladies of the Benevolent Association who stood importantly on the church steps and talked loudly to each other about "my poors." And also the truly pious, the truly charitable, and of course Mother. Father said: "You're throwing money away. They're professionals." Mother said: "Maybe not. Maybe they're really poor."

The Peking Road beggars were different. They came from the countryside, fleeing the fighting. Chiang Kai-shek, in the full flush of his Communist witch-hunt, was "scorching the earth." Large areas of land surrounding the Communist enclaves were being cleared, villages burned, crops destroyed, so that the Communists might not find sustenance. Thousands of peasants were also deprived of sustenance, of their homes and possessions, of their livelihood, but that was of no importance. So Shanghai's beggar population grew and became permanent. Where else were they to go, these dispossessed, these less-than-human beings? They came to the city in their multitudes, clinging to the sides of decrepit buses, perched on the roofs of trains, many falling by the wayside, losing hold, slipping off, dying under the flashing wheels. Perhaps those could be counted lucky. The others died too, as painfully, but slowly, ekingly.

So many, we thought then, but a trickle compared to the flood, the deluge, that was to come. They haunted the Peking Roads of the city, chased off the better streets by police batons. They crouched on the pavements, shaking their clasped fists at all who passed, pleading "do good works! do good works!"—filthy, suppurating, starving. They rushed onto the street at crossroads where vehicles were stopped by the traffic cops to beg from the occupants of the vehicles. They came to us in our rickshaw, though Runny shouted at them to go away, to leave us alone. "They're children. They've got no money. Chi, chi, chi—go, go, go." We said it too. "Chi, chi." Everybody said it. They were nuisances, clinging like flies, stinking, contaminating. If one gave money to one of them, twenty more descended, crying out, crowding around, barring the way with their extended hands.

But it was not good to feel one's heart well with pity while one's body shrank from contact and one's voice said angrily, contemptuously, "Chi, chi." We told Mother: "We must have money for the beggars." She said, "Yes." Father said: "Nonsense. They'll be swamped if they start giving money to beggars."

But it worked out. Our way to school took in only a few blocks of Peking Road, and there was only one crossroad at which we had to stop. Among the beggars at that crossroad were a boy and his sister. Their mother sat begging on the pavement, and sent the children to the vehicles held up by traffic. The boy had the proper beggar attitude. As though their misery had to be exaggerated, beggars tried to make their faces longer, their mouths more drooping, their cries more pitiful. But the girl, whom he dragged along by the hand, was too small as yet to understand her role. Sometimes she remembered and held out her tiny hand pleadingly, her mouth puckered, pretending to sob. Sometimes she forgot. Then, out of that pinched little face obscured by spikes of filthy matted hair, her black eyes might suddenly sparkle, her teeth flash in a smile. Always at Veronica. Once she even jumped, hand outstretched, and pulled one of Veronica's curls, laughing—"yeeee!" —when it bounced back. Her brother would angrily jerk her hand to remind her, and as quickly as her smile had flashed it would disappear again and she would give a big, sad sob.

This little girl became our beggar—or rather, we became her patrons. Every day Mother gave us money for her. If we were stopped at the crossroad by traffic, Veronica gave it to her. When traffic was in our favor and we went straight through, we saved the money till next day and gave her double. At first a dozen other beggars converged on us but the boy swore fiercely at them— "tsor-lor, tsor-lor"—and the mother hobbled out painfully to help keep them away. We were the little girl's prize, she had won us, and her mother and brother preserved us for her by protecting us from their own kind. Our patronage didn't solve any problems. It didn't keep the little girl alive. But no amount of individual good works such as the beggars entreated could have kept them alive. They were already dead, the beggars, although they still moved and cried. Perhaps the little girl continued to be fed a few morsels until she too no longer moved or cried or smiled.

And so we went to school every day, we three sisters, in Runny's rickshaw. School was St. Joseph's Convent, in French Town, on the edge of Nantao in the Chinese city. Fifty yards from the school door stood the barbed wire barricades guarded by French police which preserved extrality. Opposite the school door was a lovely shop, a shop I loved, crammed full of paper: piles of exercise books with double lines, single lines, squares for arithmetic;

mountains of pads of all sizes, yellow, white, blue: All of it blank, clean, faintly aromatic, waiting to be written on. Pencils too, boxes and boxes, all colors, all sharpened. Pens with indented ends into which one thrust a metal nib—a pointed nib with which one wrote finely but scratchily, or a stub nib which made one's writing thick and bold. Bottles and bottles of ink, the ordinary dull blue, but also red, green, and thick black India ink for drawing maps with. The owner of the shop was an old man with round glasses hooked over his ears with string. His wife took the money and his children served the customers, all able to add up swiftly in their heads the total of one's purchases, but none to read or write.

Inside school was the big enclosed "promenoir" in which we played when the weather was bad, the sanded playground with the lone pomegranate tree, the covered walk which led into the gloomy old building, always freezing cold in winter. On the left as one entered was the refectory with its long narrow tables and benches stained dark red with pig's-blood varnish. There, after Mass on feastdays, we would have for breakfast bowls of chicory coffee, a third of a long loaf of French bread, and two bananas. We dug out the soft part of the bread, forming a crusty tunnel into which we stuffed the bananas, then dunked the whole thing into the coffee. For lunch there would be tough, stringy, fatty meat, and if any girl left the fat it would reappear, meal after meal, in lonely congealed splendor in the middle of the soiled plate, until she finally gulped it down and was allowed a fresh meal.

Then up the scuffed wooden steps to the classrooms where we were taught English history by black-veiled French nuns. I suppose we were taught other things too, but what I most remember being taught is English history, perhaps because of Clara. We were given a homework task of looking up some obscure point about one of the interminable battles in which the English seem to have indulged. It was easy for me, with Mother to help, and two sets of encyclopedias at my disposal. The next morning, before class, Clara came to me. "Do you know the answer?" "Yes." "Well, I've asked all the other girls in our class, and nobody else knows. If you tell me, we'll be the *only two* to know!" I told her. I suppose that was part of my education too.

Thursdays were our day off from school, when we were allowed to sleep a little later and to linger over breakfast.

"It's funny," Jane said, looking out of the staircase window as we went upstairs after breakfast. "Look what Tanya's doing. She does that every Thursday."

We leaned on the windowsill and looked right into Tanya's bedroom, since her door was open. Tanya was at the window leaning out toward the right, waving her hand. We could see only the back of her curly head, her left ear, and her waving left hand.

"She's waving goodbye to her husband" I said. "What's so funny about that?"

"Just look," said Jane.

Veronica was too small to see out of the window, so we lifted her onto the sill. Luke was not interested. "Girls are so *inquisitive* and *fussy!*" He stumped off on his own concerns. We pressed our faces to the glass. Tanya was turning her head from the right to the left. As her profile came into view we saw that she had a big smile on her face. Her left hand went down and her right hand came up as she began waving to somebody on the left. She was leaning out to the left, now, waving with her right hand, smiling sweetly. Into the corner of our view of the street came a motor car. It stopped in front of the next house, a young man jumped out, walked quickly to Tanya's house, and slipped through the gate. In a moment we saw him run up the stairs two at a time and go into Tanya's bedroom. The door closed behind him.

"You see," Jane said. "Isn't that funny? She did the same thing last Thursday, and the Thursday before that. What do you think it is?"

"It's the doctor," Veronica said.

"But he doesn't have a bag. And he seems a bit young for a doctor. He *ran* up the stairs."

"Well, maybe he's a young doctor and maybe he forgot his bag."

"But why does she smile and wave at him? Did you smile and wave at the doctor when you were sick? You yelled and cried and told him to go away."

"Well, he hurt me." Veronica blushed defensively.

"He didn't hurt you. He just put a wooden stick in your mouth to look at your tongue."

"It *did* hurt. How d'you know? He didn't stick a wooden stick into *your* mouth!"

"Oh look!" cried Jane.

Another motor car was driving up, a brand new one, yellow with a black roof and shining silver-colored spiky wheels. It stopped in front of Tanya's door and Tanya's husband got out.

"He's bought a new car. What a beauty! Tanya will look lovely in it, especially when she wears her leopard skin coat!"

We were agog, admiring the car. The husband stood on the pavement admiring it too, then turned into his gateway. A moment later we saw him running up the stairs, two at a time, like the doctor. He flung open the bedroom door.

For a time there was great confusion in the room beyond. We couldn't make out what was happening. Then Veronica shouted:

"He's fighting with the doctor!"

"No, he's fighting with Tanya!"

"They're all fighting!"

We craned our necks from side to side in our efforts to see clearly. The three people were bunched together, struggling. We heard angry shouts and Tanya's piercing screams, muffled by the glass.

"Stop, Manfred, stop!"

But Manfred didn't want to stop. A few moments later, he propelled the doctor out of the bedroom door to the head of the stairs. He tried to push him down the stairs, but the doctor freed himself and on his own rushed down the stairs and out of the house. He was in shirtsleeves and had no tie on, but he didn't seem to care. He pelted down the road, jumped into his car, and drove off with a roar.

"Ai-yah!" we gasped, looking at each other.

Tanya began to yell again, and our heads jerked back to the window.

"He's smacking her!"

Veronica flung open the window, nearly falling out, and began to shout at Manfred. "Stop it! Stop it!" She waved frantically, while we clung to her. "Stop! You mustn't hit Tanya!"

Veronica had a very piercing scream when she was agitated, and suddenly Manfred heard her. He stood still in the doorway, one hand grasping Tanya's hair, the other raised for another smack, and glared at us over his shoulder. Tanya, sobbing, took the opportunity to fling her arms around his neck. He banged the door shut with a violent gesture.

We waited hopefully to see if it would open again, but it didn't. Small Amah called us. "If your mother were home, she wouldn't let you stare out of the window like that." The rest of the day we discussed the incident. We sat down to dinner still full of it, but Father started to speak first.

"I heard something from Young Ching today."

Young Ching was Old Ching's son, and Old Ching was the compradore of Father's office, the Chinese associate who acted as go-between and guarantor for Chinese customers. To be a compradore was a very lucrative and big-face profession, and to keep it in the family Old Ching had recently brought his son into the office. Where Old Ching was thin, dignified, low-voiced, formal, Young Ching was fat, back-slapping, loud, and jolly.

"He was telling me about a foreigner who made a big killing on the market last week. It was a very complicated deal. With China on the silver standard and so many countries going off the gold standard, and rumors that America and Britain will soon go off it too, the price of silver is beginning to go up in relation to foreign currencies, but not gold. Silver is still low in relation to gold. So this chap started with a ten percent cash downpayment to the brokers—Young Ching says he must have had some good introductions. With all the rest on spec, this chap sold gold bars first thing in the morning when the market opened. Of course he didn't have the gold bars—he just sold bars through the broker at the early morning price, and got a credit. With that credit he bought U.S. dollars, and with the U.S. dollars he bought silver. Of course, all on paper. By the time the market closed at noon and he had to settle, the price of silver had gone up, so when he sold his silver he made a profit, in U.S. dollars. Then he sold the U.S. dollars for Chinese yuan, and he made a profit on that too since the exchange had gone up a bit. Then he bought gold to settle for the gold he had sold in the morning, and the price of gold had gone down, so he made a third profit on that. So he made a three-way killing. Ching says he must have had excellent tips, but even then he was awfully lucky. Ching says in the middle of the morning it started to go against him and he turned white as a sheet, he was almost crying. But he held on, and by noon he was rich. Ching says everybody was talking about it—a thing like that happens once in twenty years. And by Joj! Who do you think it turned out to be? That chap next door!"

We understood only that Tanya's husband had got rich.

"That's how we bought the new car!" we shouted, and we gabbled out our story, interrupting each other. "Don't you think it was the doctor?" Veronica finished.

There was no answer. Suddenly we realized that the silence was ominous. Mother and Father exploded simultaneously. For the second time that day we were faced with confusion because they seemed to be angry for different reasons. Father, clearly, was furious because we had spied on the neighbors, we had craned out the window unashamedly, bare-facedly, no-facedly, watching our neighbors, like street children. But why Mother was upset was not so clear. It seemed to concern, not the fact that we had looked, but what we had looked at. Dinner was finished in almost total silence. From time to time Father snorted as his rage once more crested. Mother looked very pained. We were quiet as mice, trying to suppress even the clink of our forks on our plates.

10

⬡⬡⬡

Summer Time

FOR THE SUMMER holidays in 1931 we went to Kuling, which was a resort in the mountains behind Kiukiang, the fourth of the big ports up the Yangtze River. First there was Chinkiang, then Nanking, then Anking, then Kiukiang, where we got off the boat, which continued to Hankow, I-chang, and through the gorges to Chungking. The trip up-river took seven days and back down-river four days. The boat had a captain but the most important man on board was the River Pilot, who alone knew the dangerous currents of the Great River and could guide the boat through the terrible rapids of the gorges. We loved the boat, which seemed to fight its way against the river, sometimes out of sight of land, awesomely alone in the wide muddy waters, sometimes close in where we could see farmers working in the rice fields, water buffalo plodding, cart wheels turning, all in slow dreamy motion in the heat-shimmered distance. There were junks, square-sailed, scudding swiftly down-river with wind and tide, or strung out in long tows behind chugging motorboats, breasting the current up-river inch by inch. There were the narrow fishing sampans gliding on the water around us, bobbing in our wake, the cormorants perched in rows on their gunwales performing their ceaseless ballet. The big clumsy black birds sat hunched, shuffling against each other, intently watching the water. Flip—one would dive in, suddenly graceful, almost noiseless. Swoosh—it would come up again, cleaving the water, a fish in its pouched beak, a fish it couldn't swallow because of the ring the fisherman had fixed around its throat. With a deft movement the fisherman would make the bird disgorge its fish into the bottom of the boat and hop back onto its perch on the gunwale. Flip—swoosh—hop, over and over, all around, far and near, as the shifting pattern of sampans slipped by.

We were sorry when we got to Kiukiang, but soon forgot the boat as we rode through the foothills in a bumpy wooden-sided bus which deposited us at last in a wide shady glade. The sedan chair coolies were there, dozens of them, milling about, sorting out the customers they had been engaged to carry up the mountain. "Me! Me!" we shouted, but we needn't have because the coolies competed for us, the children, the small ones who, seated two in a chair, were still much lighter than men and big fat ladies.

The chairs were quickly mounted, the long carrying poles thrust through hoops in the light rattan, connected at the ends by short crossbars which rested on the coolies' shoulders. They carried in shifts of three, the resting coolie trotting beside the chair. Every two or three hundred yards they changed, the relieving coolie slipping between the poles and taking the weight while the other slipped out, never losing stride.

They rushed us up the mountain, Veronica and I sharing a chair, Luke and Jane another, Mother in a third. Up and up, the chair bouncing rhythmically with the swift, unchanging, thud-thud stride of the coolies, up steep narrow red-earth paths rutted by rivulets, buttressed by stones, shaded by ever-restless bamboos through which the cool mountain breezes sighed and rustled. Wonderful smell in the sparkling air of wood smoke, damp earth, new green leaves, old brown ones half buried in the undergrowth. Wonderful sound of streams gurgling, rushing, some unseen, some twinkling in the sunlight, some darkly mysterious in the deep shade. Our ears began to pop and to deafen, sounds humming through as though wrapped in cotton wool. The sun appeared and disappeared as we went around shoulders of the mountain, turning hairpin bends, the front coolie angling sharply right while the back one was still heading left, the chair with us in it suspended over an infinity of bamboo falling away, away, to the bottom of the mountain.

Veronica and I were suddenly alone with our coolies. Others were in front and behind but out of sight; we were alone in the infinity. "Wait," we asked them, afraid, "please wait," but they paid no attention, wasting no breath on words, no strength on a headshake, never breaking stride or pace or rhythm. Halfway up we came to a resting place. They set us down, and there were Mother and Luke and Jane, waiting for us. We were safe, after all, with our coolies. They knew where we belonged and to whom, and they would take us there at their own pace and in their own time. Wonderful. We jumped for joy and excitement. The coolies, squatting on their heels, sitting on rocks, wiping sweat with the long cotton cloths they wore around their waists or heads or shoulders, ignored us. We went into the rest house to drink tea but before we had finished the scalding smoky-tasting bowlfuls the coolies were at the door, beckoning—come on, come on, time to go. They had their schedules. Three hours to get us up the mountain, half an hour to run back down, the dismounted chair on one coolie's shoulder, the poles on another's.

It was nearly dark when we got to Mrs. Johnson's. The coolies took us onto a broad path, up a long steep flight of steps, set down the chairs, and we were there, in a small sandy garden in front of a house made entirely of rough-hewn stones fitted together. Mrs. Johnson came out carrying a kerosene lantern, a short plump lady in a long dress with hair that looked grey and fluffy in the lantern light. We couldn't see her face but we didn't like her voice or her manner when she greeted us. They were sweet-sour. Mother couldn't see any of our faces, but we knew she knew that we didn't like Mrs. Johnson because her voice had the strained note it had when she wasn't sure what we were going to do.

But that night we didn't do anything. Suddenly we were all exhausted, falling asleep over the soup that Er-Shih served us. Er-Shih was the servant Mrs. Johnson had engaged for Mother. We were to occupy half of Mrs. Johnson's house for the summer and to share the kitchen facilities with Er-Shih to cook for us. Er-Shih was a northerner, tall and strong as northerners are because they eat soybeans and drink soybean milk, and the soybean is the cow of China. He and Mrs. Johnson spoke a northern dialect which we did not understand. He was like Mrs. Johnson, his voice and manner so sweet, so gentle, but just below the surface we could feel, sleepy as we were, that he was squirming, probing, and we closed up against him as we had against her.

And how right we were. Er-Shih wasn't our servant—he was Mrs. Johnson's. She hadn't engaged him for our arrival—he had been there all along, serving her, and now he continued primarily to serve her while we paid his salary and served ourselves. We didn't have half the house—we had the dining room, which was a kind of outhouse, and two tiny dark bedrooms at the back which almost projected into the cliff behind the house. The dampness, palpable and smellable, came into the bedrooms from the always-dripping cliff, and other things too—black, hairy spiders, mil-

lipedes with red undersides and red dots on each of their thousand
legs, tiny quick lizards. We didn't share the kitchen facilities—
they were Mrs. Johnson's and Er-Shih's. He cooked meals for her
with food that Mother paid for and set some aside for us. We only
ate what Mrs. Johnson liked.

We washed in a small bathhouse with a tilted cement floor,
dousing icy water over ourselves with a tin dipper. The water
trickled into a big clay jar along a length of split bamboo which
went through a hole in the wall to the small stream outside. When
accidentally we displaced the bamboo pipe, Er-Shih told Mrs.
Johnson and she said to Mother, "I'm afraid you'll have to pay
for a new one." When we dropped the dipper and dented it,
Er-Shih told Mrs. Johnson and she said to Mother, "There's
something else you'll have to pay for." The dishes from which we
ate were Chinese bowls of cheap clay but whenever one was
broken, whether we had broken it or not, Er-Shih told Mrs.
Johnson, and the cost of a porcelain bowl was added to our bill.

It was Mother who really suffered at the hands of the Johnson/
Er-Shih gang. We were hardly ever indoors, and when we were
it was to gobble a meal and to fall, already asleep, into bed. It was
wonderful to be on the mountain. A thousand places to explore.
Five-Tiger Peak, where tigers were said still to roam and to kill
unwary people. The dark and dripping caves to be found under
almost every cliff. The cliffs themselves, some faced with square-
cut rocks which offered foot and hand holds for easy climbing,
some covered with shrubs and bracken, some bare red earth where
the land had slid. Luke climbed one of those, perhaps thirty feet
high. He scrambled up while we stood below, encouraging him.
Halfway up he overbalanced and snatched at two small holes in
the cliffside which seemed to offer finger holds. We saw his
fingers go into the holes, and then he was tumbling down the cliff

with something large and round stuck to his hand. He landed at our feet, breathless, scruffed, pants torn, mud in his hair and ears. He sat up, staring, and we rushed to see. His fingers were stuck in the eye sockets of a skull, buried fifteen feet below the surface and exposed when the landslide carried away the earth. A prehistoric skull! We ran all the way home with it to show Mother, but Mrs. Johnson screeched and told Er-Shih to throw it away.

We swam in the mountain streams and pools, sparkling clear and sweet over smooth rounded pebbles, gripping us with icy cold when we stepped into them. We went to Beggar Bridge, which spanned the biggest stream at its widest point, on which the lepers lived. They were driven out of the villages and had no place to go, so they lived on the bridge itself, which was no man's land and from which none could chase them away. They had widened the bridge and built shacks on each side of it, projecting over the water. Those whose noses or ears had dropped off did not dare leave the sanctuary of the bridge, but they sent children onto the banks to beg for money from those who passed. The children stained their finger nails bright pink with the juice of a plant that grew in abundance around the bridge. The children scampered on the bank, fluttering their hands, which looked like flowers in the pervading greenery, and called out "coppers, coppers." They did not get many, for few passed that way. Most of the food they ate came from the surrounding forest—bamboo shoots, young leaves, a small plant like cabbage. They grew yams in small clearings in the forest, and lotus in the stream itself. No one cared for them except the missionaries.

Mrs. Johnson was a missionary, and there were many others in Kuling, for the missionaries had been allowed to buy much property there. Some had homes, others came and went for their holidays and rest periods to the boarding houses maintained by the various sects. The missionaries cared for sick people and children in Kuling itself and in the surrounding villages, but they had to be converted. If, after some weeks or months of attention from the missionaries, a person did not convert, he and his wife and children were dropped from the rolls. But those who converted were welcomed in the chapels which dotted Kuling, they were visited in their homes, they were given rice and other foodstuffs, their daughters were taught to make lace by tatting on small pillows, and the lace was bought by the missionaries who sent it away to America to be sold for much more than they paid the makers, but of course the makers didn't know that.

It was clearly profitable to convert. Going to chapel once a week, singing hymns, reciting prayers, listening to sermons, was a small price to pay for the benefits received in return. "Our Chinese Brethren" the missionaries called the converts, smiling benevolently. "Rice Christians" others called them, and laughed. Er-Shih was a Rice Christian. He was smarter than most and made considerably more than average profit out of his Christianity. He knew just how to please Mrs. Johnson, and Mrs. Johnson was a big missionary. She was the widow of Dr. Johnson, who had been dead some years, but of whom the missionaries still spoke with reverence. He held, it appeared, the record for converting Our Chinese Brethren.

But to be pampered by the missionaries one also had to be patronized by them. Mrs. Wei was in their bad books. She was a Scotch lady whose husband was an engineer building roads for the government in the interior of China. The missionaries regarded Mrs. Wei askance because she had been foolish enough to marry a Chinese. They would still, however, have patronized her in the spirit of Christian charity if she had been willing to be patronized, but she was not, so they ostracized her instead.

"We go to the Methodist chapel sometimes," Thurda Wei told me, "but as soon as the service is over we leave quickly—we don't give them a chance to snub us anymore."

Thurda was fifteen years old to my thirteen, but we were the oldest of our group of children and we naturally gravitated toward each other. Her younger sister was Sally, pretty, bright, flirtatious and, even at ten years of age, successfully so. Luke was her slave. He would never carry any of our towels or bathing suits, but Sally had only to bat her eyes and he would carry anything for her. He even tried to carry her once when she stumbled and hurt her ankle, or pretended to. Thurda would never think of pretending anything, but nobody would think of trying to carry her either. Sally constantly took advantage of her and, even when she realized she was being exploited, she complied with good nature. I was pleased that Thurda took me for her friend, but at the same time I felt rather patronizing toward her.

"The missionaries don't like us because Pa is Chinese," she told me, not resenting it. "Ma would like to live in Shanghai, where we could meet people who aren't missionaries. Living here all year, it's only in summer that she can have a friend like your mother. And it gets awfully cold here in winter. But we have to live here because Pa's salary is so small, and it's cheap here, especially in winter."

"But your Pa works for the government, doesn't he? Maidie Chang—she's a girl in school—her father works for the government and he's awfully rich."

"Well, you see, Pa never takes squeeze. Ma gets mad with him sometimes because he always gives everything back. And even Ma —he makes her send the things back too. When we lived in Changsha people were always sending Ma things—since Pa wouldn't take anything, they thought he was hinting for them to give things to Ma instead, so he couldn't be accused of graft. People just can't believe that Pa doesn't take squeeze. Once somebody sent Ma a whole bolt of silk, a case of oranges, and a huge basket with bottles of wine and brandy all tied up with ribbon. In the middle of the ribbon was a red envelope—you know the kind for giving money in—but there was no money in it. There was a diamond, all wrapped up in silver paper! Another time a car company sent Ma a car! She didn't mind giving back the other things, but she did want to keep the car. But Pa just won't take anything, so we have to live on his salary, and that's not much!"

We were climbing uphill and it was very hot. We went to a little stream and sat on its bank, dangling our feet in the water. Everything was very green and cool among the bamboos. The cicadas, which we called "yang-stars," were happily making their earsplitting noise.

"Will you promise not to tell anybody if I tell you a secret?"

I crossed my heart and hoped to die.

Thurda whispered, just over the noise of the cicadas:

"I think that in his heart Pa is a Communist."

"A Communist! But Chiang Kai-shek will chop his head off!"

"Oh, I don't mean a fighting Communist. I mean—well, I mean, it's in his heart, he's a believing Communist. He believes, for instance, that people have rights just like government officials."

She paused and looked at me searchingly.

"You won't forget you hoped to die?"

"I really won't."

She nodded in her accepting way. I thought how lucky for Thurda that I'm truthful.

"Well—I'm going to marry Ling-tsze as soon as I'm seventeen years old. Ling-tsze is Pa's assistant. In June, when Pa came to visit us, he came too. We've known him for ages, of course. He started working for Pa when he was fourteen years old, and now he's twenty-one. Ling-tsze asked me to marry him when I'm seventeen. I said yes right away, I like Ling-tsze very much, but he said to wait before saying yes, he wanted to explain something to me."

I had forgotten the heat and the cicadas. I was all ears.

"Ling-tsze said, when he started to work for Pa, he thought he could simply work for China in whatever job he had. But he soon saw that would be impossible. He said Pa is such a good man, he works his heart out for China, he lives on rice and tea and he makes us live on not much more, because that's the faithful way, but everything Pa does is for nothing. Ling-tsze says to try and work for China in Pa's way is like trying to empty the ocean with a wine cup. You know, Pa is the Number One road engineer, and he decides what equipment and what kind of trucks and cars to buy. That's why everybody wants to give him squeeze, because an awful lot of money is spent on his say-so. I told you Pa will never take the squeeze, but Ling-tsze says that the squeeze he doesn't take is grabbed by the others.

"You see, when Pa buys anything he has to authorize the bills for payment, and then they go to the Finance Ministry to be paid. Everybody knows that Pa's bills are honest and if they go through as they are nobody will get any squeeze. So the clerks in Pa's own office pad the bills before sending them to the Ministry. When Pa found out what they were doing, he fired them, but they were just shifted to other jobs in the Ministry, and the Ministry sent Pa some new clerks who went on padding the bills more than before. Ling-tsze says that some of the companies Pa buys from even gave blank invoice forms to the clerks, to make it easier for them to pad the bills.

"Then, when the bills get to the Ministry, they delay paying

them until they're sure that the companies know what they're
supposed to do. Then they pay them, and the company invites a
man from the Ministry for dinner and gives him a box of oranges
or something like that, and underneath the oranges is the squeeze,
all in cash, that the company is paying back to the Ministry. And
it's split among the people in the Ministry and Pa's clerks."

"Ai-yah!" I gasped. Thurda nodded vigorously.

"You can't imagine all the things that Ling-tsze told me! He
says that's why Pa is always so silent and sad. He sees us living
all year in Kuling, he knows the kids at the missionary school are
mean to us, he knows Ma isn't happy, but the only way he could
make us live somewhere else would be to take squeeze, and he
won't do that, but at the same time he knows it's all for NOTH-
ING! Ling-tsze doesn't want to be caught like Pa. He says it's not
enough to be a believing Communist. He wants to be a fighting
one. He wants to run away and join them, and he wants me to
go with him."

"Are you?"

"Of course. I'll go wherever Ling-tsze goes. But we'll wait until
I'm seventeen and we're married."

"Do your Ma and Pa know?"

"Yes. We told them. Ma cried, but Pa is happy in a sad sort
of way. He said Communism is a name, like Christianity. What
it really means is a way of life. China must have a new way of life,
like Sun Yat-sen said. A life where all the people will have justice.
And whoever works for that can be called a Communist or a
Christian or whatever, it doesn't matter what he's called, he's a
good Chinese and a good man. He said Ling-tsze is a good man
and I will be a good woman. When he said that, Ling-tsze and
I kow-towed to him, and he blessed us."

I was so impressed that, for once, I was speechless. Thurda, whom I had benignly despised, whom Sally bullied because she was slow and unsuspecting, whom the smaller children teased because she was timid and clumsy. When she hesitated before one of the stream-crossing bridges made of two slim bouncing bamboo poles lashed together, the kids chanted "Thurda Wei is no good, chop her up for firewood," and she giggled and hopped nervously from one foot to the other and said, "I know I'm a coward, but would you please hold my hand?"

Suddenly I saw in her gaucheries her great simplicity, which the unknown Ling-tsze had channeled into a shining sureness. Thurda! Thurda! I gulped a big breath. She hugged me.

"I'll never tell, I'll never tell! How brave you are, Thurda!"

"I'm not brave. I'll go with Ling-tsze."

"But . . ." The implications struck me. "If the Communists are working for justice, what's Chiang Kai-shek working for? Why does he say the Communists are bad? Why is he exterminating them?"

"Ling-tsze explained to me that it's like the opera. You know —when an actor lifts up his left leg, he's supposed to be mounting a horse. Then he waves a stick and he's supposed to be riding somewhere on the horse. And when he lifts up his right leg he's getting off the horse. Well, Ling-tsze says that when Sun Yat-sen died and Chiang Kai-shek came onto the stage of China, he lifted up his left leg and he mounted China. China is his horse. He's riding China. And he'll never of his own accord lift up his right leg. His own people in the Kuomintang won't make him because they're riding along with him getting lots of face and making lots of money. Only the Communists can make Chiang Kai-shek lift up his right leg, and that's why he hates them. He hates them so much that he's not paying attention to anything but the Communists.

"Ling-tsze says—look at Manchuria. The Japanese have been trying to grab Manchuria for years, and soon they'll just march in there—they'll find some excuse like saying the Manchurians attacked them. And when they've got Manchuria they'll put Pu Yi in as puppet emperor. Pu Yi is living in the Japanese concession in Tientsin, and a few months ago the Japanese gave him a present—a silk fan with symbolic writing on it. Something like "From the Emperor of Japan to his fellow Emperor." You know, Pu Yi really was Emperor of China in the Manchu time. He was only a child, but he was Emperor until the Revolution, and that's only twenty years ago. Lots of old Chinese still believe that Pu Yi is the Son of Heaven and that it's right for him to be emperor, and they'll think the Japanese are right. Ling-tsze says that's why the Japanese are so dangerous—not only are they much stronger than China, but also they know how Chinese think. All Chinese should be getting ready to fight the Japanese, but Chiang Kai-shek keeps on fighting the Communists, he keeps on trying to exterminate the Communists, and he lets the Japanese do what they like."

In a short hour I had received a whole new education. I walked back to Mrs. Johnson's full of it, turning it over and over in my mind. It was already dark, but by then we could have found our way blindfolded around our part of the mountain. I climbed the steep steps to the sandy garden and sat on the low stone wall, dinner forgotten, loving Thurda, envying Thurda, being ashamed of myself, sorry for Pa Wei, proud of Ling-tsze, furious with Chiang Kai-shek.

Dimly, the sound of voices in our dining room came to me. Mother's voice, tense and strained. Mrs. Johnson's. I went in. Er-Shih was there too, humbly bowed forward, wearing his humblest smile.

"Er-Shih says one of your children broke it," Mrs. Johnson was saying.

On the table lay the remains of the big acetylene lamp, the only one that gave enough light to see properly by. The other lamps were small smoky kerosene ones.

"I don't see how they could have," Mother said.

"Er-Shih says Luke did it. He saw Luke climbing on the table this morning."

I said: "Luke climbed on the table because there was a spider building a web up there, one of those big hairy ones. He hit it with a magazine and killed it. But he didn't touch the lamp."

"I'm sorry." When Mrs. Johnson said she was sorry with her lips pursed up like that, one always had the feeling that she was very pleased. "I'm sorry, but Er-Shih doesn't lie."

"Nor does my daughter!" Mother said sharply.

"Er-Shih tells stories," I said. "Maybe that isn't lying."

"Impertinence!" she snapped. "Er-Shih is a Christian!"

"He tells stories," I said sweetly, "and he takes squeeze."

She could have slapped me, and Er-Shih could have too. He didn't understand what was being said, but he knew it wasn't good for him.

"You'll just have to pay for this lamp." Mrs. Johnson sounded vicious. "I cannot afford to stand the cost of damage done by your unruly children. Really, I wonder what kind of upbringing they have had!"

Tears came to Mother's eyes. "Don't cry," I said fiercely inside myself, "don't cry!" Mother blinked them back and bit her lip, summoning a reply. Outside it was pitch dark. Suddenly I caught a glimpse of bobbing lights just below us on the mountain path. I rushed to the window. The lights were candles shielded in the long thin oiled-paper lanterns that the mountain people carried.

They were bobbing toward our house. They were slung from a sedan chair. Faintly came the call that Father always made: "yooo-hooo, yooo-hooo."

"It's Father!" I shouted. He was supposed to come and fetch us home at the end of summer, but somehow he was here already, here he was, at exactly the right moment.

Mother's eyes shone as she hurried to the door. She looked back at Mrs. Johnson.

"My husband will deal with you, Mrs. Johnson, *and* with Er-Shih," she said in a perfect imitation of Mrs. Johnson's voice and manner. It was the first time I had ever known Mother do a thing like that. I burst out laughing and together Mother and I rushed out to meet Father.

II

෨෨෨

Fighting Time

SHANGHAI WAS once again in the grip of winter—wind slashing at one's face, gnawing at one's frozen fingers. Slush underfoot oozing into one's shoes. Overhead the leafless trees stood stark against a leaden sky and the sun seemed lost forever. Streets choked with traffic, pavements choked with people, hurrying, huddled. Here and there, the beautiful shapes of water turned to ice as it gushed out of burst hydrants.

Any time is a bad time for fighting, but especially winter time. Once again the city was shrouded in barbed wire and criss-crossed with barricades. Armored cars and tanks rumbled through the streets at all hours. Within the city, military deployment was for precaution, to guard against the infringement of the sacred rights of extrality. Without, it was for real.

The Japanese, their unopposed infiltration of North China well launched, deployed a splinter force which attacked at Shanghai in January 1932. The Chinese 19th Route Army, in rest camp near Shanghai after taking part in the Third Communist Extermination Campaign, spontaneously engaged them without orders from Chiang Kai-shek. For weeks the battle raged, to the vaulting pride of the Chinese and the astonishment of the world. The worm had turned. Exhausted from chasing Communists, inferior in armament, outnumbered, outclassed, the 19th Route Army stubbornly fought the Japanese.

In the city, under the continuous rumble of guns, we went through what was becoming a routine. Inhabitants of the less secure parts of the city fled to relatives and friends in the more secure parts. This time we were not refugees—but we received numerous relatives who were. We pushed the furniture together, laid mattresses on the floor, queued up to use the bathrooms, had meals in shifts. We hurried through the early darkness to get home before curfew, often waiting our turn to file through the narrow openings between barricades, scrutinized by watchful sentries. Like everyone else, we hoarded rice, sugar, soap, fuel, as supplies grew scarce.

Outside the city, the soldiers of the 19th Route Army fought, fell, bled, hailed around the world as heroes, which they were, for their main ammunition was valor. Chiang Kai-shek did not want them to fight the Japanese. He wanted to exterminate Communists first, so he cut off their supplies. When their bullets ran out, they pitted flesh against steel, blood against bombs. The Japanese, superior in everything but courage, pursued and butchered them in the narrow, tortuous streets of the Chinese city right to the frontier of French Town.

One group, separated from its commanders, retreating step by step, found its back against the barbed wire barricades. In front, the advancing enemy. Behind, the inexorable protectors of extrality: no sanctuary for you, you may not enter here, it is extraterritorial soil.

Father Jacquinot, our parish priest, could not stand it. Taking care of souls was fine in peace time, but this was fighting time.

"We cannot let them die on our doorstep to protect a principle!"

Brandishing his single arm—the other had been lost in some other fight—he threw himself into finding a solution, his red beard jutting. The Japanese commander had been a student of Father Jacquinot's: he agreed not to pursue if his old teacher could arrange an internment camp for the Chinese soldiers. The city fathers agreed to a small camp. The Chinese agreed to lay down their arms before entering it. On its scale, it was a miracle of diplomacy. Father Jacquinot made himself responsible to see that everyone kept to their agreements. He himself stood at the narrow gap in the barricade through which the soldiers entered the internment area, one by one, handing their arms to a contingent of Shanghai Volunteers. The battle was still raging in other sectors farther from the city. Big guns boomed, snipers' fire pinged. A block away, bombed out docks along the bank of the Whangpoo River were silhouetted in grotesque twisted shapes. Unseen, the Japanese pursuers lurked among the ruined houses on the Nantao side of the barricade. As the last Chinese soldier passed through, a Japanese, furious with frustrated bloodlust, leaped out of hiding, rushed to within ten feet of Father Jacquinot, dropped to one knee, and deliberately aimed his rifle at the priest's head. It was a moment etched in time. The ruined street. The kneeling man, intent on killing. The priest with his flaring beard, motionless, facing his killer. Then the Japanese keeled over, his rifle clattering to the roadway. A stray bullet out of nowhere had found its target in his head.

We all helped take care of Father Jacquinot's soldiers. If Father Jacquinot was your parish priest, you couldn't be uninvolved. He saw that their wounds were attended to, that they were fed, and we all helped to find food for them. Luke helped to gather and transport it, making endless trips on his bicycle, baskets and bags tied to the carrier and hanging from the handlebars. They stayed in their internment camp a few weeks, until May, when Chiang Kai-shek signed a peace treaty with the Japanese creating a neutral zone around Shanghai in which he immobilized the Chinese on their own soil.

Father's friend, the Editor, sat in our parlor, newly refurbished after the departure of our refugees, and wept for his country. He was an unusually tall man, very thin, dressed conventionally in western style in a dark suit, white shirt, black tie. He always wore dark glasses, and we watched the tears stream down from under them. Mother brought tea. Father sat and waited, saying nothing, which was a thing that Father could do.

After a while the Editor took a folded handkerchief from his pocket and wiped his eyes without removing his glasses, slipping the handkerchief under each lens in turn. He took the cup that Mother handed him and sipped tea.

"I'm glad you dropped in," Father said.

The Editor bowed. He and Father always spoke English. His English was impeccable. But they always called each other "Old Friend" in Chinese.

"Old Friend, I came to tell you that I'm going away. You know, after the peace was signed, I wrote an editorial?"

"The one condemning the peace? Yes, I read a translation of it. It was excellent."

"It was truth. But it was not wise. Or perhaps very wise. In any case, the order came today to close down my paper. The police came and sealed my presses, confiscated all the type, and sent my staff home. I've been ordered to pay all of them off."

"But that means nothing! In a month or two you can reopen under another name. It'll mean a few gold bars for the police and the magistrates, but you'll be able to start publishing again."

The Editor shook his head.

"But of course you can! It happens all the time!"

The Editor smiled. "I don't mean that I can't reopen. I mean that I don't want to."

Father opened his mouth but only said, "I see."

For a while they talked of other things. Then the Editor rose.

"I must go. A week from today I'll leave for Naziang, where my family has its home. Come and see me. Naziang is beautiful and peaceful. Its only two hours away by train from Shanghai North Station. Bring your wife and children and spend the day. There is much I wish to say, Old Friend, but I cannot say it now. At this moment it's my stomach that's thinking, not my head."

The stomach, not the breast, is the seat of the emotional heart, so we knew what the Editor meant. We rose and bowed to him, thanking him for his invitation and for including us in his tears. Children think more with their stomachs than with their heads, so there is no reason to exclude them from scenes and happenings. Father and Mother accompanied the Editor to the gate. He bowed once more and walked away, a not-so-old man, walking slowly and deliberately, holding himself straight, although it seemed that his shoulders were bent.

"Poor man!" Mother said when they came in again.

"By Joj!" Father said. "Its a damn shame! Closing his paper like that. But it had to come. For months before that editorial he'd been calling for unity against Japan. In fact, come to think of it, I'm surprised they didn't close him up sooner."

In school, Maidie Chang was both envious and indignant.

"You know him? He went to your *house?* How lucky you are! I wish I knew him. I wish I could have worked for him—just clean his brushes and ink plate, or empty his wastebasket, or anything.

But it's too late now! It's getting worse and worse every day. Everybody is scared of saying what they think. Why should Chinese fight Chinese while the Japanese are taking China away from us under our noses! I'd like to go to Chiang Kai-shek and tell him 'Teh nung va ze ngiung! Tsung-sang! Tsung-sang!' "

"Shhh!" I said, alarmed. To tell Chiang Kai-shek that he wasn't human, that he was an animal, an animal, seemed excessive even for the rich and spoiled Maidie, even if we had not been in the hallowed precincts of the Sacred Heart Convent.

We had changed school. The bishop had had a bright idea. At St. Joseph's the school had been divided in two, physically by a high wall, morally by a deep problem. On our side of the wall were the girls for whom parents paid school fees. On the other side were the girls for whom no fees were paid, the orphaned, the abandoned. We had almost the same curriculum, but we couldn't be taught together. We were the rich girls, they were the poor. They hated us, and we hated them because they hated us and because, if they were inferior, that made us superior. There were bitter, angry, contemptuous exchanges whenever poor girls and rich girls happened to meet. "Charity," we were counseled— don't be angry with them, they're poor girls, you must be charitable. "Humility," they were counseled by the same counselors— don't be envious, accept your station in life, be humble.

The new bishop had discerned something wrong with all that, and had invited the Sacred Heart nuns to open a school in Shanghai. St. Joseph's was now entirely a poor school and Sacred Heart was a rich school, with some girls very much richer than others. My sisters and I barely qualified, the fees were so high. Maidie was one of the richest. But outwardly we all looked the same: no jewelry, no make-up, the same uniform, white blouse, navy blue skirt. The skirt had to be long. Even for girls in the baby-class it had to measure four inches on the floor when one was kneeling. Our biggest problem now was that the girls in Public School wore tunics above the knee and laughed at us whenever we met.

"I mean it!" Maidie said passionately. "My father has a fit when I say it at home, but I don't care. He'll have to tie me up and gag my mouth to stop me from saying it!"

And, a year or two later, that is exactly what he did. He tied Maidie to her bed, gagged her when she shouted, locked her bedroom door, forbade the house to her friends, and threatened her mother and the servants with a severe beating if they let her out when he was not home.

For Maidie joined a student demonstration, was arrested, and spent the night in jail. That morning she came to school as usual in her chauffeured car, removed her gold carrings and neck chain in the cloak room, put them into her school bag, and went demurely to English class. At 10:45 we had a fifteen minute break before math, and she whispered to Jane and me: "I won't be at math, I'm going to sneak out."

"Where to?"

"It's a secret!"

"Be careful, Maidie!"

"I'm tired of being careful!"

We never saw her again at school. The next day was Friday, the day for Exemptions, when the whole school assembled and, class by class, formed a semicircle before Reverend Mother, curtsied, and stood, feet in the third position, to hear the conduct notes given them by their teachers for the week. "Very good" was the best note. "Good" was bad. "Fair" was terrible. "Indifferent" meant expulsion. I was a green-ribboned monitress and always "very good." So was Veronica. Jane, who was a chatterbox and very inventive, was often only "good" and once even "fair," but

that was when she sneezed twenty times in a row in chapel. She
was asthmatic and couldn't help it, but nobody believed her.

That Friday, Maidie Chang was absent but all the same her
note was read out—"Indifferent". There was a low gasp from the
assembled students. What had Maidie done? After Exemptions,
Reverend Mother spoke. Maidie would not be coming back to
school. The girls who had been friendly with her were advised to
drop her. She had done something "unacceptable."

Weeks later we met Maidie in the Wing On Department
Store. She was with her mother, not the woman whom her father
took to functions and who appeared with him in photographs on
the social pages of the papers. That one was his fourth concubine,
a young and very pretty woman who had been an actress. This was
Maidie's real mother, her father's first wife. She was short and
dumpy, with a very pleasant smile. She was being conciliatory and
Maidie was being sullen and indifferent. They were buying linens,
beautiful embroidered tablecloths, and sheets.

"Maidie marry soon," her mother told our mother. "Marry
foreign style. Maidie very happy."

Maidie glared and snorted.

"Who is she marrying?" Mother asked.

"Very big man. Government. Very nice man. Plenty money."

Maidie said in a voice of inhuman patience:

"My father has arranged a marriage for me, to one of his friends
in the Executive Yuan. He's forty-eight years old and has daughters older than I am. His first wife is dead, so luckily I will be
Number One. That's the only lucky thing about it."

She turned passionately to Jane and me:

"You know that day I sneaked out of school? I went to join a
student demonstration. I carried a banner which said "Unity
against Japanese Running Dogs." We marched in Chapei with

a band in front and a band behind. Some policemen tried to stop us, but we went on marching and singing. But finally a lot of police came in a van and they made us all get into the van and they took us to a police station and locked us up in a sort of cage. We stayed there all night still singing and shouting "Unity against Japanese Running Dogs." Father came in the morning and got me out. He was furious. He hasn't let me out of the house all this time, and now he's making me get married!"

She told us all about it, glaring at her mother, who smiled nervously and patted her hand with quick little pats.

"Maidie like get married. Maidie daddy give plenty money, buy pretty thing. Look, Maidie, you like that one?"

She pointed to a pillow case, elaborately embroidered in pink and orange. Across the face, in red, was stitched the phrase in English: "Victory for You."

Maidie burst into tears.

12

Marriage of Ah-May

WITH MAIDIE CHANG in mind, I was more than ever determined that Ah-May should not marry Small Amah's son. Maidie, at least, would be rich in that mysterious way in which rich Chinese were rich. Squeeze we had always known about, and Thurda had explained how squeeze worked, but still it seemed incredible that some people should have so much money—money for many cars of the latest models, for beautiful jewels, for silks and brocades, for huge houses behind walls topped with jagged broken glass as protection against kidnappers.

Maidie would have that kind of money. The house in which her father had locked her up had parquet floors, deep scarlet rugs, lush pink velvet curtains, mother-of-pearl inlaid blackwood furniture, French chandeliers, Belgian crystal, Italian marble, English silver, huge Siamese elephant tusks set upright in gilded teakwood bases, each pair meeting in an arch high above one's head. That was only one of her father's houses—the one in which she lived with her mother and her father's oldest concubine. He had two or three others in which his younger concubines and their children lived. Maidie said they were all decorated in more or less the same manner. In all his houses he employed nearly a hundred servants, who were fed and sheltered, given two new sets of clothes every Chinese New Year, and no money. Their cash income came from the tips that her father's friends gave them whenever they came to drink tea or eat dinner or play mahjong. It was the custom among the rich not to pay their own servants but to tip lavishly those of all their friends, thereby obtaining much face.

Maidie would be rich in that incredible way. But not Ah-May, who could not even keep her two dollars a month. For a long time now, Ah-May had accepted the principle of breaking her betrothal, but she still refused actually to do it.

"Doo-bebe, its no use to tell Small Amah before its necessary," she insisted. "Think, Doo-bebe. If I tell her, what would happen? Do you think she'd just say 'all right'? Do you think she'd agree and continue as though nothing had happened? Of course not! She'd call men from the village to carry me back, and she'd make the marriage immediately. She'd tie me up so I couldn't run away!"

"She couldn't do that!"

"Of course she could! Who could stop her? You couldn't stop her, nor could your mother and father. She'd just wait until one day nobody was home, and she'd let the men in and they'd carry me away. What could you do? Could you get the police to follow me? For you, Doo-bebe, they'd do that. But not for me! No, no, Doo-bebe! Its impossible to tell her beforehand."

"Then when will you tell her?"

"I don't know. When the time comes. We'll have to wait and see what happens."

"But when a thing must be done, it should be done quickly and finished with!"

"Ai-yah, Doo-bebe!" Ah-May laughed in the way she had, throwing her head back and crinkling her bright button eyes. Her pigtails had been cut off and her hair hung straight, secured by two bobbie-pins behind the ears. "You're always so impatient. Always quick-quick-quick!"

For three years the matter had remained like that. Ah-May was right to be cautious, I had to admit, but I was impatient— impatient and disquiet. So many things were changing, but not the things I wanted changed. Now only Jane and Veronica shared Runny's rickshaw. I was in graduating class and had to go to school early every morning to prepare for the Cambridge Matriculation exams. I took the bus by myself, leaving the house when it was barely light. Again it was winter, and my breath steamed around my head as I walked, crunch-crunch, in last night's snow. The sky was pale gray, the snow gleaming white. Few people were about at that hour and they walked hurriedly, secretly, hunched over, their hands tucked into their sleeves for warmth, each with his own breath-cloud hovering over his head. We had moved to French Town, to a quiet side street. On our own street the snow was still almost virgin. I walked along carefully, trying to make clear footprints without scuffing. On the main road the snow was already sullied, churned up by wheel marks.

The wheezing bus came along, a dusty dark-red color, black smoke pouring from its exhaust. Why couldn't French Town have nice double-deck buses like the Settlement? I climbed in, stepping on old debris of cigarette butts and discarded tickets, and sat on a seat with broken springs. All the other empty seats were the same. The conductor came up yawning in his dirty uniform, took my money and gave me a ticket, tearing it carelessly from its place on his clipboard. Opposite me sat an elderly man in an old-fashioned long gown. He was looking meditatively out of the grimy window, plucking at the sparse grey stubble on his chin with a pair of copper coins. He held them between thumb and fore-finger, probed for a hair, snapped the coins together over it and jerked it out. I watched him, fascinated. By the time I reached my stop, he had finished half his chin.

The cold shocked me again as I stepped out. A small crowd stood watching a dog fight. Four scrawny mongrels snapped and snarled, each trying to gnaw at something on the ground while preventing the others from doing so. I stepped into the street to avoid them, and glanced at what they were trying to eat. It was a baby's foot. The baby was clasped in its mother's arms, Madonna and Child lying dead in the snow.

I attacked the dogs with my school bag, hitting right and left, shouting, furious. Furious with the dogs, the people watching, the snow, the wind, the city, God. The dogs turned on me snarling, then slunk a few feet away to wait. Some of the people walked away, some gaped at me vacantly as they had at the dogs, two nudged each other, giggling. I rushed at the dogs again. They slipped by on each side of me, back to their meal. The gigglers giggled more loudly, slapping their thighs.

"What are you laughing at?" I raged. "Is it funny? Is it funny for dogs to eat babies?"

They went into a paroxysm of mirth. A large crowd had gathered, staring at me, at the dogs, at the bodies. I stared back, too angry to be afraid. An old man who looked like the Editor came to me, taking his hands out of his sleeves.

"Sior tsia. Young miss. They are laughing at your actions. You are angry. You are shouting. But there is nothing you can do."

"How can they laugh! How can they laugh!"

He took my elbow and led me away. The crowd parted.

"It is not seemly, of course. But they are ignorant. The woman and child died of hunger, and the dogs are hungry too. It is a natural thing. You are going to the school? Go quickly."

The tears froze on my cheeks as I went.

"And the dogs were eating the baby's foot!" I told Ah-May that night. "Ah-May, everything is changing. You remember Mother used to give us ten cents every day for the beggar girl on Peking Road?"

"She died too."

"I suppose so. But we gave her ten cents every day. When they're dead you can't even give them ten cents."

"Doo-bebe, there are too many. You could give them all the money you have, all the money your parents have, and perhaps you could keep them alive for one more day. For what? So they can die on Tuesday instead of Monday? Today, before you came home, a family was sitting outside on the curb. The father and mother, one little son and two daughters. They were trying to sell the daughters to people who passed by. Your mother sent me out with food and money and told me to ask them to go away. They went. But they'll try to sell the daughters on another street. If they can, whoever buys the daughters might be kind to them and feed them, and they'll have a bit of money to feed themselves and the son a little longer. But after that, what? They'll die. If they can't sell the daughters, they'll all die sooner. There's no help for it, Doo-bebe. There are too many."

I felt sad and afraid and a little brave, a little adult.

"There are dead bodies on the streets every morning. It says in the papers that the police drive around in vans and pick them up by the dozens. But I never saw one before."

"Now you have seen one."

"Yes."

I thought of the ragged Madonna in the snow, and of Maidie's father's concubine, exquisite, silken, dripping jewels.

"Ah-May!"

She looked inquiring.

"Ah-May. Maidie Chang is going to get married. She's sixteen, like us. Small Amah might soon begin to think about *your* marriage. When are you going to tell her?"

Ah-May suddenly looked shy.

"Doo-bebe, I was going to ask you. I've been thinking about it for some time. You know Little Bell, your uncle's driver?"

Little Bell. He had been Uncle Bill's rickshaw puller, promoted to driver when Bill bought a car. A handsome young man, who refused to wear a driver's uniform because when he was alone driving the car with Bill's old homburg on his head the girls thought he was the car's owner. Once I had asked him, "What would you do if you were to win the lottery?" and he had answered, "I'd buy a car and sit *behind.*"

Yes, I knew Little Bell.

"Well, Doo-bebe. I like him. His family owns rice land in Zose, and his father wants him to go back and help them with the rice. His parents are getting old. Their other children are all gone. He's the youngest son. And—I like him."

"You want to marry him, Ah-May? But he must be married!" He was about twenty-five years old. No Chinese man at that age could still be unmarried.

"He's not married. I know he isn't. Whenever your uncle comes here, he sits in the kitchen and talks to Dahsoo, and I've heard him tell Dahsoo why he's not married. His parents arranged a marriage for him, but when he was eighteen, just before the marriage, the girl died. Her parents had no sons, only twin daughters. His parents had three sons, and the parents were very good friends—they had mutual ancestors. So his parents had agreed that he should go and live with her parents and become their son, instead of the other way around. When the girl died, the families arranged for him to marry the twin sister. They buried a doll with the dead one so the spirits would think that both had died and wouldn't come to get the one who was still alive. But she died too! And then nobody in Zose would let their daughters marry him. With such terrible bad luck, everybody thought of course that he must be inhabited by a devil. He lost so much face that he had to leave Zose. He came to Shanghai and got work with your uncle. But he's still not married. I know he's very handsome and lots of girls would like to marry him because of that, but there's nobody to arrange the marriage for him. He tried once or twice—he paid a middle-woman, but she found out about him, and the girls' parents refused. So he's still not married."

I must have looked doubtful because she went on with a rush.

"Don't you see, Doo-bebe? His parents want him to go back to Zose, and since they're alone now he must go back, otherwise they'll lose too much face. But if he goes back still not married, *he'll* lose face. So I thought maybe that's a good reason for him to marry me. I don't know—maybe he does have a devil inhabiting him; after all, both the twins died. But that's long ago, and I'd take a chance on it. And anyway, your mother would say there's no such thing as devils inhabiting people and I believe your mother. Your mother is my mother. She's more than my mother, and I'd believe her."

I must have looked happier, because she began to smile.

"And, Doo-bebe, if I were to marry him and go to Zose to his parents' home as their daughter-in-law, they'd have to protect me, and I'd be safe from Small Amah."

I'm sure that then I beamed. Ah-May, as usual, was right. In fact, she was brilliant.

"Oh Ah-May! Who'll arrange the marriage? Shall I ask Mother to ask Uncle Bill to ask Little Bell?"

"That's what I thought." Ah-May and I hugged each other. "Quick-quick-quick, come. Let's find Mother."

We whispered to Mother for a long time behind the closed doors of her bedroom. She was horrified to learn of Ah-May's situation but doubtful about the solution we proposed.

"Of course he doesn't have a devil! But do you think he'd make a good husband?"

"I don't know. But I know Small Amah's son won't."

That was clear. Mother made up her mind and went immediately to phone Bill. There passed some days of suspense. Then Bill phoned. Little Bell had agreed. In fact, Bill thought he was secretly delighted. He had said that Ah-May was ugly, but he had seen uglier girls. The girls who thought he owned the car when he drove it alone hatted in the homburg were often beautiful but out of reach and perhaps stupid. Ah-May was not stupid. In fact, Little Bell thought Ah-May might be as intelligent as the more stupid men. Finally, Ah-May looked well fed and strong, and that would please his parents. What they needed was help with planting and threshing the rice. Weeding, which was not very hard work, he would do himself.

And so it was arranged. There was no wedding ceremony. In the village, the bride would be fetched from her parents' home to ride in a curtained sedan chair to her husband's parents' home, all alone, usually tearful, sometimes trembling with fear. Rice would be thrown for the cock god to peck at, to distract him from deflowering the bride before she reached her destination. In front of the sedan chair the bride's trousseau would be carried displayed on litters—bedding, chests of clothing, and, in a prominent spot, the chamber pot. If the family were wealthy, food might come first, festival food—black eggs still covered with mud and straw, slices cut from the lotus pod looking like Gruyere cheese with holes where the seeds had been removed, a ham with the pig's foot still on the end of it pathetically curled, all topped by a roast suckling pig.

Ah-May was fetched in Uncle Bill's car. Little Bell was driving. In the trunk was a cardboard suitcase with the new clothes Bill had given him, and in his pocket three months' salary.

Mother had sent Small Amah out on a long errand. As soon as she had left the house, we packed Ah-May's trousseau into the trunk of the car. We had bought it in small installments and stored it in Father's wardrobe, which Mother locked so that Small Amah would not see it. A box with three sets of new blue cotton trousers and jackets, and a fourth set for winter with cotton wool padding. A beautiful wedding jacket of red satin brocade with matching pink silk trousers. The bedding—Father's special gift. Two quilts with threshed silk wadding—"ss-mee"—which is far warmer than cotton. The threshers stand over a low table on which the raw silk is spread out. They have big bows like archery bows and stand for hours twanging the bow-strings into the silk fibers, which fluff up enormously. The threshers die young because lots of the fibers get into their lungs, but the result of their work is a wonderfully light and warm padding material. Ah-May's quilts were covered in silk brocade, one pink, one green. They were obviously ss-mee, not cotton, because they were so puffy. Ah-May, Little Bell, and his parents would gain much face from those quilts.

Then the chamber pot, my special gift. Like a small wine barrel stood on end, of wood stained dark red with pig's blood varnish, highly polished, with a cover and a bright brass handle.

Mother clipped her special gift into Ah-May's ears. Small hoops of twenty-four-karat gold from which dangled jade drops.

Not bright green jade. That would have cost a fortune and would have been inappropriate. Dark green jade, what the jewelers call "brother of jade," but still the most face-giving gift that could be imagined for the village of Zose.

Bill took the wheel of his car. Little Bell was installed behind. Ah-May stepped into the car and stepped out again immediately. Her bright face faded. She looked at me, frightened, bewildered, dumb—the same look she had had that first day, sitting on the stool in the kitchen trying to hide her face from us.

"Go, Ah-May," I said. "You must go before Small Amah comes home."

She stood rooted.

"Ah-May! We'll always be here. If you don't like it in Zose you can just run away and come back to us. We'll always protect you. Here is your home, here there's always rice for you and bedding. But you must go now with Little Bell. You must at least try the life in Zose. Chi, chi, chi. Quati, quati, quati."

Go, go, go. Quick, quick, quick.

Ah-May's face lit up again. She laughed out loud, head thrown back, eyes crinkled.

"Doo-bebe! Always quick-quick-quick!"

She jumped into the car and sat down on the back seat as far as possible from Little Bell. Bill turned the ignition key, the motor roared, Bill waved, Little Bell lifted his homburg, Ah-May hid her face, and they were off to the Creek, to the boat landing from which it was quickest to reach Zose by tow boat.

13

Broken Rice Bowl

WHEN SMALL AMAH came back, there was hell to pay. In her prissy way she came up to Mother complaining genteelly that she had had to go far afield to match exactly the thread that Mother had wanted. Although it was usually Mother who dealt with the servants, especially Dahsoo, this time she had insisted that Father must help, and Father was quite prepared to do so. He loved Ah-May, her brightness, her giggle, and he had always hated Small Amah, whose gentility irritated him almost beyond endurance. Usually he ignored her, but when Ah-Ching had gone away Small Amah had had to serve table for a while, and Father had tormented her to our great amusement. "Just watch," he would say in English, head bent over soup, "she's going to bump into something any minute now," and, as though he had hypnotized her, she would. The soup tureen would tremble violently in her hands and Mother would say, "If she spills the soup I'll never forgive you." Small Amah suspected that Father had somehow caused the bump, and she would look at him reproachfully and glare at us when we laughed, especially at me.

Now, he attacked. Mother had reminded him that in betrothing Ah-May to her son and thereafter adopting her, Small Amah had broken no laws and no customs. Father had said he had no objection to that, but he did most certainly object to the fact that Small Amah's son had benefited from Father's pocket to the tune of two silver dollars a month for seven years. Mother had thought that they should speak to Small Amah privately to preserve her face, but Father had said, "What face? Stealing Ah-May's money? She's got no face left to preserve!"

Now he brushed all the thread to the floor and spoke to Small Amah in his most menacing voice, and when Father was angry he could be terrifying.

"What happened to all those silver dollars you've been taking from Ah-May?"

She turned pale, then bright pink.

"What do you mean, Tung-kah?"

"What do you mean what do I mean! Tah-tah gave Ah-May two dollars every month for the last seven years. You've been taking them away from her, haven't you?"

"I was keeping them for her. She's very young and might spend them foolishly. I've been keeping them for her."

"All of them? Ah-May never spent any? In that case you should have nearly two hundred of them around somewhere. Let me see them."

"They're in the country, in my village."

"Good," said Father. "In that case, just leave them there. You can keep them as compensation. Because Ah-May is not going to marry your son. As a matter of fact, she just married somebody else half an hour ago."

Small Amah's eyes popped.

"WHAT IS THAT THING YOU ARE SAYING?"

Mother motioned to Father to be quiet.

"Yes, Small Amah. I arranged it with Uncle Bill. Ah-May is married to Little Bell, Uncle Bill's driver, and she has gone to Zose with him. She will not marry your son."

Small Amah then literally had a fit. It lasted a good five minutes. At first she simply stared at Mother, eyes popping. Then her face became dark red. Her mouth opened and froth started to pour from it, but no sound came. She snatched at her hair, which came loose in wild tangles. She stamped one foot, then the other, in quicker and quicker rhythm, beating her fists against her thighs. At last sound came from her mouth: "Ai-yah! Ai-yah!" over and over, louder and louder, while her fists beat on her thighs and her feet stamped, while her popping eyes glared, sightless, and the froth ran down her chin. It was awesome.

Suddenly she rushed at me, fingers clawed.

"It's Doo-bebe! It's Doo-bebe's fault!"

I had grown much taller and stronger than Small Amah, and I easily caught her hands. She fought me, struggling to claw my face, my eyes, hissing "Devil! Devil!" The froth from her mouth spattered me and my stomach heaved with disgust. Everyone was shouting. Father was trying to hold her from behind, but she flung herself about so violently that he could not. Dahsoo came running, already sliding up his sleeves in preparation for the role of arbiter, but when he saw what was happening he turned tail and scurried back to the kitchen. At last Father wrestled her away from me and sat her down heavily on a chair. She went on screaming, her voice so ragged that it seemed to be tearing.

"It's Doo-bebe! Ever since I brought Ah-May here, Doo-bebe has been teaching her bad things! Doo-bebe is a devil! She has broken my rice bowl!"

Father helped Small Amah to stand.

"Go back to your room now," he said quietly. "Tomorrow, go

back to your village. You'll find another wife for your son. We'll give you money. Go now and rest and pack your things."

She hobbled to the door but suddenly swung around again.

"Your daughter broke my rice bowl!" she screamed at Mother.

"Was Ah-May your rice bowl? Ah-May is a person. Nobody's rice bowl."

"Her marriage to my son was my rice bowl! I nourished her and taught her since she was a baby to be a good wife to my son."

I could no longer contain myself.

"Why didn't you teach your son to be a good son? You never let Ah-May learn to read and write, but your son's been in school since he was little. How old is he now? Twenty-two years old? And still in high school! At that age he should be in university, but he's still in high school because he's stupid or idle. And you gave him Ah-May's two dollars every month to help him to be stupid and idle! Ah-May told me when you had famine in the village, you sold the gold chain her parents left for her, and you gave him the money so he could stay in the town and buy food and be stupid and idle! And you made Ah-May eat bark and leaves from the trees!"

"That's what I ate myself! How do I know high school, university, whatever words you say! School is school, and I sent my son to school because I didn't want him to be a tenant farmer like his father. That's the way to misery and early death. Work, work, work, and pay, pay, pay. Pay the landlord, pay the policemen, pay the soldiers, pay the taxes. They say you owe so-much, you don't know how to add it up, you don't know how to write it down, you just pay! I wanted my son to learn how to read and write, how to add, so he could work for the government and *collect* the taxes instead of paying them! How do I know what Doo-bebe says— high school, university! How do I know! I only know I sent him to school to get the paper that says he is educated! He is my only son to support me in my age!"

She tore at her tangled hair.

"And now it's finished! Now he'll lose face before the whole village, he'll go away when he's educated and leave me alone! And everybody will laugh at me and I'll starve!"

I felt horrible. I saw suddenly that there could be no foreign-style reasoning with Small Amah. I had indeed broken her rice bowl. Little Bell was going home triumphantly with a wife, even an ugly pockmarked one. Small Amah's son would do what Little Bell had done: he would run away.

Small Amah was leaning against the door frame, keening softly, head bowed, hopeless.

Mother said to me: "Never mind, you did right."

To Father: "We'll have to give her enough money to last her a long time—many years. That'll help to restore her face, as well as feed her. But let's send her back quickly, at least tomorrow morning if not today."

She put her arms around Small Amah and led her toward her room, gently, patting her with little, soft gestures.

Dahsoo peeped out of the kitchen and tiptoed to Father. He whispered:

"I know one of her relatives who works in the city. Shall I phone her to come and fetch Small Amah back to her village?"

"Yes, yes." Father nodded and gestured toward the telephone.

Dahsoo tiptoed to it, cautious, important, the arbitrator, rolling up his sleeves.

That night Jane and I discussed it at great length, whispering in the dark of our bedroom. Finally Mother came in to end the discussion.

"Sometimes nothing is clear. Sometimes there isn't any yardstick to judge by. Then you just have to do what you yourself think is right. You thought it was right to encourage Ah-May to break her betrothal and marry somebody else of her own choice. Therefore it was right. It was right. So now stop worrying about it, and go to sleep. Both of you."

But still, sometimes, I think perhaps it was wrong.

14

♋♋♋

Sing-Song Girl

I GRADUATED from school and had one more wonderful girlhood summer holiday, during which I became a young lady victimized by my siblings. Whenever they could, Luke and his great friend Toby confiscated the letters I received daily from an Italian pilot, one of a team training the Chinese Air Force at its Loyang base. They sold the letters back to me for the price of tickets to a movie, or whatever it was they wanted at the moment. Once, with the spoil from three black-marketed letters, they went to Kiessling & Bader's tea room, spread the money on the table, and told the waiter to keep on bringing them chestnut cream cake until the cash was all used up.

Veronica's voice was exactly like mine and, coached by Jane, she took my phone calls when I wasn't home and made dates with any and all young men who called for any time and anywhere they suggested. Sometimes they told me and sometimes they forgot, so half the time I was scurrying to keep inconvenient and unwanted dates, or trying to explain why I hadn't shown up.

One of the dates they made on my behalf was with a young man to whom I was much attracted, to meet at 8 P.M. for dinner at the Sukiyaki Shop in Blood Alley. They didn't tell me until the last moment, too late to call and change the meeting place or request to be fetched. I was torn between going and not going. He was really a most attractive young man, but my parents would highly disapprove of him. They would be shocked to know I so much as knew the names of such places as Blood Alley.

When my Italian pilot flew to town on weekends, I dined elegantly off cutlets à la Kiev at D.D.'s or stroganoff at the Renaissance, and danced to the strains of an evening-suited balalaika orchestra, in an atmosphere of Imperial Russian splendor, bowed to by grand dukes acting as headwaiters. With lesser mortals, the brothers of girl friends, I went to movies, danced at the Cathay or the Ambassador, and dined at Jimmy's. The Jimmy's restaurants were owned by an American ex-sailor called Jimmy who had jumped ship at Shanghai with his winnings from playing stud poker all the way across the Pacific. He opened his first restaurant on Nanking Road. It had unvarnished wooden tables, each with a collection at one end of paper napkins, salt and pepper shakers, mustard, Worcestershire sauce, ketchup, and sugar in a kind of pourer. It had a menu consisting mostly of hamburger steak, eggs any style, sandwiches, pancakes, and ice cream. It caught on immediately and made Jimmy a rich man. He opened other branches in other parts of the city, but the Nanking Road branch was his favorite and there he could be found almost any night, short, neat, blond, slightly cross-eyed, watching the girls, watched by his pretty Chinese wife.

The Cathay was our favorite dance hall. The trumpeter was extra special and the dance floor magnificent. People who loved to dance went there solely to dance so it had no need of embellishments, just that expanse of shiny, polished floor, the great band, and square tables covered with red-and-white checked tablecloths.

But Blood Alley! It was a short street off Avenue Edward VII close to that part of the Bund where ships docked. It was frequented by sailors of all nationalities, and naturally by girls. The Tanyas of the city predominated, but there were also Chinese, Koreans, Japanese. The street was lined on both sides with restaurants, bars, cabarets, and nightclubs. During the day they looked shoddy and frightening. At night they changed miraculously. They glowed with colored lights, beckoning, inviting. I had never been inside them. The street got its name from the frequent knife-fights that exuberant shore-leave sailors picked for any reason, but usually over the girls.

And the Sukiyaki Shop! It was famous, not for its sukiyaki, which tastes much the same anywhere, but for its ambience and its beautiful Japanese waitresses.

Should I go? Should I not? Finally I decided to go. I phoned secretly for a taxi, waited at the door, and rushed out when it tooted so that Mother wouldn't know I wasn't being fetched. The taxi man drove quickly, too quickly for me. I wanted to be half an hour late, but it was only 8:20 when I got there. They were all there already, however, Kurt and his friends, standing on the street waiting for me. We stepped into a courtyard with a bonsai pine tree in a big pot, surrounded by flat white pebbles, soothingly lit by a bronze lamp. On three sides of the courtyard there was a low wooden veranda on which we sat to take off our street shoes and put on felt slippers supplied by the management. We ducked through a doorway, under a fringe of curtain made of strips of dark blue cotton on which white characters were printed—Welcome. Somehow the tiny curtain seemed to keep out the noise of the street. Inside, we stepped immediately onto tatami, the thick padded mats covered in the finest woven straw which covered the entire floor of the restaurant. There were our waitresses, blue-black hair dressed high, smiling mask faces white with rice powder, gorgeous rainbow kimonos, bowing low to show us into our tiny room closed off from its neighbors by sliding paper screens. There was a low round table and flat cushions spread over the tatami, on which we sat cross-legged.

The waitresses, smiling, cooked the sukiyaki over the charcoal fire on the table and served us, the men first, of course, with graceful studied gestures. I sat beside Kurt, happy, unhappy. He offered one of the waitresses a cigarette. She smiled and refused. He offered her saki from the lovely porcelain wine june. She smiled and refused.

"You don't smoke? You don't drink?"

She smiled and shook her head slightly. More of a shake would have toppled the hairdo. She delicately wriggled her shoulders so that the collar of her kimono slipped backward, revealing more of the nape of her neck, the sexiest part of the female body.

"I no smoke, I no drink, but I very bad girl."

She simpered behind her hand. Everybody laughed. I couldn't imagine why. For me, badness held an essential connotation of enjoyment, and I couldn't imagine her enjoying anything.

From the Sukiyaki Shop we made a tour of nightclubs and cabarets: Blue Heaven, New World, Celestial Delight. They were all more or less the same. As dark inside as they were bright outside, crowded with customers, some in shirtsleeves, some tieless, at small tables around an inner ring of tables edging the dance floor at which the taxi girls sat, sipping pale tea from champagne or whisky glasses. The girls were of all shapes and sizes —vivacious, bored, elegant, gamine, genteel, vulgar—but all business conscious. The Filipino bands played short numbers in quick succession. The customers bought tickets from the utterly indifferent cashier and paid the girls with them, some handing out whole rolls to grateful, laughing girls, some tearing them off carefully one by one after each dance and getting cold glances from their partners. The more cautious customers tried to make dates with the girls for after closing time. The more liberal bought up the rest of the girls' time and left with them immediately, arms draped over bodies, clinging, nuzzling. I was both disappointed and uneasy. It all seemed at the same time very tame and very rough.

At Celestial Delight Larry was drummer of the band. A slight, handsome Filipino, husband of my friend Eleanor. He had music in his feet, his fingertips, in all his body. He was pleasant in a good mood, dangerous when he lost his volatile temper. He and Eleanor lived in a residential hotel. When I visited Eleanor he was usually at home, since he worked nights. In the room below theirs lived the Second Secretary of the Greek Embassy, whom we had met a few times in the dining room. He always left the door of his room open and one day when I was going up to Eleanor's, he stopped me with a proposal that he made standing politely in his doorway while I sat on the stairs.

He thought I was too flighty, partly because I was still very young, but also because it was in my character to be so. On the other hand, he himself was too serious, too heavy. Therefore, he proposed, we should be engaged for a period of two years, during which we would act on each other as moderating influences. I would of course learn Greek and he would be promoted to First Secretary. After that, we would be married. I thanked him and said I would consider the matter, and went upstairs, quite awed, to tell Eleanor. Larry produced a flick knife and was at the door before Eleanor and I caught him. He was raging. In this hotel I was under his protection! How dared that Greek so-and-so make me a proposal!

"He wants to *marry* her, Larry!" Eleanor shrieked, clinging to his belt. "For goodness sake don't make a fuss here or we'll be thrown out again!"

She finally persuaded him to put away the knife, but ever since he had felt himself my special protector. Now, in Celestial Delight, when the band took a break, he came over to our table. He didn't like Kurt, who was a head taller, and Kurt didn't like him. I sat between them on tenterhooks, trying to make conversation.

"Let's go somewhere else," Kurt interrupted me. "I don't like it here."

He stood up brusquely and pulled me up. I looked apprehensively at the scowling Larry, but fortunately at that moment the band filed back to its dais and Larry was obliged to go. Kurt pulled me along with him, leaving the rest of our party, to the bar next door. It was very dark, very noisy, full of half-seen men, gesticulating, shouting their conversations, thumping mugs and glasses on tables. There was a tiny dance floor, but no taxi girls and no band, just a piano played by a sad, tired man, whose music was almost drowned out but he didn't seem to care—he played for himself. Kurt plunked me down at a table, yelled an order for drinks into the ear of a waiter, and frowned silently at the stained bare wood until they came. The waiter, as usual, put the chit for the drinks into an empty glass in the middle of the table. When one left, the chits in the glass were collected, added up by the light of the waiter's flashlight, and paid, or signed if one had credit. Kurt gestured toward the floor where no one was dancing. I shook my head. He pulled me up again and I was forced to go with him, reluctant, furious. We danced for a minute but could not hear the piano over the roar of the drinkers and went back to our table.

Where the single chit had been rolled up in the glass on our table, there were now several. Somebody had foisted the chits for his drinks on Kurt. Kurt glared around. Nearest us was a table of French sailors having a wonderful time. One of them looked up at Kurt and saluted gaily. Without hesitation, Kurt swung at him. In a moment there was pandemonium. It seemed that every man in the room jumped up, shouting lustily, and started to fight. Chairs and tables crashed, glasses went flying, their contents spraying all over. I cowered against the wall, making myself as small as possible. The lights flashed on brightly. The piano player suddenly made the piano heard. I glimpsed him between swaying bodies. His eyes were closed, his face had the same tired, patient look, quite unrelated to his flying hands pounding out the "Marseillaise." The fight died down as suddenly as it had begun. The French sailors began to roar out their national anthem. The non-French who didn't know the words roared out the tune anyway. Everybody slapped backs, righted chairs and tables, yelled for more drinks. As the lights dimmed again, I saw the doorman and the bouncer carrying out Kurt's unconscious body.

Heart pounding, mouth dry, I tried to make myself even smaller and crept toward the door, sticking to the wall. Suddenly a hand was on my arm, a man bending over me, saying, "Mademoiselle, I will take you home."

I went with him helplessly. He called a taxi, gave my address to the driver, sat beside me reasonably far away, and talked calmly all the way home in English with a strong French accent mainly about the French navy. When we arrived he took my key, unlocked the door for me, and bowed over my hand.

"You are not afraid anymore? It was only a small fight. That piano player knows all the national anthems, and whenever a fight starts he plays the anthem of whatever sailors there are most of in the bar. He is very successful in stopping fights before they get dangerous. Nevertheless, Mademoiselle, I would advise that in the future you do not go to such places. Do your parents know you were there?"

I shook my head.

"Ah!" A very speaking sound. He stepped back, saluted, and went to the taxi.

Next day I told Veronica and Jane that if they ever again made a date on my behalf with Kurt I would have their skins. Jane said, "Don't be silly. We'll make dates with him for difficult places, and you don't keep them." It seemed almost as brilliant as Ah-May's ideas. The first time it worked. The second time he was angry over the telephone and Veronica almost hung up, but with Jane's urgent encouragement she managed to make a date at a cinema away across town. The third time she hung up immediately after saying "Hello, Kurt," and finally, after the tenth consecutive call in as many minutes, Jane took the phone off the hook.

A few days later, Veronica met me when I came home, goggling with excitement.

"That French chap, it must be the one who brought you home the other night—he's in the parlor with Mother. He brought flowers! Not for you, for Mother!"

I rushed upstairs to tidy up, and came down sedately, my heart in my mouth. Was he going to mention Blood Alley?

He was not.

"Mademoiselle, do you remember me? We met a few weeks ago, at the reception at the French Club for my ship?"

He handed me a card. Mother had the same one in her hand. Lieutenant Gonzague de Pirey, Officier d'Ordonnance, of the French flagship *La Motte Picquet*.

"My ship is now assigned on duty to the French Legation in Peking. My admiral is paying a courtesy call to our ambassador in Shanghai. I have taken the liberty to pay a call on your mother to see if she will have the kindness to allow me to escort you to a party."

Mother was clearly very pleased. Here was the sort of boyfriend she thought proper. My run-of-the-mill boyfriends were tongue-tied young men who shook hands bashfully, made agonized small talk until I was ready, and then said "Let's go!" with great relief. My Italian pilot didn't even know Mother—I had never asked him in to be introduced; he clearly wasn't interested in parents.

Now the lieutenant explained that while the mayor of Greater Shanghai was entertaining his admiral, the French-speaking deputy mayor had been instructed to give a dinner for senior officers of the *La Motte Picquet.* It was to be a Chinese dinner at the Park Hotel, and the officers had been asked to bring lady partners. Would Mother allow me to go with him?

I thought for a moment that Mother was going to say "yes, certainly," and send me upstairs to wash my face. At the last moment she remembered my new status and said graciously:

"If my daughter would like to go, I have no objection."

I was very pleased with Mother, and told the lieutenant I'd love to go. The date was for the following week, and I got a new dress for it, a lovely wine red heavy silk long dress, with a two-inch border of sequins across the neckline and shoulders and around the sleeveless armholes. Mother thought it was much too sophisticated. I thought it was great.

The lieutenant called for me and came in to present his respects to my parents, with chocolates for Mother and an orchid corsage for me. Father looked astonished and said, "What's that for?" Mother replied acidly, "As though you never gave me flowers when we were young!" Father said, "But . . ." and then suddenly looked sad. "Flowers for Doo-bebe?" he said wistfully.

I went off with the lieutenant, and half an hour later I nearly went home again without him. The dinner party was for men only. The officers had been asked *not* to bring lady friends because sing-song girls were to be present after dinner.

The lieutenant was red with embarrassment. There was the round table laid for ten people, with damask cloth, crystal glasses, finest porcelain dishes, ivory chopsticks resting on silver holders. There were ten men, including himself, and one young lady. Everyone was standing still, bottles poised over glasses, glasses halfway to mouths. Then, with ineffable Chinese courtesy, the deputy mayor came forward. He was very happy I had come. Of course I must stay to dinner. There were no other ladies, but that meant more gentlemen to see to my wants. No, no, I could not leave before dinner, he would not hear of it! But if I wished to leave *immediately* after dinner, the lieutenant would take me home and come back for the entertainment, which would not interest me in any case, he thought.

I was swept to the table on the wave of his politeness. The waiters had already laid another place, although eleven is awkward for a Chinese meal. The dinner started to be served. It was magnificent—not very big, only sixteen courses, but each a gem of its kind. Four dishes each of the four main categories of food —from the skies, from the mountains, from the plains, from the waters. The wine flowed, warmed just enough. The talk flowed, directed and sustained by the deputy. The officers relaxed, savoring the food, appreciating the finesse of the host.

As befits the host, the deputy sat with his back to the door, the most dangerous place. I had the place of honor opposite him, facing the door where I could see instantly if an enemy were to come in. What I saw, when we were on the fourteenth course, was not an enemy but the sing-song girls. The contretemps about my arrival had delayed the dinner, and the sing-song girls, arriving promptly, were too early.

They came in anyway. Sing-song girls were members of a respected profession, not to be kept waiting at the door. They swept in, five of them, like characters onto a stage, doll-like with their shining black wings of hair and brightly made-up faces, chins high over tall stiff collars, bodies slim in colorful gowns split on each side up to the thigh. The waiters, quick as magic, produced chairs for them, placing one between each pair of men. One of the chairs was placed between me and the Lieutenant, and a sing-song girl seated herself beside me, graceful, gracious, proud, a little disdainful.

I said hello in Chinese. She stared.

"You speak Chinese?"

"Yes. How are you?"

She dropped her party manners and leaned across the table toward her colleagues—a girl, only a little older than I was, excitedly calling out to other girls:

"Hey, hey look—she speaks Chinese, she speaks excellently!"

As one, the other four girls stood up and came around the table, signaling the waiters to bring their chairs. I explained how I came to be there.

"Ai-yah! Indeed you speak Chinese like a Chinese!" they said to me.

"She speaks Chinese like a Chinese!" they said to each other.

The lieutenant was looking embarrassed again. The other officers were looking, some resentful, some amused. The deputy was looking reproachful. Then suddenly he smiled and shrugged his shoulders. What could he do? There was no help for it! He signaled the waiters to continue serving dinner.

I felt guilty and said to the girls:

"I was supposed to leave before you got here, and I'd better go now. You're here to entertain the gentlemen."

"No, no, no!" they said. "We'll be paid anyway. Its the mayor's party, isn't it? He wouldn't dare not pay us. Stay! We never met anyone like you before."

I stayed. I'd never met anyone like them before either.

They were insatiable in their questioning. How old was I? Was I married? Who supported me? My parents? And I had a brother and two sisters and my parents supported them too? How fortunate! Each of them was helping to support parents and to send younger brothers and sisters to school. I must have wealthy parents! Oh, not so wealthy. I would be earning my own living pretty soon. What was I going to do? Well, I'd start by being a secretary. What was that? It was a profession having to do with correspondence, typing letters. Oh, then I must be able to read and write very well? How fortunate! Three of them could read and write a little. Would I be typing letters during the daytime? What time did I get up? At seven! In the *morning?* How unfortunate! What time did they get up? Oh, three or four in the afternoon, whenever the hairdresser came. They each had their own hairdresser who came every day, and when he came they drank tea with him and heard the news of the day. Then he did their hair, they bathed, and they ate dinner with their families. Their parents were home by then, and their brothers and sisters from school, and they spent an hour or two with their families, gossiping and relaxing. At about eight in the evening they started to make up and to dress for the appointment of the night. How they dressed depended on the appointment. For instance, tonight the mayor had engaged their services, so they had each got a new gown— he would pay. They had—well, how many gowns? Thirty? Forty?

Now the sixteenth course had been served, and rice was being brought to the table. Nobody ever ate rice at a Chinese dinner in a restaurant as grand as the Park Hotel's. Everybody touched a grain or two and left it, to show how full their stomachs were, thereby complimenting the host. Chinese guests belched loudly. Luke was expert at producing the loudest belches, but I couldn't, I didn't know how. Seeing the rice, I tried again to keep my tacit promise to the host.

"Now, really, I'd better go. Dinner is finished."

But they wouldn't let me.

"No, no, stay! There are only foreign men present tonight, and that will be very dull and aggravating. They'll think we're prostitutes. Foreign men never understand. They never give us credit for all the training we went through to become entertainers. Anybody can be a prostitute, like those poor girls standing on the street corners in groups, with an amah to bargain with the men on their behalf. We had to *study* to be entertainers!"

Did they have girl entertainers in foreign countries too? Well, I wasn't sure—they had them in Japan. Oh, Japan! They didn't mean Japan—they meant foreign countries, western countries. These men, for instance, what are they? They're French. Oh— France is a western country, isn't it? Well, ask them. Ask this man here. Ask him if they have entertainers like us in his country.

I asked the lieutenant. He said well, no, not exactly, and certainly not as beautiful. I translated. They were delighted and smiled graciously around at all the officers, who smiled back and looked a little less bored.

Did I know any Americans? Yes, I did. Were they nice? Yes, some. Not all? Well, in every nationality there were some who were nice and some who weren't. But especially not Americans? No—Americans could be very very nice. Truly? Yes, of course. They looked at each other. Well, maybe. But what about Mei

Our grandmother—the lady from Ningpo (circa 1910).

Luke and Doo-bebe in the garden of our house in Dixwell Road (photo taken by my father).

Luke, about seven years old.

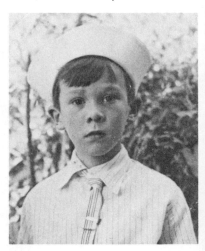

Luke and Doo-bebe astride a stone horse at the park gate (photo taken by my father).

Veronica—a sweet and tender fifteen.

Jane at nineteen.

A weekend "bag"—six wild boar and eighteen deer. The Old Boss (right) with friend (circa 1905).

Mother (right) with Father's oldest sister in Kuling.

Author (right) with friend in a "Moon Gate"—at a pleasure spot outside Shanghai.

On a picnic in the countryside near an ancient stone bridge.

Author (extreme right) on a zigzag bridge leading to an amusement house in Chinese City, outside Shanghai.

Father.

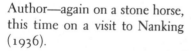

Little Bell, with the Ching-meis and a small friend.

Author—again on a stone horse, this time on a visit to Nanking (1936).

Ah-may (left) carrying the baby Small Ching-mei, with friends.

Author, getting her fortune told by Chinese City fortune teller.

Jane with son Christophe and daughter Danielle on *Marine Angel* enroute to France after the evacuation from Shanghai (1946).

Author making a homerun in a softball game on a race course (courtesy of North-China Daily News).

Mother, with a friend's children, being ferried across a creek on a picnic in the countryside.

Luke and Yvonne's wedding in Shanghai in 1948. Both have been residents of Sacramento, California since 1955.

Author (right) with Mother, outside our final residence in Shanghai—No. 22 Avenue Victor Emmanuel.

Ling? Their friend Mei Ling. She was a very lovely girl but unfortunate, misguided, perhaps haunted by a devil. She fell in love with an American and left the honorable profession of sing-song girl to become his mistress. Yes, poor girl. They had argued with her, they'd even got up early to go to the temple and burn incense for her, but she had been blinded by love, absolutely blinded.

What happened to her?

Well, this American, he had been a boss in an oil company. Perhaps not a very big boss, though he acted like one, because he had been sent away to Wuhan, and that's not Shanghai, is it? It's a small place, up the river. Anyway, she went with him. Can you imagine it? She was so blinded by love, she trusted him so much, that she left her family and her profession and went to Wuhan with him. He had his own house there, which belonged to the company, so he didn't want her to live in his house with him. He got her a small house nearby, and at first it was very nice. He gave her enough money so she could send for her mother to come and keep her company, and her mother did the cooking and washing, and she had a private rickshaw coolie who took her to his house in the evenings whenever he wanted.

But after two years he was recalled to America. And what do you think! After two years he gave her only fifty dollars as a farewell present! In his own money that was only about twenty dollars! Can you imagine how much face she lost! Poor Mei Ling! She ate bitterness then! Everybody in Wuhan was laughing at her. Her mother got up at four in the morning to go to market; she didn't dare go at the usual time, she'd lost so much face. Even her rickshaw puller was ashamed! Oh, it was terrible! What bitterness she had to eat!

What did she do?

Well, of course, she asked him for more money. She asked him many times, but he paid no attention. He was giving many parties to say goodbye and he was very busy, and drunk all the time. So a few days before he left, she went to his office. It was on the main street, near the market, and everybody passed there. She went early, with her mother and the rickshaw coolie, and sat down on the steps outside. And she told her story—she told what had happened, how she had come to Wuhan with this American two years ago, so stupid and so blinded by love. And her mother told how she had come to keep her company and keep the house for her. And her rickshaw puller told how he had taken her to his house and waited for her and taken her back home again four or five nights a week. And she told how he liked to make love, with tricks, and she had always cooperated, and she had been faithful for two years, and now he was leaving and had given her only fifty dollars as farewell present.

Of course, people stopped to listen. All the cooks of the foreign bosses in Wuhan were going to market, and they stopped to listen, and the drivers of the foreign bosses' cars, and many others. Even some people who worked in the office came down to listen. New people came all the time, so she had to start her story again three or four times. All the listeners were talking to each other and giving her advice. Nobody was surprised—foreigners don't know about face.

But finally Mei Ling's boss understood. He sent down somebody from his office with a big white envelope and inside it was another fifty dollars. She opened the envelope and counted the money for everybody to see, and everybody laughed and cheered.

I felt like cheering myself, but the lieutenant caught my eye and looked pointedly at his watch. I looked around. The officers were extremely bored. The deputy was smiling in a strained way. "Would you like to go home now?" he asked me gently.

"Oh yes!" I nearly said "I'm sorry," but instead I said politely but haughtily, in Chinese, not French, "I'm rather tired."

15

❧❧❧

Quest for Mao Tse-tung

WHEN LUKE, JANE, AND VERONICA went back to school, I went
to Mr. Farmer's Institute of Shorthand and Typewriting. Mr.
Hugh Farmer was an Englishman who reminded me of Superintendent Red Face of Big Park. Purplish, puffing, strangulated by
his collar. All day long while he dictated to us in his loud, hoarse
voice, he sipped from a big bottle of what looked like tea and milk.
The more he sipped, the more elaborately he pronounced, and the
more colorful his face became. Every day at 11 A.M. and 3.30 P.M.
he left us, and Mrs. Farmer took us over for typing. Students who
happened to see him on the street at those times reported that
he made straight for the bar of the Palace Hotel across the road.

Mrs. Farmer had a long, thin nose, a tight mouth, and a voice
like a crow. "Look up, look up," she insisted while we pounded
at the typewriters, "you're supposed to be learning touch typing."
The phone rang. She answered, looked harried, told us to keep
typing, and hurried out. The girl nearest the window craned her
neck and reported, "She's going into the Palace bar." As one, we
rose and rushed to Mr. Farmer's desk, where the bottle always
stood on the right-hand corner. It was half full, tightly corked.

The girl who reached it first worked out the cork and sniffed. "Yeck!" She nearly threw it from her. "It's *gin!*"

And so it was, almost pure gin, with a little tea and milk to camouflage it. The braver among us tasted it gingerly. It was unbelievably horrible.

Mr. Farmer didn't come in for a few days after that, and when he did he looked paler and his collar seemed to fit him better. But he and his wife were good teachers. Prospective employers trusted them and phoned them when they needed secretaries. In a few months I was in my first job, earning money.

On my first payday I rushed home feeling wealthy, to find that Thurda Wei had come to see us with her husband Ling-tsze and their baby, a roly-poly gurgling boy called Didi, Little Brother. They were in the parlor with Jane and Veronica. Luke wasn't home yet, Mother was out, and Father never came home from his office before dinner time.

Thurda looked different. She had always worn foreign dresses, belted, short-skirted, like all of us. Now she was in a Chinese gown of plain blue cotton, ankle-length, baggy at the waist because it was straight and unfitted, but hobbling at the knees because it was slit only a few inches up the sides. She had on flat-heeled tie shoes and carried no purse. Her handkerchief was tucked into the pocket of her gown under the fastening, from where it peeped out. She wore no make-up. Her straight, light brown hair was cut short and tucked behind her ears. She looked so different, almost like one of the evangelists the missionaries sent out, who were truly converted and not Rice Christians. But when she spoke it was the same Thurda—the same soft, rather hoarse voice, gentle brown look, wide smile. She carried Little Brother straddled across one hip, country-woman style, and introduced me to Ling-tsze, shyly, happily.

Ling-tsze was lean, unsmiling, with startlingly sharp eyes. I felt a little afraid of him. He was a man on guard—determined, wary, with anger somewhere deep inside him.

Conversation was difficult. Thurda spoke English and Mandarin. We spoke English and the Shanghai dialect. Ling-tsze spoke Mandarin and the Shanghai dialect, but no English. Ling-tsze was very silent, however, and soon we found ourselves speaking only English while he sat, watching Thurda, holding Little Brother fast asleep on his lap. When Jane and Veronica had to go to their homework, Thurda turned to me quickly.

"Before your father and mother come home, I want to tell you. Ling-tsze and I came to say goodbye. We're going away. We're going to follow the Communists."

It swept over me, dreamlike. The hot afternoon on the mountainside under the bamboos, our feet dangling in the cool stream. But that was years ago now. The Communists were finished, exterminated. All the newspapers said so. Nanking was jubilant. Chiang Kai-shek's Fifth Extermination Campaign was a great success. We would no longer be troubled by the Communists, their strikes in the cities, their revolts in the countryside, their troublesome agitation of the otherwise peaceful people, peacefully growing rice in the fields, peacefully working in the factories.

"But Thurda, the Communists are wiped out, aren't they?"

"No, they're not! It's true that the Kuomintang armies have destroyed the Communist bases in Fukien and Kiangsi, but quite a lot of Communists got away. About a hundred thousand. And they're marching west in small groups—west and north. The Kuomintang soldiers are chasing them, but they're getting through. They're making for the far north. There's a new leader now. His name is Mao Tse-tung."

At the sound of the name, Ling-tsze broke in, leaning toward me, fixing me with those eyes. He spoke rapidly in a low voice in the Shanghai dialect:

"Thurda should not have told you, but she was too young then and it was too much for her to keep in her stomach. You have not told anybody about us?"

I shook my head. To Thurda in English: "I've never told a soul."

Ling-tsze looked at me searchingly, then nodded, satisfied.

"We are going now. We've already waited too long, waited for Thurda to be seventeen before we married, waited for Little Brother to be born. We must go immediately. Now is the time that the party most needs us, and now is the time that China most needs the party. Mao Tse-tung is the only hope for China."

"But the newspapers say that peace is coming to the country-side."

"Peace! What is peace, the Kuomintang peace!" He almost spat the words. "It's peace for the rich thieves to enjoy their riches, to build their great houses and close their thick shutters so that they cannot hear the groans of the poor, so that they cannot see the miserable peasants working in the mud of the rice field while the landlord tramples on their backs, tramples their faces into the ground, tramples them to death!"

He saw my face and continued more quietly.

"It's true. China is stinking rotten with corruption and injus-tice. Do you know how many taxes the peasant has to pay? Forty-four different kinds of taxes! And do you know where the money goes? To the new villas of Kuomintang officials in Nan-king. To the generals who say they have 50,000 troops when they have 15,000. To the landlords, who lend the money back to the peasants for 10 and 15 percent interest per month. The peasant is at the bottom. He carries the whole country on his back. The

only one who will restore to the peasant his rights—his *rights*—
is Mao Tse-tung. So Thurda and I are going to find Mao Tse-tung
and join him. Thurda's father said it: Communist is only a name,
but it is the name of those who will clean the filth out of China,
who will bring back honor to the Chinese people, and that can
only be when China's peasants are no longer animals, and when
the Japanese no longer defile our land. There will be no peace,
not in the cities, not in the countryside, until then!"

His face shone. I stared at him, hypnotized. I had not understood all his words, but his meaning was clear. Thurda touched
my knee.

"Ling-tsze could talk like that all night," she said comfortably.
"He worships Mao Tse-tung. Mao is somehow getting the remnants of the Communist army to a new base in the north—
Yenan, they say. Ling-tsze gets word from friends now and then.
At first the Communists were trying to take things with them—
bedding, even furniture. That slowed them down terribly and
made them an easy target for the Kuomintang troops. But Mao
sent word to all the groups to throw away everything, to travel
quickly with nothing but the clothes on their backs, to find food
and shelter where they can along the way."

"And you're going like that, Thurda?"

"Yes, we're going. I'm afraid we've told a lie to everybody.
Ling-tsze told Pa he's got a better job in the west, in Kweiyang.
He left Pa ten days ago—Pa's still building roads in middle China.
I'm sure Pa didn't believe him. He cried when Ling-tsze said
goodbye to him." Her own eyes filled with tears. "Then Ling-tsze
came to fetch me in Kuling, and we told Ma and Sally the same
story. We had to come to Shanghai to say goodbye to Ling-tsze's
parents, and we told them the same thing too. I feel so bad to
lie like that. But it's too dangerous to tell the truth. We're telling

you because you already knew about it, and because—well . . ." she looked very sad for a moment ". . . because I want *somebody* to know where we're really going. We'll probably never see our parents or any of you again." She smiled at me, lips trembling. I gulped a big, big lump in my throat. After a moment I asked, "Are you taking Little Brother?"

"Yes, of course. It's easier to take him now than if he'd been a little older. He's still such a baby that he sleeps most of the time, and we won't have to try and find special food for him. I'm still feeding him, and I have plenty of milk. Besides, he's a Communist too, I suppose."

"Thurda, are you really a Communist?"

"Me? I'm Ling-tsze's wife."

She smiled, a beautiful smile. Her whole face lit up.

Ling-tsze's wife. Ling-tsze says. Off to the west, the north, because Ling-tsze says. No home, no roof, foraging for food, running, hiding, looking for someone called Mao Tse-tung who would restore justice and dignity and honor to China.

"Oh Thurda! Take care!"

"Of course we'll take care!"

She laughed and hugged me.

Mother came home, and then Father and Luke. There were more introductions, more admiration of Little Brother, more talk of Pa on the road, of Ma and Sally in Kuling—maybe they would come to Shanghai next winter—explanations about Ling-tsze's new job in Kweiyang. When they rose to go, Ling-tsze kowtowed to Mother, saying that Mother was Ma's most beloved friend, asking Mother to look after Ma and Sally if they should need it. Mother was surprised by his intensity but said of course she would. We all kissed and hugged Thurda and Little Brother, and wished them good fortune. I went with them to the gate and watched them down the road, tall Ling-tsze and short, plump Thurda, Little Brother on her hip—watched them go off to join what history now knows as The Long March.

Thurda. Is she alive still? Will she read this and know how much I loved and admired her?

That night I went to bed early but couldn't sleep. There was too much to think about. At last I rose and went down to the kitchen to boil some milk. Dahsoo was still there, for once alone, pottering about his dishes.

"Aren't you going home tonight?"

"Not yet. I feel like making music."

Among his other accomplishments, Dahsoo played the Chinese fiddle. He produced his instrument now, a short fat hollow bamboo tube, from which three catgut strings were stretched to a thin crossbar. The bow was another strip of bamboo to which catgut was attached. He sat on a kitchen stool, the instrument held vertically in his lap, and began to scrape from it screeching sounds in wildly varying tones. I winced but didn't stop my ears as I would have liked. He sang to his own accompaniment, in the high-pitched nasal artificial voice that the Chinese use for singing. After a minute he stopped singing and said to me:

"That Chinese man who came today—he's a Communist, isn't he?"

"What!" I turned, astonished. "What gave you that idea?"

He smiled and went on playing, eyes closed, head bowed over his fiddle.

"You don't have to answer. I know."

"What do you know?"

"I know what Communists look like. They have angry eyes."

A long, contemplative screech.

"I don't say they are wrong. Perhaps they are right."

"Will you stop that noise and tell me what you mean?"

He stayed his bow.

"Doo-bebe. Many years ago, when you were small, I told you that the Kuomintang party was good. I thought so then, and perhaps they were good in the beginning. Perhaps they were. But now—now, why is Chiang Kai-shek fighting the Communists instead of the Japanese? Why should Chinese fight Chinese while the Japanese are taking our mountains and our rivers? They say that the Communists are bad, that they're always making trouble. I don't know. Maybe they're bad. But if so, then all China is going bad, because I *know* that the Kuomintang is bad. I know that now."

He bent his head again and drew an excruciating screech from the fiddle.

I took my milk and went back to bed, but even the milk did not make me sleep.

16

⊚⊚⊚

The Filthy Rich and the Filthy Poor

IN OUR OFFICE we dealt all the time with various branches of the Kuomintang government in Nanking. Our biggest business was in tires and inner tubes for cars, trucks, buses, airplanes, for civilian use as well as for the army. The business was so big that all the tire companies got together and agreed not to cut each other's throats in competition. Each would have a turn to take a piece of business, when all the others would quote higher prices. It worked quite well for a time but broke down when one company manager, quoting a high price and never thinking he would get the business, promised a big squeeze to the government official who phoned him about it. Lo and behold, to his astonishment and chagrin he got the business, and lost money because the squeeze he had promised was bigger than his profit. That set everyone to cutting each other's throats again, and everyone found it very difficult to convince government officials that they really could not keep on paying squeeze at that one-time level.

At first, it had all been very interesting, but after a year or so it became dull. I amused myself by setting time targets for myself and trying to beat them: so many minutes to type a page transcribing from shorthand notes, so many points deducted for each error. I became expert and very quick, which left me time to read the newspapers and, if our bosses weren't in, to talk with the compradore, whose name was shown in the English language company register as Mr. Z.T. Shih. The bosses called him Z.T. or Mr. Shee because his surname in the Shanghai Chinese dialect was unpronounceable to them. It was like the letter S long drawn out —a hissing sound: Ss. I called him that and, in the Chinese style, I always added "si-sang" to his name—"born before me," thus "older than I am," a title given to people, older or younger, whom one respected.

Ss si-sang had three sons and was very worried about them. Madame Chiang Kai-shek was promoting the New Life Movement, to which all young people were exhorted to subscribe. It invoked all the ancient Chinese virtues: filial piety, chastity, modesty, honor, loyalty. With great joy, Ss si-sang had called New Life to the attention of his sons, and was hurt and bewildered when they laughed.

"They laugh!" he told me. "They say, 'Father, we respect you, we respect mother, we respect all those who are aged. We behave honorably. We are modest.' I say 'Then why do you laugh?' and they answer 'Because who are they in Nanking to tell us to do good things?' They say 'Look, father, look at this list of New Life virtues: brush your teeth; button your clothes; dress neatly; do not spit on the streets; do not take bribes.' And they laugh!"

I began: "Ss si-sang . . ." but he interrupted me.

"There, you see! Although you don't need to do so, you call me 'si-sang.' But my children, who should refer to those in authority as 'si-sang,' they call them 'tsung-sang' instead!"

The same word that Maidie had used about Chiang Kai-shek: animal.

I said: "Ss si-sang, don't be angry with your children, and don't be angry with me if I remind you: here you are working and earning a percentage of the profits. Don't you know about those nice boxes of oranges and candy that our bosses sometimes take to the government officials? Don't you know what lies underneath the oranges and candy?"

He swung around, alarmed, and hissed at me:

"Sshhh! You should not speak of such things. It is dangerous!"

"Ss si-sang. That's why your children laugh."

He was called to the telephone then, and began as usual to shout over it. The clerks said that he didn't need the phone—if he shouted out the window, the person at the other end would hear him. Later he came back to me.

"But these are the people who are in power!"

"That's right," I said.

"There's nothing I can do about it!"

"That's right," I said. "I'm not saying you should or could do anything. I'm just saying that's why your children laugh."

He leaned over and whispered: "Do you think my children are Communist?"

"Are they here, in Shanghai?"

"Yes, they're all here."

"Then I don't think they're Communist. At least, not real ones. At least, not yet."

He sighed.

"The worst thing is to be Communist! Communism is a terrible thing. The Communists want to disrupt business, to make strikes, to make everybody poor."

"Are you rich, Ss si-sang?"

"I'm not rich at all!" He denied it hastily. "My family has a little land in the south that we rent to peasants. My father has a rice shop and my brothers have a small rice-milling business. I work here but I don't make much money, as you know. I'm not rich, but the little I have the Communists would take from me!"

He went back to his desk, shaking his head.

The little land, the little rice shop, the little rice-milling business. The peasants grew the rice and paid Ss si-sang's family land-rent in rice, the brothers milled it and no doubt acted also as middlemen buying up padi, unthreshed or unharvested rice, at cheap prices from farmers desperate for cash, and the father sold it. Rich enough, I thought.

The phone rang, this time for me. It was the lieutenant, whom we now called Gonzie. His ship was in Shanghai again for a few days—could he come to dinner? Indeed he could! It would make a welcome change.

Life was still gay, but somehow it didn't taste as good as it used to. We could no longer have a wonderful time for a few dollars dancing at the Cathay; it had closed up. It had been too simple —just good music, good floor, good dancing—it couldn't make money anymore. Cabarets had proliferated all over town and were beginning to move out of town where they could openly conduct roulette and chemin-de-fer in upstairs rooms. Floor shows had degenerated—in some nightclubs, where patrons threw silver dollars at the showgirls they preferred, one felt squeamish about watching them. There were more pretentious night spots, but they too were tawdry behind their glittering façades. They catered to a new clientele. New legions of the world's outcasts were coming to our free city, where passports and identity papers were not demanded of those who entered. Many came as to a haven, but others were predators, scenting deterioration, seeking the quick dollar, the easy prey. They were to be seen in increasing numbers, unsavory, brushed and toilet-watered but not washed.

Our parents deplored them—what is our city coming to!—and we shunned them with distaste.

There were dozens of new restaurants, some big and showy, some small and intimate, each specializing in a different kind of national food. The Chinese restaurants also specialized: Peking duck, roast suckling pig, piquant Szechuen food, Cantonese dishes, the typical Shanghai dishes, including "Eight Precious Rice" which I have never had elsewhere. Gourmets even took the trouble to line up outside coolie-food shops at the times when "pao-tsze" came steaming hot from the ovens: those light rice-flour dumplings, filled with juicy bits of pork, running gravy when one bit into them, which were steamed in large, globular clay ovens, stuck in rows to the curved inside walls.

Gonzie adored Chinese food and usually ordered too much of it, more than we could eat. Once, at Sun Ya on Nanking Road, sitting with an absolutely full tummy before dishes still half-full of delicious meats, bowls almost full of rice, I asked the waiter for a cardboard box from the restaurant's cake counter and filled it with the left-over food. When we left, I gave the box to the first beggar I saw, just outside the door of the restaurant, a woman with two small children. At first she wouldn't take it. She wanted money. What suspicious thing was I trying to hand her? I lifted the cover, and she saw the food. Without a sound she snatched the box from me, plumped down onto the sidewalk, pulled her children down beside her. In a split second they were wolfing the food, shoving it into their mouths with both hands, gulping, not tasting, not chewing, just getting it into their stomachs as fast as they could. Gonzie took my hand and we quickly walked away.

And so we lived.

Jane was out of school and having her go at Mr. Farmer, who was still guzzling gin-tea-and-milk. Jane reported that he was now leaving for the Palace Hotel bar at 10:30 each morning, and poor Mrs. Farmer was looking cadaverous. Luke, as the sole son of the family, was slated for university in Hongkong next year and was meantime gaining fame as a sportsman. Veronica was still in school, a sweet and tender fifteen.

We learned from a letter written by a professional scribe at the behest of Little Bell that Ah-May had had a girl child, and were relieved by his observation that his parents were happy to have a grandchild at home, even a girl.

We read every day for weeks and months that Generalissimo Chiang Kai-shek had exterminated the Communists. The news was praised, rejoiced in, laughed at, mourned, scorned. Then the official admission: a few thousand Communist renegades, including the archtraitor Mao Tse-tung, had escaped the Kuomintang dragnet and were holed up in the mountain caves of Yenan, a nest of vipers. Another Extermination Campaign would be necessary. The Generalissimo's brothers-in-law, H.H. Kung and T.V. Soong, high up in Kuomintang circles, cajoled more enormous loans from the United States, while every day our money became more inadequate because of the way prices were shooting up.

Uncle Bill was among those who made fortunes dealing with Japanese businessmen in the south, while in the north Japanese soldiers descended to the gates of Peking. Rumor had it that the Kuomintang Defense Minister had signed a treaty with the Japanese generals and had withdrawn all Chinese troops from the north. A new edict had been issued: it was a capital crime, punishable by death, to maintain that resistance to the Japanese was more important than extermination of Chinese Communists.

Japanese entrepreneurs and their Chinese counterparts were flooding China with cheap opium. We saw a group of coolies, those ever vulnerable scapegoats, dragged to the place of public execution, ropes around their necks, for having violated New Life by smoking opium. Ruined effigies of men, nearly naked, glassy-eyed, stumbling, beyond humanity.

We went to Maidie Chang's simple Methodist wedding—like the Generalissimo, her husband had professed Christianity—and to the magnificent reception for five thousand guests that followed at the Park Hotel. And daily read of the students who were risking their heads by following in Maidie's footsteps, carrying banners and shouting for unity against Japan.

We ate the good food both in restaurants and at home, cooked by our Dahsoo, who had completely resigned his politician role and now played the fiddle to his guests in our kitchen. We danced and went to the movies. In summer we played tennis and softball and we swam. In winter we rode horseback, played badminton, and stood in freezing winds watching our famous brother play football.

And all around us, all the time, the filthy rich and the filthy poor.

17

Prediction

FATHER HAD A LETTER from the Editor: Old Friend, when are you going to keep your promise to come and see me in Naziang?

We went one lovely Sunday in early June, all of us except Luke, who was at Hongkong University. The wang-mei-ti was over—that dripping month when the rain drizzled constantly and our shoes grew disgusting rims of mold inside the toes. The sun shone that day, not yet too hot, from a gentle sky. We took the train at Shanghai South Station, a chuffing train that ambled through the green countryside, stopping at small stations where there were sudden frantic melees at the train doors, people pushing to get out and pushing to get in. It was the custom to push—people could stand, sit, squat for hours, calmly waiting, but the moment there was a door to get through people pushed and shoved as though evil spirits were after them. Now, after struggling into the train, mussed and panting, they sank onto seats, beaming, friends choosing seats at opposite ends of the carriage and shouting to each other for the rest of the journey in their loud country voices.

Naziang lay in the sun, a small town open to the sky, no tall houses to obstruct nature. A main street, dusty and yellowish. A marketplace, vegetables piled high, fish with bulging dead eyes lying among chips of melting ice, pig carcasses hanging from hooks, butchers wielding their great choppers, cut meat laid out, every part of the animal from the pathetic little trotters to the blank-eyed snouts to blood being caught in wooden buckets under the counters. Flies buzzing in clouds. People buying, selling, bargaining, pretending to walk off with outraged gestures, turning back when the vendors gave in and lowered their prices. Children underfoot, intent on their games. Dogs sniffing, mules and donkeys patiently waiting, twitching their ears, lifting their tails to let out lumps of dung which lay unnoticed, steaming gently, beside the food stalls.

We found the Editor's house easily, just beyond the town. A bridge led to a high wooden door, closed and barred, over which a mirror hung, reflecting us in glints of sunlight. We were welcomed through a side door into a cemented courtyard, filled with birds in cages of all shapes and sizes. Then through a moon gate into the first house, the house for receiving guests. Behind it alternated more courtyards and more houses, all one-storied. In older times the Editor would have had concubines occupying the houses, each separate but all together in his compound. Now the houses were occupied by the Editor's family, his mother and old relatives, his wife, his sons and their wives and his grandchildren.

The guest house was surprisingly comfortable. The Editor had upholstered armchairs and sofas instead of the usual blackwood torture chairs. He said pleasantly that he would rather forsake custom than be uncomfortable.

But the Editor himself was hard to recognize. "I believe in comfort, as you can see, so I have gone back to Chinese dress, which is much more comfortable than the foreign style." He wore a thin black silk Chinese robe, the long sleeves of which overhung his wrists, over white silk trousers bound at the ankle, and soft cloth shoes. On his head, in the old fashion, was the little round cap of black satin, a red button on the top. He had grown a beard, long, gray, and straggly. The nail of the little finger of his left hand was almost two inches long and curved inward. With the Chinese clothes he had reassumed the Chinese manner, slower, more graceful, more elegant, more stylized than his manner when he had worn foreign clothes. Only his dark glasses were the same, and his fluent English.

We were served a gorgeous Chinese lunch, more than twenty different kinds of delicacies, steamed or fried, ending with long-life noodles. Their entire length had to be lifted high with the chopsticks and lowered into the mouth, not bitten off, to symbolize good wishes for a long life for guests and host. The Editor was the only one of his family who ate with us. His sons were out, and his wife, a twittering woman who supervised the serving of lunch, would eat later with the other women and the children.

The conversation at lunch was general, the Editor talking gently about his birds, which were aired in the courtyards every fine day, taken in at night to rest with padded coverings buttoned over their cages, and even taken for walks. He carried selected ones to the tea house on its artificial lake so that they might be near water for a while. He walked every day, he said, very early in the morning, to the field behind his house where he and some other older men performed the slow, studied movements of Chinese gymnastics. They did not speak or acknowledge each other's presence. In the misty quiet of the predawn, each did his gymnastics silently and alone, so as to achieve the necessary tranquility of spirit. But still, they were together, and if one should fail to come he was missed and asked after later, and that too was as it should be, for are we not all brothers?

During the day, the Editor studied the classics, wrote poetry, played with his grandchildren, taught them calligraphy. Calligraphy was becoming a lost art, he thought, and that would be a great pity. There and then he sent for his brushes and rice paper, cleared the table in front of him, wet the ink stick and ground it onto the black slate block until he had ink of the consistency he wanted, and wrote for each of us three sisters a Chinese name, the brush held upright between his fingers, its tip flicking lightly over the paper. We learned what we had not known before—that the family name of Father's mother, the lady from Ningpo, had been Ma. What Ma ideogram was that, the Editor asked. Father said the one that meant "horse" in English. So, with the family name Ma, the Editor gave each of us the name he thought suitable. For Veronica, "Delicate Blossom" ("she is about to bloom," he said while she blushed scarlet). For Jane, "Precious Stream" ("streams ripple prettily on the surface, but they have depths"). For me, "Beautiful Brocade" ("brocade is woven in many colors—the same piece looks quite different in different lights—but it is all one and the same piece").

When the sun had moved toward the west and the house cast some shadow in the courtyard, we went outside to admire the birds, to drink more tea, this time mixed red and green with jasmine, and to eat sweet cakes stuffed with black bean curd, studded with sesame seed. When we were settled on the stone benches, Father said:

"Old Friend, I wonder you didn't retire earlier! It's a thousand times better to live here than in Shanghai!"

"Yes. I'm enjoying it. I'm enjoying it as much as I can, and for as long as I can."

"You're a young man yet," Father laughed, "and your health seems to be excellent."

The Editor smiled and stroked his beard.

"I'm not thinking of my health—that, fortunately, is good. I'm thinking of other things, of the changes that are coming in China."

"You mean the Communists?"

The Editor looked up and out over the walls of his courtyard to the paling blue sky. He extended his arms and slowly slid his sleeves up, first left, then right, until his wrists were exposed. He looked ineffably Chinese then, the essence of the old, gentle, scholarly, philosophizing China.

"Communists! Nationalists! Japanese! And beyond them, what? Beyond them is China, our vast beloved suffering country with its two-thousand-year-old civilization. Sometimes I think that's what is really wrong with China. We have been civilized for two thousand years, but that makes our civilization two thousand years old! Obsolete. Outdated. We still revere Confucius, ignoring the fact that nobody really knows what he himself wrote and said, and what was said and written in his name by disciples many years after his death. Worse still, the basis of his teaching was that only the ancient is good! Is it any wonder that in many ways we seem to be going backwards instead of forwards, worshipping ancestors, placing on youth the solemn duty of caring for the old, even if it must be at the expense of the new generations? For example, a father can't afford to send his children to school because it costs him so much to feed and clothe his old relatives —not only parents, mind you, but uncles, aunts, cousins, who come along and make a claim. It's by no means unknown for a young man overburdened with ancient and demanding relatives to give them opium to smoke. A small outlay in opium, and they'll die quickly and uncomplainingly, happily drugged. That's the kind of solution we Chinese instinctively seek. We are irrelevant to the present day!"

He laughed and looked around. We murmured a response. It

was true, I thought, that the preoccupation of many Chinese with their two-thousand-year-old civilization was irrelevant. The Editor spoke of it with gentle mockery, but many did so with pride and nostalgia, as though nothing could be better for the future than more of the past. The proprietor of my favorite silk store would shake his head sadly over foreign tourists standing at the counter of his shop who wanted to buy a yard or two of silk in the ten minutes between tours. "Ah!" he would say coldly, turning them over to his most junior assistants, "you are in a hurry. You come from a *young* country." The proper way to buy silk was to spend a whole morning sitting at one of the marble-topped tables set around his big shop, chatting and sipping tea from eggshell porcelain cups, while assistants displayed bolt after bolt of silk and brocade, draped over their extended arms; finally, to buy at least one bolt of ten or fifteen yards, after conducting with finesse and humour the ritual of bargaining about price. Anything less, the proprietor seemed to say, frowning at the tourists who were paying without question his atrociously high first asking prices, was uncivilized.

Father and the Editor were talking about the Unequal Treaties, the treaties which gave to foreigners the revenue from China's salt tax, the right to administer the Salt Monopoly, and the right to fix and collect Customs tariffs.

"Of course," the Editor was saying, "when the treaties were concluded early in the century they were guarantees for repayment of the loans that the foreign nations were making to China for purposes like building railroads. If all the money had been used for such purposes it might have been a different story: enough internal development might have been generated to repay the loans in a reasonable period. But in the usual Chinese way a lot of the money was diverted to purposes like maintaining the armies of warlords! The treaties are disastrous to China. They're depriving us of two of our most important sources of revenue. We hoped they'd be abolished after the first world war and were bitterly disappointed when they were not. But they and extraterritoriality will have to be abolished soon. They're anachronisms from the bad old days. The way the world is moving, the way China is moving into a new order, I doubt they can endure into the second half of this century."

Father said that a lot of foreigners were working hard to maintain them. The Editor laughed.

"You mean the 'open door' policy? The foreign nations getting together and agreeing among themselves that they'll leave the door to China open for each other! No single exploiter should be allowed to grab all the spoil! That's a bald way of putting it, but it's the fact. Well, the Japs are closing the door now. When they first walked into Manchuria they were still pretending to subscribe to that policy, but now they've come down into North China they're beginning to close foreign firms—American, British, German. Soon the foreigners will want to get the Japs out of China almost as much as the Chinese do!"

His voice sharpened and he turned to face Father directly.

"Nanking closed down my paper because I called for unity against Japan. There weren't many of us calling for it then— mostly students marching in the streets making more noise than impact—but they had nuisance value, if nothing else. Today the call for unity is rising louder than ever. More and more people are speaking out. The Kuomintang can't close down all the newspapers, they can't put all the people in jail. I tell you, Old Friend, the time is coming when *both* the Japanese and the westerners will be out of China, when China will be Chinese again!"

His voice rang. The dark glasses glinted in the sunlight, seeming to throw our gaze back at us, making him mysterious, almost frightening. The gentle philosopher was gone.

"And at that time, the only relevant question will be: Kuomintang or Gungtsetang? Nationalist or Communist? All this talk of exterminating the Communists—rubbish! Chiang can never exterminate Mao. In his own domain Mao is already far stronger than Chiang in his. Mao's domain is still small—just a slice in the north—but it will grow! And in the end, the two of them will struggle to the death—the Titans, Chiang Kai-shek and Mao Tse-tung."

He gestured with his slim, long-fingered Chinese hands.

"Think of a peasant who has always been at someone's mercy, who has always been cheated, beaten, thrown into prison without recourse, forced to hand over the major part, if not all, of his crops to the landlord, to 'the government' which he knows only in the person of the tax collector. A peasant whose *life* can be flicked away like a fly's. Take a man like that and recognize him as a human being. Give him a say in the conduct of his own life. Let him vote. Send to his village a teacher who will teach his children to read and write, as he cannot. That, Old Friend, is what Mao is doing up there in the north, in his own enclaves that he's established in the teeth of Chiang Kai-shek's armies. When the time comes to choose, who will that peasant choose, fight for, give his life for, that the inheritance of his children will not be the bitterness of his forefathers? Of course—who could doubt it!— of course, Mao Tse-tung!"

There was silence in the courtyard except for the twittering of the birds. The sun still glimmered on the gray pavement, the stone benches, the shrubs and bushes growing sparsely in their pots.

"And when the time comes"—the Editor was still twanging

like a taut wire in a high wind—"I will be prepared to move out of my houses and my courtyards, to live in whatever austerity Mao Tse-tung decrees. I will be quite prepared!"

We all seemed to sigh together. The Editor sprang up, handed around more sesame-seed cakes, called for more tea, was jovial. We responded feebly, as though still trying to emerge from a spell.

"I'll show you something," the Editor cried, suddenly thinking of it. "We'll make an experiment!"

He clapped his hands and a servant came running, to whom he spoke in an undertone. The servant went away and came back leading a very old woman. She glanced around with milky-white eyes, seemed to sense that there were strangers present, gave us a vague smile, hobbled to sit on a bench in a patch of sun, and raised her face to the warmth. The servant came forward and placed beside her a basin of water and a bowl containing a few grains of raw rice.

"This old lady is one of my ancestors," said the Editor. "My mother's aunt, my great-aunt, and one or two more greats for my children and grandchildren. She is a natural seer. I'm going to ask her now to try and show us something about the future of China, and we'll see what she can do. Like all true seers, the power is not hers to command, only to use when it comes to her. We'll see if it's with her today."

Mother spoke politely, although we knew she was outraged. "Editor, I'm astonished! You dabble in the occult?"

"Madame, for us it's not dabbling, and its not the occult! The powers of my great-aunt are part of the interchange that goes on constantly between the spirit beings and the human beings that co-inhabit China."

"Nonsense," Mother said sharply, although she smiled.

The Editor answered quizzically:

"Think, Madame. If you ask how many Chinese there are, you'll be told between four hundred and five hundred million. That's an average of fifty million difference in the range. Fifty million people! In a western country, fifty million people would have billions of dollars worth of services: electricity, gas, running water, telephone, telegraph, roads. These things are built by redesigning the face of the earth, digging into it, inserting pipes, moving hills, filling in valleys. All of which disturbs the Yin and the Yang and infuriates the spirits, but eventually drives them away because they can have no kind of rapport with bulldozers and earthmovers. But here in China fifty million people aren't even counted. We have almost none of those modern things. And the spirits still live with us."

He smiled at Mother, half teasing, half serious.

"Mostly, I'm afraid, spirits to be feared, at least we fear them. You saw the mirror over my front gate? It's there because a spirit trying to enter would see himself reflected and would run away, terrified by its own hideousness. And it couldn't enter by the side doors because, as you noticed, the path to the side doors curves sharply and spirits can travel only in straight lines. That's also the reason for the zig-zag bridges to the tea house—spirits can't manage zig-zags."

Mother smiled, thin-lipped.

"Oh yes, the spirits live with us! When somebody dies in Naziang, his body is never carried out of the front door of the house because his spirit would be able to recognize the way back home and might come one night to fetch a relative to keep him company. Dead bodies must be carried out of a side door, or a window, even if one must be specially cut, so the spirit won't be able to recognize the way back. And, to make quite sure, strings of firecrackers are set off while the body is being carried out to frighten the spirit so he won't be noticing the way. And we burn things for the spirits of the dead to use. Paper rickshaws. If we are rich enough, even paper motorcars. Paper figures of servants. Silver paper folded to look like silver bullion to use for money. We burn these things, and the Tao priests jump back and forth over the fire to bestir the spirits of the paper figures and urge them to move off into the spirit world. We hope they'll make our dead relatives comfortable and encourage them to stay away."

"Oh, Editor!" Mother had a hard time remaining polite. "You don't believe all that rubbish!"

"Oh yes I do!" Teasing, serious. "At any rate, let's make this experiment, and we'll see what we will see."

He went to his great-aunt and spoke into her ear. She opened her eyes and peered at him, smiled tremulously, nodded. He put into her hand the bowl containing raw rice. With shaky fingers she picked up the grains and put them into her almost toothless mouth. She chewed for a while, chin moving, eyes closed, and then swallowed with an effort. A few minutes, and her body began to slump slowly, her chin to fall forward onto her breast.

"She's going into a trance," the Editor said in his normal voice.

"Here? In the sunlight?" Father was incredulous.

"Oh yes! True seers have no need of darkness and mumbo-jumbo. That's for the seers who work for pay. Sometimes, even if they are true seers, they have to resort to trickery because their clients are paying money and insist on results. If the power does not come, what can the seer do about it? Nothing but play a trick of some kind to give the client what he's paying for."

The great-aunt began to breathe stertorously.

"She's in full trance." He turned to me. "Beautiful Brocade, will you go and look into the basin of water?"

I did as he asked. The water was clear, still, blankly white against the white enamel of the basin. I stared and stared into it, unconsciously holding my breath, while the ancient beside me breathed loudly. The water remained clear. Something bumped against my leg—a big red ball. Two children, six or seven years old, came running out of the house chasing it, scrambling about my feet to recover it. Standing again, they saw the basin and looked curiously into the water. The smaller child laughed delightedly, pointing into the water.

"Papa! Papa!"

"It's not Papa!" the other child said reprovingly. "Its somebody else. Papa doesn't have so much hair!"

Then she too laughed and pointed into the water.

"Look! Look!"

She thrust her head forward, narrowed her eyes, opened and shut her mouth as though speaking earnestly, tapped the fingers of her right hand into the open palm of her left as though emphasizing points. Evidently she was mimicking a scene that she saw in the water.

Somebody called from inside and the children ran away. The old woman sighed softly, relaxed, leaned back, raised her face again to the sun and slipped into sleep.

The children had spoken in Chinese, but of course we had all understood.

The Editor sighed.

"I myself have never seen anything in the water. My wife has sometimes seen things, but vaguely. My youngest daughter-in-law is the only one who, quite regularly, sees things in the water. Once before she saw something like what my grandchild has just played out. She says the face of the man is strange to her, so it cannot be the face of Chiang Kai-shek, whom everyone recognizes only too well." He shrugged. "Who knows?"

Father wanted to discuss the matter, but Mother rose and said it was time to go home. Her smile was stiff. We said our goodbyes, and the Editor took us to the gate where, gently, he detained Mother.

"Madame, I've read about the Catholic miracles—the ancient ones, and modern ones too. Hasn't there been quite recently a report of a spirit appearing to three children shepherding flocks on a mountain slope? And haven't there been many reports of saintly persons being levitated while they prayed? Would you say it was possible for a spirit without any visible agency to raise and hold in the air for an hour or more the body of a kneeling human being? But that it was impossible for another spirit, through the agency of my great-aunt, to show us a little scene in the water— perhaps a scene of the future?" He smiled warmly, whimsically. "Who knows?"

As we walked away through the gathering dusk, he called after Father:

"Old friend, take care!"

18

Battle of the Shanghai Delta

"WELL . . . ," SAID BILL, coming in as we sat at dinner. He interrupted himself to look critically at the food on our plates.

"Is that turtle? Great! I'll have some if there's any left. Your Dahsoo is the best turtle cook in China. Well—it's war!"

We went on calmly eating turtle.

"What d'you mean, war?" Father said when he had swallowed. "It's been war for the last ten years."

"That was civil war. In the family. Chiang Kai-shek chasing Mao Tse-tung around the family compound. Now its War with a capital W. International war. War between China and Japan."

"Oh, come on, Bill!" said Father. "It's six months since the Young Marshall kidnapped Chiang Kai-shek and nothing's happened except a lot more pious declarations."

The Young Marshal was Chang Hsueh-liang, son of Marshal Chang Tso-lin, former war lord of Manchuria, whom the Japanese had wooed in 1925 and blown up in 1928 after he jilted them, having first taken their money. The Young Marshal had inherited the warlordship of Manchuria, been wooed in turn by Chiang Kai-shek, joined the Kuomintang, and lost his province when the Japanese seized it in 1931. Now he was in Sian, in northwest China, assigned to fighting Communists. In December the previous year, 1936, the Generalissimo, not at all satisfied that the Young Marshal was doing his best, had flown to Sian to reprimand him—and had been kidnapped by him and his generals. The Young Marshal and his Manchurian army did not want to be fighting Communists when they might be fighting Japanese ensconced in their homeland. For two weeks the Generalissimo had been held in Sian and had been forced to meet face to face with the Communists. When he returned to Nanking he had given orders for the Sixth Extermination Campaign to be dropped because, so we read in the newspapers, the Communists had repented their wicked ways and had begged for forgiveness. The Generalissimo had generously forgiven them, had allowed them to remain in their enclaves in the north. Now, so we read in the newspapers, the Generalissimo, freed of the necessity of exterminating Communists, could at last turn his attention to the Three Principles of Sun Yat-sen, which he would forthwith implement throughout the land. People dutifully applauded while they raised their eyebrows and whispered: did Chiang remember what the Three Principles were? And what about the Japanese? The Japanese, squatting up there in the north of China?

Now Bill said again:

"It's war. They're shooting at the Marco Polo bridge near Peking. You'll see it in tomorrow's papers. I just got it from Newsreel Wong."

"It's another incident," said Mother.

"Not this time! This time it's going to be war. That's what they really agreed to up there in Sian six months ago. It's never been said and it's never been written, and it may never be said or written, but I'll bet my right arm that that's what it was. Chiang

Kai-shek was forced to give up his Communist witch hunt and forced to agree to a united front against Japan."

"Have some more turtle," Mother said. "There's plenty."

That was the evening of 7 July 1937, the last time we ever had Dahsoo's famous turtle stew. For a long time afterward there was no turtle to be bought, and when there was we couldn't afford it anymore. "It's three million dollars for a small one," Dahsoo told Mother sadly.

Bill was right. It was war. At first we only read about it, sitting secure and far away in our extraterritorial city. The Japanese army was marching from the north—one column from Peking through the Nankow Pass and down through Shansi Province with its rich coal and iron fields, another column down the railway from Tientsin toward Nanking. Japanese tanks commanded the northern mountain passes and valleys. Japanese planes ruled the northern skies. The warlords, who were only nominally Kuomintang but had nevertheless elected to fight for China, were breaking before the advance like pricked balloons.

Then, on 13 August 1937, the day on which our own world shifted into its last long downward spiral, the war of the Shanghai delta broke out.

We were at a birthday party—a swimming party at a private pool. On one side of the pool there was a snack bar serving a continuous supply of sandwiches, hotdogs, hamburgers, cakes and pastries. On the other side, a drinks bar with everything from orange juice to champagne. Sixty or seventy guests played about in the water and on the turquoise-tiled terrace surrounding the pool. Veronica had just learned to dive and was splashing in and out of the water, beaming, plunging again and again so as not to forget how.

Suddenly one of the young men appeared at the side of the pool in his street clothes instead of swimming trunks. His nickname, I shall always remember, was Mimi.

"I've got to go," he shouted. "I've just been telephoned to. The Volunteers have been called up."

One by one the young men disappeared, waving goodbye: "I've got to go, I'm sorry, it's a great party but I've got to go. The Volunteers have been called up."

Half an hour later there were only girls and women at the party, and a few fathers and uncles who were not members of the Shanghai Volunteer Corps.

"What's happened? What's up?"

"Don't know, but they've called up the Volunteers. There must be fighting somewhere around Shanghai."

Indeed there was fighting—savage fighting that turned the Shanghai delta into a torch and, when the armies passed on three months later, left it a scorched shambles. The Generalissimo, watching the Japanese phalanxes descend inexorably from the north almost to the banks of the Hwang Ho, the Yellow River, watching the riff-raff armies of the war lords scatter before them like puffs of dust, had decided to broach war in his strongest arena, the valley of the Yangtze River. At Shanghai, on that night, he flung against the Japanese garrison his own best troops. These crack German-trained divisions held for a time, while the Japanese concentrated their navy and air force and shelled and bombed the hell out of the Shanghai delta. When they fell, they were succeeded by wave on wave of Chinese flesh: uncounted hundreds of thousands of Chinese peasants turned soldier were fed incessantly into the trenches to die in the bloody ooze, to be trampled by the Japanese hordes. Chiang Kai-shek, against the pleadings of his own generals, stubbornly refused to withdraw from the useless, spectacular battle which held the attention of the world, which he hoped, it is said, would draw to himself the aid of the world. At last, in November, he ordered a retreat and the Shanghai delta fell to the Japanese.

At first we thought it was another incident—at least, we hoped so. A few weeks of refugee-ism, the usual barbed wire barricades, sandbag shelters, foreign troops and Volunteers patrolling, to prevent trespassing on extraterritorial soil. Then back to normal life.

But then, bombs dropped inside the city. A lone Chinese pilot, his plane crippled, tried to unload his lethal cargo into the Whangpoo River and hit instead, with his whole stick of bombs, the huge entertainment complex called Dah-ss-ka, the Great World, in the heart of the International Settlement.

Everybody, excited, alarmed, awed, indignant, poured out his experience:

"I was just about to leave the office—I'd worked late—when I heard the crash. I wondered what had happened but I'd decided to walk home, so I walked anyway, along Race Course Road. I thought it was awfully empty for that time of the evening—everybody must have rushed off to gape at Dah-ss-ka. Then I saw this dark pink stuff running in the gutters, and I thought that the dye factory must have blown up—that must have been the big explosion I heard. But it was *blood!* Blood from the Dah-ss-ka bombing, so much of it that it was running in the gutters four or five blocks away!"

"I was driving by Dah-ss-ka when the bombs dropped. In the car next to me were Tom and his wife. Just before the bombs dropped, he tooted at me and we waved to each other. Then, just as we were coming to the traffic lights on the Dah-ss-ka corner —that series of bangs! I was just under it and I tell you I thought I'd go deaf! I was shaking like a leaf! The traffic light was just turning red, and I stepped on the gas and went right through it. But Tom stopped for it, and they were incinerated! The car and both of them, all black, incinerated by the fire!"

And then, the "lost battalion." Everybody was calling them that. They were holed up in a building just across the border of the Settlement, on the further bank of the Soochow Creek. A Chinese battalion.

"We took a walk down there at lunchtime today. They're still shooting. My boyfriend, he's a Volunteer, he's assigned to that district. He was there that night last week when they went into the building. He said they flooded in. It was dark, but there was a moon and the streetlights. It was like a dark wave, he said. Heads bobbing, bobbing. They began shooting from the windows, and it was hard for the Japs to get at them from the other side without shooting into the Settlement. But now the Japs have set up guns on this side of the Creek, our side. They can, of course—they've got extrality. And they're shelling them from this side. It'll be over soon, poor devils!"

And then the bombs that screamed down onto Shanghai North Station, hurling great lengths of railway track helter-skelter through the air to come crashing and clanging back to earth. The buildings roared, spurted bricks and shattered concrete, and collapsed into piles of smoking rubbish. Arms and legs, blood and brains, rained down and splattered everywhere. Newsreel Wong took a photo which made front pages around the world: a small child, sitting unharmed in the midst of havoc, looking around for its mother, just beginning to cry.

In the city the patrols were more vigilant than they had ever been, the sandbag walls higher, the barbed wire more lavishly strung. All around, the mortars boomed constantly, the machine guns rattled. The people looked harassed, anxious, almost furtive.

They scurried for shelter when showers of glass came tinkling sweetly down from high windows, followed seconds later by the reverbrating crack of the bomb, falling outside the city, that had shattered it. A haze of dust hovered around the periphery, rising from collapsed roofs, broken walls, bricks and stones lying loose in the narrow streets of the ruined Chinese city. Smoke and flame spurted fiercely as fire took hold, or puffed lazily as fire spent itself in leisurely fashion. The flow of meat and vegetables petered out, markets were empty, Dahsoo called on old friendships to get us a cabbage, a pound of beef, a dozen eggs.

For us, the final sign that this was war come to stay, come to change our lives forever in ways we could not guess, was when the Old Boss came to live with us, the Old Boss who had never before abandoned his beloved house. Veronica said, "I've got goose pimples," and shivered.

The Old Boss was one of Father's brothers, bristle-haired, bristle-browed, gruff, dogmatic. Once in his youth when he was laying down the law in his barking voice which squeaked when he got excited, his father had said laughingly, "Tay, tay, Lor-pe" —"Right, right, Old Boss"—and ever since he had been known to everybody by that name. The Old Boss was a bachelor who had lived for thirty years in his bare, ascetic bungalow in Kiangwan, outside the city limits, with his cook, his hunting dogs, his guns, his boars' heads glaring down from every wall, and his Packard. He had utterly refused to leave his house during previous incidents, although it had been hit by stray bullets in 1927 and narrowly missed by a shell in 1932. But now he gave his cook six months' holiday, boarded his dogs with a vet, barricaded his house, and came to us driving his Packard with a big trunk and three suitcases in the back.

"Thought I'd better get out while I could," he barked at Mother. "You've got room for me, I suppose. Just for a few weeks while those bloody shit Japs are bombing and shelling around my place."

"The Old Boss is here," Veronica told me in a hushed voice when I came home. "Mother put him in Ah-May's old room. You should see what he brought with him!"

We went up together and peeped into his room. At first we could see nothing but newspapers. The whole room seemed to be full of newspapers hung at eye level, like cafe curtains, entirely obscuring the view. Then, under them, we caught a glimpse of the highly polished brown boots that the Old Boss always wore.

"Old Boss?"

"Humph." His usual grunt, coming from the midst of the newspapers.

"What are you doing?"

"What d'you think? Tidying my things, of course."

"Oh."

Veronica and I began to giggle. Hastily we shut the door and went to find Mother.

"Did you see all those newspapers in the Old Boss's room? What on earth is he doing!"

Mother sighed.

"The wardrobe in Ah-May's room isn't anywhere near big enough for all the clothes he brought. I offered to empty out one of the wall cupboards for him, but he wouldn't hear of it. He says its too damp for his clothes in a wall cupboard. So he got some thick wire and strung it all around the room. Not around the walls, mind you. From the middle of one wall to the middle of the next, so it fills the whole room, and he's hanging his clothes all around the wire and covering them up with newspaper to keep the dust off and absorb the damp, he says! I believe he's brought every shred of clothing he owns!"

At dinner that night the Old Boss said with satisfaction:

"You see, no need to clean out any cupboards. No need to bother about me at all. I've got everything fixed up nice and tidy."
I said:
"But can you see to get to your bed and back out again?"
"No trouble. No trouble. My things are too good to put into a wall cupboard. Damp. Too damp there. My things are most excellent. Pure wool. British wool suits, Jaeger underwear. Most excellent."

When Lane Crawford, the English department store, had closed down the previous year, it appeared that the Old Boss had gone every single day to their liquidation sale. They had reserved for him one of the enormous storage drawers behind the counter in the men's department and in it, day by day, he had stored what he bought. He had priced everything, knew exactly the things he wanted, and bought them up by the dozen as the prices were progressively reduced.

"You see. Clever thing to do. Clever. Most excellent things. And ample. I've got ample. Last me till I die."

And indeed they did last him till he died in 1974 at the age of ninety-six. The Old Boss, who moved in with us for a few weeks while those bloody shit Japs were shelling and bombing around his house, and stayed with us for the next thirteen years until we all left China. He never went back to his beloved house in Kiang-wan. It was a ruin in the war zone controlled by the Japanese after the Shanghai delta fell, a bleak waste of rubble and shell holes criss-crossed with barbed wire, patrolled by bloody shit Jap soldiers who shot on sight.

The Shanghai delta fell in November 1937 and the war swept on toward Nanking. The Kuomintang government moved its seat to Hankow, up the Yangtze River. Nanking fell at the end of the year and the Japanese army rested for a time on its laurels—the bestial Japanese army, looting, sacking, murdering, burning, raping until its lust wore thin.

In the spring of 1938, the Japanese marched again. Hankow fell and Chiang Kai-shek moved his government further up-river to Chungking. Canton fell, and the Japanese held the entire coast of China, the deltas of the three great rivers, both banks of the Yangtze as far as Hankow, much of North China, and Manchuria. The Chinese armies were contained in the interior of the country. By early 1939, the armies faced each other on a front of two thousand miles across a belt of no-man's land where, for the next six years, the war see-sawed back and forth in campaigns of savage ferocity which gave victory to neither side. Towns and villages changed hands half a dozen times as the armies skirmished, now gaining, now losing. But the peasants lost all the time—their villages destroyed, their homes burned to the ground, their cattle seized, their fields ravaged, their lives in pawn. Where the Japanese army advanced, peasant women hiding in the tall grain were flushed out by cavalry for rape, men were stripped naked and hitched as beasts of burden to munitions carts. Where the Chinese army held sway, men were conscripted by the million, snatched off the fields, kidnapped on the roads by press gangs to be sold to recruiting officers responsible for supplying Chungking's insatiable demand for manpower.

The Chinese peasant was not afraid to fight for his country and did so with fierce courage, but he feared and hated his government and its total power over him. The history of the Kuomintang's conduct of the Sino-Japanese war is sprinkled with examples of monumental cruelty, corruption, and stupidity. Recruiting officers quoted standard prices at which recruits who could afford it bought their freedom. The rest were forced into training camps, many to die of starvation and brutality before they ever reached

the front. Soldiers trudged, sometimes for weeks, to reach the
front, barefooted, half starved, pitted by disease. Three or four
men shared a rifle and a few bullets. Regiments toted to battle
a few mortars left over from World War I and a few shells.
Ammunition was hoarded, hoarded so preciously that in 1944 a
cache of 50,000 tons of it was blown up by an American demoli-
tion team to prevent its falling into Japanese hands. Generals
bickered jealously while their men moved to battle aimless and
leaderless, infantry with no artillery support, artillery sitting on a
hill undefended. Troops fended for themselves on foot while their
commanders fled, using army vehicles to move their families and
possessions. The Chinese soldier was a nothing man. He usually
fought until he died, unknown, unhonored. Wounded, he was
patched up to fight again or, if he was beyond repair, given a pass
to drag himself away from the front on his own, with nothing to
live on, if he survived, but beggary.

In Honan province in 1943 occurred one of the most terrible
famines in China's age-long history of famine. Parents were killing their children because they could no longer bear to hear them
beg for food. Yet the Kuomintang government still demanded of
the Honanese peasants their full quota of the grain tax. Peasants
eating tree bark and peanut shells, whose entire crop had gone in
taxes, were forced to sell their oxen, even their land if they had
any, to buy more grain at sky-high black market prices to meet
their tax quota. The land they sold was bought up cheap by
profiteers who rushed in from other provinces. The grain they
bought was their own, looted from tax reserves by army and
provincial officers and put back on sale on the black market.
Money for relief came from America, and with it relief administrators bought grain from the hoarded stocks of the same officers
at fifty or sixty times the price of grain in America. Grain was

plentiful in neighboring provinces, but the Kuomintang government made no move to order it into Honan lest the provincial
governors be offended and the fragile balance of power on which
the Kuomintang rested be disturbed.

From their own observations, foreign correspondents estimated
that three million Honanese had died of starvation and another
three million had fled the province, but these eyewitness reports
were blandly dismissed by Chungking—exaggerations, figments
of the imagination of overly emotional foreigners.

In 1944, when the Japanese marched an army of sixty thousand
men into Honan, the Chinese Honan army of three hundred
thousand disintegrated in a few weeks time, many disarmed by
their own countrymen, by the peasants who had survived the
famine with implacable hatred in their hearts for their own government, who turned to the Japanese for vengeance.

In the winter of 1937, the first bitter winter of the war, the
unity Chinese had so passionately desired came to pass for a while.
The Japanese army had rested that winter, believing that news of
its savagery at Nanking would spread terror and weaken Chinese
resistance. But the will to resist had fed on hatred, had run like
fire through the interior of the country. At Hankow, Kuomintang
and Communist sat side by side making joint plans for the prose-
cution of the war. Warlord armies from the south, the east, the
west, marched to join the government. In the north, where the
Japanese were entrenched, where they thought the war was over,
the war went on. Communist soldiers and guerrillas, Communist-
organized peasants, blooded Japanese entrenchments, faded into
the landscape, emerged again to ambush patrols and blow bridges.
Throughout that first winter, unity sprang from the very earth like
the rice itself.

But it soon died. While the grim old order persisted in the

Kuomintang-dominated areas, while the peasants strove to provide the wherewithal of war, in the fast-expanding Communist-
dominated areas a new social order was being established and total
partisan war was being broached in which everybody participated
equally. Inevitably, friction arose between the old and the new.
Bands of Kuomintang and Communist soldiers began fighting
each other as early as the fall of 1938. In 1940 agreements were
made to demarcate the fighting areas between the Kuomintang
and Communist armies which required the Communists to withdraw north of the Yellow River. While in Chungking Chiang
Kai-shek was assuring Chou En-lai that all arrangements had been
made for a smooth withdrawal, a superior Kuomintang force
attacked and massacred a small headquarters detachment of the
Communist New Fourth Army.

It was the final blow to unity. From then on, two Chinas fought
the Japanese and, sporadically, viciously, each other.

19

How to Make a Million

WHILE THE WAR was being fought in the mountains and plains of China, our extraterritorial city stood almost intact in the midst of the carnage of the Shanghai delta, focusing exclusively on its cardinal concern: the making of money. The city had never been so full of people, and more people poured in daily—Japanese businessmen hurrying in the wake of their armies, Chinese from interior cities paralyzed by war, Europeans fleeing the Nazis, entrepreneurs, gamblers, adventurers of all nationalities. And everybody had business. Everybody was buying, selling, scrambling to make a living, scrambling to get rich. In every cafe people sat over coffee cups and beer mugs whispering urgently to each other, passing quickly hidden papers, handing over mysterious packages. Tiny offices sprang up bearing such names as All Asia Agencies and Universal Resources, Inc. In the hallways of the dignified old firms, scruffy looking people gathered and were received into sanctums from which a few years earlier they would have been forcibly ejected. Everyone and everything had a price.

Ss Si-sang came to me one day in the office, glowing with excitement. He whispered to me in English, his habit when he wanted to reduce the risk of being overheard by the clerks.

"My friend coming today from Hongkong. He like see big boss. I fix."

"What's it about?"

"Big business. Very big business."

I looked uninterested. If I asked him to tell me, he would go on making an important mystery of his big business. If I ignored it, he would tell me.

"My friend very big man."

"Umm."

"Very rich."

"Umm."

"Before very poor, now very rich. You know how he make money?"

"Umm."

In a very low whisper: "He buy tungsten from interior China, bring to Hongkong, sell to America, England, Japan. Plenty profit."

"How does it get out of China?"

"He very clever man. He know how to do. Pay some people— some Chinese, some Japanese."

"Oh, you mean he's smuggling it out?"

"Shh! You no say this word!" He glared at me for a moment, but could not resist his triumph. "Not smuggle. Only pay some people, ore come out. Now he think—same way, something can go in. He think—tires! Chungking want plenty tires for army. So he come see our big boss, buy tires. I fix. He pay me commission." He beamed.

"Why doesn't he buy them in Hongkong?"

"He try. Factory don't sell him. Factory say our company agent China and Hongkong. He must buy from agent. So he come here."

"And he's going to smuggle them from Hongkong to the interior?"

"Shhhhh!" Ss si-sang hissed angrily. "I already talk you no say this word! This very good business. Chungking must have tires for army, for make war against Japanese."

"But Chungking also must have tungsten for make war against Japanese. Now your friend sells to Japanese for make war against Chinese!"

"Shhhhhhhhh!" Ss si-sang wailed. "You no talk this fashion! My friend make business. Somebody like buy, he sell." He frowned at me furiously, then smiled again. "I make big commission. After big boss ask you write letter to factory, you write very quick, very good, I give you present." He raised his eyebrows delightedly, nodded at me quickly three or four times, and went away.

Ss si-sang's friend came in the afternoon. A small Cantonese in a worn-looking western style suit, a humble forward thrust to his head, an ingratiating smile on his face. Ss Si-sang ushered him into the front office, hovering like a hen. The friend stayed in there the rest of the afternoon, Ss si-sang running in and out for tea, papers, his abacus. When he passed my desk with the abacus he gave it a small shake, rattling it like a tambourine.

"Is that your friend? You said he was rich?"

"Of course rich! He no like show. He show rich, maybe after kidnap!"

The next day I was called into the front office, the door was shut carefully, the letter was dictated to me in a low voice, and I was warned of its utter confidentiality. When I went back to my typewriter, Ss si-sang looked at me inquiringly. I nodded. He beamed.

There were then two ways of sending letters to the United States. By boat to Mukden, the trans-Siberian railway to Europe, boat or air to the United States, which took four or five weeks. Or by boat to Hongkong and from there by air, which took two weeks or less, but the letters were subject to censorship in Hongkong.

I typed this interesting letter explaining to the factory in Akron, Ohio, why a buyer in Hongkong, where the consumption of tires was small, wanted to buy twenty thousand tires of large sizes. It was complete with details of how they were to be smuggled from Hongkong into China through the Japanese naval blockade and the Japanese army lines, and how bribes were to be administered. I gave it to the boss to sign, sealed it into an envelope marked "Air Mail via Hongkong," and gave it to the office boy to post. Then I put on my coat and left for home.

In the small hours of the morning, I started awake from a horrible nightmare. I lay staring into the dark. What was it? The letter! I had sent it via Hongkong, where the censors might well open it and read its contents! I leaped out of bed. It was 5:30 in the morning. I could scarcely wait for the light before I rushed to the office, typed a facsimile of the fatal envelope, and hurried to the main post office.

"I want to see the Commissioner of Posts," I announced.

I announced it stubbornly many times to many people before I was finally led into the room of the Assistant Commissioner. To him I said that I had to get back a letter that had been posted the evening before, like the facsimile I showed him. He was coldly sorry. It was impossible. I burst into tears. He regarded me distastefully. I leaned over the desk and, between sobs, whispered that the letter concerned an action against the Japanese and I had made a terrible mistake in sending it via Hongkong because it absolutely must not be seen by the Hongkong censors.

"Against Japanese?"

"Yes," I sniffed.

Not a muscle of his face changed. It still held its "impossible" expression. He rang a bell. An underling appeared.

"What is the status of last night's Hongkong mail?"

"Sir, most of it went on the S/S *Chinkiang,* but four sacks were too late and came back. They're going today on the S/S *Foochow.* "

"Open those four sacks."

The underling stared.

"Open them?"

"Yes. And help this young lady to look through the contents to find a letter that looks like this. If it's there, give it to her."

The underling's eyes boggled.

"Yes, sir. But who will break the seals?"

"Ah, yes. I will come and break them myself."

We went out in solemn procession. On the way the underling phoned instructions. We descended to the basement. Fourteen other underlings stood around four huge sealed sacks. Somebody handed the Assistant Commissioner a pair of scissors. He went around and clipped the strings that held the seals. The sacks were overturned in the middle of the floor. Four sacks of mail made a huge pile. I showed the facsimile to the underlings. We all squatted around the pile and began to search. Twenty minutes later, one of them stood up with a grunt of satisfaction and handed me my letter. I burst into tears again. The Assistant Commissioner took me to the entrance and bowed me out, the "impossible" expression still on his face.

I walked across the Szechuen Road bridge. On its apex the barbed wire barricades, now three years old, rusted away. Sand from tattered sandbags heaped itself in the gutters, scrunched underfoot. Below the bridge was the bulky building of Carlowitz

& Co. whose haughty Prussian boss, disdaining the Nazis as gangsters, was employing Jewish refugees when it suited him.

I turned into Yuen Ming Yuen Road. It was lunch time and food was being carried into the office buildings. Most Chinese companies gave lunch to their employees, and each day it was delivered by waiters who carried the dishes in round bamboo baskets slung from shoulder poles. After the employees had eaten, they carried the soiled dishes away again. By custom, beggars had the right to any remnants of food in the dishes. Though there was never much left, beggars clustered around the doorways waiting to pounce on the scraps. As the carriers came out, they set their bamboo baskets down on the sidewalk and stepped back quickly to avoid the rush. For a minute or two around each basket a mob of beggars pushed and fought, the quick children snatching and running off with their morsels before they could be snatched away again by their elders. The carriers waited and, when the beggars fell back, casually picked up their baskets and walked off.

I stood outside the door to my office building and waited for the daily fight to be over, then went up and found Ss si-sang anxiously awaiting me.

"Why you no come this morning?"

"I came very early, before you got here. I did a silly thing! I sent your letter via Hongkong . . ."

He turned absolutely pale. His eyes goggled.

"It's all right, Ss si-sang! I got the letter back. Look, here it is. I'll post it again right now via Siberia."

He leaned weakly against a desk.

"I'm so sorry, Ss si-sang! But really, don't worry, it's all right. It'll go via Siberia, right now!"

He nodded feebly, still speechless.

"Don't worry, Ss si-sang. You'll be rich yet."

Richer, I added to myself. Bill was another one of those who were getting richer. With my new knowledge of the fertile field of smuggling, I asked him the next time he came over what business he was doing.

"Business with the Japs, of course. Those bastards!"

"But you're making money?" the Old Boss inquired sardonically.

"You're damn right I am! I'm going to screw every penny I can out of them."

I pressed Bill for details about his business, but he was evasive —no doubt, I thought, for most excellent reasons. He had once again taken to carrying a small handgun in the inside pocket of his jacket. That day, he was also carrying several gold bars. He showed one to Father.

"Better get hold of some of these. Money's going to hell."

Father laughed. "How? They're not giving them away, are they?"

Unlike Bill, we were getting poorer. Father was no Bill. He was Old Faithful, working long hours accounting for the money of his English firm, never dreaming of making any for himself apart from his salary. With Luke in university in Hongkong and Veronica at Mr. Farmer's, we were having a hard time in spite of the contributions that the Old Boss and I, and Jane, who had just started work in Father's office, made to the household expenses. Prices were blowing up. Most things cost five or six times what they had, and many things for us were unbuyable.

We ate more simply than we ever had before, and more than ever appreciated Dahsoo, who could make poor ingredients taste almost as delicious as good ones. We traveled by bus and tram. Rickshaws had been replaced by pedicabs, three-wheelers which the coolies pedaled instead of pulling, but they were too expensive for every day unless one felt like spending ten minutes haggling with the coolie to bring the price of a trip down to what one could afford. So we took pedicabs only when it rained, and the rest of the time walked long blocks to the crowded trams and buses. We took our shoes to be resoled as long as the uppers lasted, and put together parts of old dresses in order to have a new-looking dress for a party.

The rare parties were "bottle parties," for which the hostess provided food and the guests the drinks. The parties had to last all night because of curfew, so they were getting rarer because few people had the desire or the stamina to stay up all night in a small room dancing around the furniture to the music of a record player. We didn't go to cabarets any more. They opened their doors at 3 or 4 P.M., some closed at 8:30, some stayed open all night. All were sleazy and still going downhill. Restaurants were still crowded with people who had learned to dine earlier, but who could afford them? It was almost a condemnation to be seen dining in the more expensive restaurants. "Profiteer!" people said contemptuously.

Most of our time after office and before curfew was spent at home or in the homes of friends. We dropped in on each other for those few hours and socialized as cheerfully as we had in a gayer time. Occasionally someone remarked, "Isn't it amazing how quickly one gets used to things!" but most of the time nobody noticed it. It was natural to rip old sweaters and knit the wool again, to sew torn sheets "sides-to-middle," to drink weak tea instead of something more exotic, to walk instead of riding. Young men fetched girls from friends' houses to walk them home in time for curfew, and romances developed as favorably or unfavorably during walks home as they had on the dance floor or during car rides.

Jane got engaged during a walk home. Her fiancé had refined

curfew-breaking to an art. He knew all the back roads and alleys where patrols rarely circulated, and restricted walking on patrolled main roads to Avenue Foch only. Avenue Foch was the boundary between the Settlement and the Concession. Its north side was patrolled by one set of police and its south side by the other, and each set had no jurisdiction on the opposite side. Unless it happened that patrols were on both sides of the road at the same time, one could escape arrest for curfew-breaking by simply crossing the road. Jane claimed that she had been proposed to in three stages, because patrols had unexpectedly appeared on each side in quick succession, and her fiance had had to interrupt his proposal to rush her across the road.

But the main subject of everybody's conversation was the Index, that magical yardstick by which people's salaries got increased. It was in connection with the Index that Mother and Dahsoo had their moment of fame. When prices first started skyrocketing, employers had increased salaries when and if they felt like it, or were forced to. Some never did. Then the Hongkong and Shanghai Banking Corporation agreed to be responsible for producing a definitive cost-of-living index as the standard for salary increases.

From the time of her marriage, Mother had every single night without fail settled accounts with Dahsoo. In her cupboard were forty or more exercise books filled with meticulously written accounts of Dahsoo's daily expenditures in the market—items, quantities, and prices. Somehow the managing director of the bank learned of them. He wrote Mother on embossed stationery: he understood that she had accounts showing the price of food for the last twenty-odd years. Would she lend them to the bank? They would be of inestimable help in establishing the Index. Mother lent them. She told Dahsoo. After that, every time we got an increase of salary, one would have thought that Dahsoo had personally bestowed it.

20

Peking Winter

Ss SI-SANG's "PRESENT" was an air ticket to Peking.

A few months after the letter incident, when the sale of the twenty thousand tires had been completed and they were on their way to Hongkong, Ss si-sang handed me a red envelope as I left the office one evening, my name on it in big black letters written with a Chinese brush and ink.

"What's this?" I asked.

"You look, you see." He glanced at me enigmatically, shaking his head, smiling with downturned lips. "You very clever girl!"

When I got home I slit the envelope and found the airplane ticket. Shanghai and Peking and all the coastal cities between being under Japanese control, air communications had been established.

That night I discussed it with Veronica, the two of us sitting on my bed. I told her the whole story, except what Ss si-sang's "big business" was.

"What shall I do? I'll have to give it back to him tomorrow. I hope his feelings won't be hurt, but how can I accept it? And I can't understand why he gave it to me!"

"Why didn't you say 'no' when he first said he'd give you a present?"

"Because I never dreamed of anything like this! He knows perfectly well he doesn't have to *bribe* me to type letters! That's my job—I'd be fired if I didn't do it. I thought at the time—he was so happy and excited, bubbling over—I thought he just wanted to be nice to me. I thought he'd give me oranges or something like that. It would be nice to have a few oranges around here for a change, so I didn't say anything. And now this!"

"He said you were a clever girl?"

"Yes. And he looked pleased—admiring almost. But at the same time I thought he looked a bit rueful."

"You know," Veronica said, "I bet you anything he did mean at first to give you oranges. But when you told him that you'd sent the letter via Hongkong and got it back, he didn't believe you. After all, it is extraordinary to get a letter back from the Assistant Commissioner of Posts after its been posted. He got an awful fright and I bet he thought you'd made the whole thing up to frighten him into giving you a bigger present than oranges. And that's why he's admiring! He's rueful because it's costing him money, but he's admiring because he thinks you're smart enough to know how to squeeze!"

She ended in a shout of laughter, and we both collapsed on the bed.

"But I'll have to give it back," I managed at last.

"Oh, you *can't!* You can't do that! Now he admires you for being smart enough to parlay a couple of oranges into an airplane trip to Peking, and if you get stupid again and give it back he'll be terribly disappointed!"

We laughed some more. When, in another time and another

country Veronica died at the age of only forty-two, what I missed most was her lovely laughter.

Mother came in to find out what was going on. She didn't think I should use the ticket, and anyway she didn't want me to go off to Peking alone. Father joined the discussion, and finally the Old Boss. Jane was dodging about on Avenue Foch with her fiancé.

The Old Boss settled the matter. He produced his wallet and shoved some money into my hand.

"Here, that's for the hotel in Peking. Of course you must go! It's not every day you get a free trip to Peking! Of course you must go! Stupid not to! Stupid not to!" His voice squeaked up into the higher registers. That made us laugh again.

So, on a bright morning in December 1940, Bill—who of course still had gasoline—drove me out to Lunghwa airport and I got into my first plane. It had two propeller engines which roared deafeningly, an on-and-off heating system, twenty seats full of Japanese men, and no toilet. I discovered the last fact when the plane landed at Chinkiang, its first stop. My fellow passengers hastily descended and ran onto the field to stand in a circle around the plane, backs turned, relieving themselves. I had not thought about a toilet until then, but now I wanted one. I didn't dare leave the plane for fear that it would take off without me—it didn't stop long. So I sat huddled in my seat all the many hours to Peking, enviously contemplating the backs of the Japanese as they carried out the same ritual at Tsingtao and Tientsin.

It was dark when we reached Peking. Lights twinkled below us like diamonds. The plane landed with the usual bumps, and all the Japanese rushed forward. But this time I pushed, elbowed, burrowed, and was first at the door when it opened. I almost fell down the short ladder and raced into the reception building. No need to ask where the toilet was. There was the open door through which men were coming and going, lifting or settling their gowns, buttoning or unbuttoning their flies. I rushed in like a whirlwind, shoved past a man who was entering the one and only closed stall, and slammed the door in his face. It was filthy, of course, and smelled to high heaven, but I couldn't have cared less. It was exquisite. Sometimes now when I suspiciously inspect the impeccable bathrooms of expensive hotels, I burst out laughing to think how Veronica would laugh.

The hotel for which the Old Boss was paying enchanted me. It was built like the Editor's house, only much bigger. Courtyards and low houses succeeded each other in a long row from the entrance on one hutung right back to the hutung behind. From the rickshaw coolie who took me there I finally understood that "hutung" meant a small road. I was enchanted because I had so much trouble understanding his Mandarin, enchanted with its rolling *r*s and its soft *sh* sounds. He wanted two military yen for the trip. I said "liang kwei?" in Shanghainese. He said "urrrr kwai." It sounded wonderful. At the airport I had changed the Chinese money we were still using in Shanghai for the military yen that the Japanese had introduced in the north, paper money without any backing beyond Japanese bayonets. The rickshaw coolie picked out notes from the handful I showed him and went off saying "shay shay," where I would have said "zia zia"—thank you.

The hotel boy led me through four courtyards and bowed me into my room in the fourth house. It had a foreign style brass bed, a thick Chinese carpet, a round blackwood table with a marble top, some blackwood stools around it, a curtained recess for clothes, and a huge iron stove in which a fire roared. It was beautifully warm and peaceful. Frozen by my rickshaw ride, exhausted by the plane trip and all the excitement, I lay on the bed to relax for a moment.

I woke up choking, each breath searing my nostrils and lungs.

I stumbled to the door and out into the courtyard, gulping the pure, fresh, knifelike air.

A voice beside me said in American: "You too?"

It was a girl.

"It's those stoves. They give out such gorgeous heat but they dry the air until its like breathing powder. Tomorrow we'll have to ask for pans of water to put on top of the stoves. Its awfully dry in Peking. We're not far from the Gobi Desert, you know."

She was a student of Asian history who had saved for years to make the trip to China and had decided to make it anyway in spite of the war. She had arrived the day before from Hongkong.

"Let's sightsee together. It's much more interesting and it's cheaper. We can share all the expenses, rickshaws, tips, meals." She hesitated a moment. "We could share rooms too, if you like."

I said I liked my own room, which my uncle was paying for, but thought it would be a fine idea to sightsee together. And it was. She had in her handbag a little black book in which she entered every military yen and military sen spent while we were together. At the end of the day she added it up, divided by two, and insisted that we settle the account on the spot. If I owed her forty-three military sen and didn't have change, I had to go to the hotel desk and get it.

But she knew far more about Chinese history than I did. I had only been born in China and lived there all my life until then. She had studied it. We bought the best guidebook we could find (that was one thing she didn't want to stint on) and wandered about, dispensing with guides, spending as much or as little time as we wanted on each site.

A millennium before Christ, Peking existed as the city of Chi, capital of the Yen kingdom. Two thousand years later, after many destructions and rebuildings, changes of name and of rulers, it was the capital of Kublai Khan, founder of the Mongol dynasty. The plan of the modern city originated in the fifteenth century under the Ming emperors. We wandered around the towering walls of the Inner City, through all of its nine deep gates, each one forty feet thick where it pierced the wall. We explored the Imperial City set squarely in the middle of the Inner City, and squarely within that the moated Forbidden City where in the Hall of Supreme Harmony the Manchu emperors had sat on the Peacock Throne.

Here was the marble boat of Tzu Hsi, the Last Empress, who had once seized the entire budget of the Chinese navy. As a concession to the purpose for which the money had been allotted, she had built the marble boat in the lake in the Imperial City and used it as a pavilion for drinking tea. Tzu Hsi had started life as a third-grade concubine in the harem of the third-to-last Manchu emperor. The son she bore him was the heir apparent and, on the emperor's death, she became regent for her young son. While he was still in puberty, she encouraged the eunuchs of the harem to pander to his awakening vigor. In due course he died, exhausted. His pregnant widow died too, after eating certain cakes sent by her sorrowing mother-in-law.

Next to ascend the Peacock Throne had been Kuang Hsu, nephew of the Last Empress. Him she had kept virtually imprisoned until she finally broke his spirit by having his favorite concubine drowned in a well, into which my friend and I peered nervously.

Last to sit on the throne had been the grand-nephew of the Last Empress—Hsuang Tung, whose personal name was Pu Yi. He had become emperor at the age of three years when the Last Empress finally, reluctantly, died, and been dethroned at the age of six, in 1912, when the Manchus had been overthrown and the

Republic established. Pu Yi now sat on the ancient throne of Manchuria, puppet emperor of Japan's puppet empire Manchukuo. It all seemed very recent, very close.

From the Forbidden City we walked all the way down the arrow-straight road which led through the Money Gate, through the Outer City, directly to the Temple of Heaven where, once every year, the Emperor had stood on the Altar of Heaven, the center of the universe, to report to Heaven the state of his empire.

We took buses out of the city to explore the Summer Palace, to dawdle on the broad roadway on top of the Great Wall of China, to walk over the eight-hundred-year-old Marco Polo Bridge with its multitude of carved stone lions, to marvel at the tombs of the Ming emperors, to view the Temple of Heavenly Peace, to picnic in the Western Hills sitting in a patch of sunlight on a blanket filched from the hotel.

Ten days passed in a flash. On the last day, with the money my friend had saved for me by her strict economy measures, I bought a silver ring set with a huge uncut aquamarine weighing four hundred karats, and a padded dressing gown of turquoise colored brocade. She came with me to the East Station outside the Money Gate to say goodbye. When I had gone to the airport to confirm my return passage on the plane I had been told "so sorry," many Japanese businessmen were traveling and it appeared all of them had priority over a non-Japanese girl, even one with a seat reserved weeks earlier. But I could exchange my plane ticket for a first class sleeper on the train, changing at Nanking for Shanghai. I exchanged it, not wishing to remain in Peking indefinitely until a gap in the throng of Japanese businessmen left an empty seat on the plane for me.

The train started with a jerk. I was alone in my two-berth sleeper. I didn't know who was going to share it with me. The

stationmaster in Peking hadn't been able to tell me. "A woman?"
I asked. He shrugged. "Maybe woman, maybe man, I don't
know."

We chuffed all day through the frozen countryside. In the
afternoon I left my compartment to find the toilet. The narrow
corridor was full of Japanese soldiers, lining the walls on each side,
standing, leaning, sitting on their packs, sprawling on the floor,
most of them asleep, snoring and grunting with mouths open.
They didn't move to allow one to pass. One had to push by them,
step over them, smelling their ripe smells from close up. When
I found the toilet I couldn't believe my eyes. It contained five
soldiers crushed in body to body. Three shared the toilet seat,
propping themselves on it by thrusting their legs against the walls.
Two balanced on the washbasin, clinging to each other. All were
asleep. How could they sleep in those positions? I called out.
None of them stirred, and those outside the door began to laugh,
highly amused. I pushed my way back to the compartment, de-
feated. It wasn't possible! Not again! And the trip to Nanking
would take two days and a night! In the evening I tried again.
Nothing had changed. The five were still sleeping noisily.

When, miserably, I got back to the compartment, my fellow
traveler was arriving. Inevitably, a Japanese businessman, short,
stocky, uncouth, arrogant. Two friends with whom he had obviously been drinking accompanied him. They roared out good-
nights in the harsh way of Japanese males, their bursts of words
sounding as though they were being hawked up and spat out.
When the friends left, my compartment mate didn't even glance
at me. He started to undress. I stood up and tapped him on the
shoulder. He looked around, scowling at my insolence. I pointed
to the upper berth and then to myself. He shook his head. "I-ye!"
No. He wanted it himself. He hung his overcoat, jacket, and pants

on a hook and, in long gray woolen underwear, climbed into the top berth. A few grunts, a few nose and throat clearings, and then snores.

I wrapped myself, still fully clothed, in my new turquoise dressing gown and lay down on top of the blankets in the lower berth, utterly miserable, sure I wouldn't sleep. But sometime later I woke with a start. The train was slowing down. Through the window beside me I saw the lighted name panel of the station as we slid past: Tsinan, where I had been told we were to change military yen for Chinese currency. The train stopped with a tremendous jerk and a loud clanging. My Japanese businessman in his long gray underwear tumbled out of the upper berth onto the floor. He sprang up, whirled around, shook my shoulder.

"Chinese fight train"—a loud, tense whisper—"You no fear! I take care you!"—pounding his chest, glaring protectively.

I wanted to giggle with relief, but managed to say politely:

"Thank you, but I think it's the station for changing money."

"Hah!"—surprised, staring out of the window—"Sssssssss"— long descending Japanese hiss of deprecation. "Very sorry! Very sorry! I wake you up?"

"No, no, I was already awake."

"Very sorry! Sssssssss! Very sorry! I change money you?"

"Oh, thanks."

I gave him the little I had left, he threw on his overcoat over the underwear, rushed off, rushed back, handed me notes.

"Very sorry! Very sorry! I help you anything?"

I had a brilliant thought. "Yes! In toilet many soldiers. You can wake them up, tell them go away little time?"

"Hah! You come!"

In ten seconds, with harsh Japanese shouts, he cleared the toilet and stood on guard outside while I used it. Next day, which he spent with friends elsewhere on the train, he came every three hours to conduct me to the toilet. Every time he said "Very sorry!" and I bowed and smiled graciously and said everything was fine. I felt quite regretful when he left the train at Nanking with a final "Very sorry!" and I changed to another train for Shanghai.

21

Occupied City

In DECEMBER 1941 three important events occurred in what had become a very monotonous existence. Since my return from Peking a year earlier, life had been a series of increasing restraints, dull and wearisome. The amenities were shrinking out of sight. Our house was almost unheated—the big stove in the parlor which used to be alight twenty-four hours a day all winter was now lit only from five to nine in the evenings and the whole house was chill, the bedrooms icy. Getting into and out of bed required heroism. We didn't have coal for the big hot-water heater. Kettles of water were boiled all day on a small Chinese clay stove and poured into thermos flasks, cheap ones with a rattan outer sheath which burst regularly. We each had a thermos flask of hot water to wash with in the mornings, and in the evenings we bought hot water. The hot-water shops got coke from the gas works and with it kept huge cauldrons of water boiling all the time. Buyers got two large wooden bucket-loads toted to their homes on a pole across a coolie's shoulder. Two bucket-loads were enough for two baths, and we took turns. The joy of life was reduced to whether it was one's turn for a hot bath.

The only interesting event had been Jane's wedding in June. She was married in a short white dress concocted from an evening gown that she had worn only once because somebody had burned a big hole in it. We arranged for the hole to be on the right side of the waist and embroidered a flower over it as camouflage. The dress really looked very nice, and with it she wore a short white veil made of mosquito netting and the wax orange blossoms from Mother's wedding veil. Her French husband had the most impeccable formal manners, but at the same time a mind which rejoiced in fantasy. His oldest friend, who was his best man, told us seriously: "He has his feet well planted in the air." We were all very fond of him.

Then, in December, three things happened: on the seventh, Ah-May came back to us. On the eighth, the Japanese, in a small but neat sideshow to their action in Pearl Harbor, seized the International Settlement and the French Concession, thereby effectively ending extraterritoriality. It was to be abolished after the war, but the Japanese were the ones who really ended it. On the eighteenth, Bill, having carried out his threat to screw every last penny he could out of the Japanese, slipped out of town, not to be seen again by us until the war was over.

On the seventh I was alone in our parlor, knitting and reading, when Ah-May came back. I heard "Doo-bebe" and the familiar giggle. She stood in the doorway, grinning broadly. Behind her was Little Bell and behind him two little girls.

"Ah-May!"

Everyone came running at my shout. Luke was back from Hongkong University with his civil engineering degree. Only Jane was no longer with us.

There was rejoicing and lamentation. The farm in Zose had had to be abandoned. Zose was a backwater in which there had been no fighting, but it was important because of the excellent rice that grew there. As the war seesawed back and forth, both Japanese and Chinese had extorted rice from the peasantry. The peasants had hidden their rice, what was left after paying taxes, in caves in the hill which gave Zose its name—Snake Hill. They had buried it in silos dug deep into the ground. In spite of their efforts, they had seen much of their rice swallowed up into the maw of army trucks. Still, they had managed to subsist until this year.

This year Chungking had ruled that peasants must pay all their forty-odd taxes in grain. Money had become reliable in one way only: it could be absolutely relied upon to lose value from day to day. In Chungking, the Finance Minister, the Generalissimo's brother-in-law H.H. Kung, had begun his policy of meeting the government's ever-escalating demands for money simply by putting more of it into circulation. By 1944 he was releasing five thousand million new Chinese dollars every month in beautiful crisp notes printed in America. But in 1941 Chungking had already decided that it didn't want its own diminishing money coming back from the peasants in payment of those taxes that they had been paying in cash. Only grain, Chungking wanted, rice or wheat, in quotas fixed for each province. So in 1941, foreshadowing on a small scale the disaster of Honan two years later, the peasants of Zose had been cleaned out of rice.

Little Bell, still handsome, told us on a sign from Ah-May how all the rice had disappeared, how Ah-May had decided that the farm must be abandoned for the time being. His parents had both died. There was nothing to hold them back. Ah-May had decided it was time to come back to us.

Ah-May was smiling, tears running down her cheeks. To Father and Mother:

"Tung-kah. Tah-tah. We couldn't stay any longer. There was nothing to eat. So I told him we must come back to you."

"Of course, Ah-May! Of course!"

She wiped her eyes on her sleeve, the smile twisted.

"Doo-bebe," she patted me. "Doo-bebe."

"Ah-May."

We laughed. We all laughed, patting Ah-May while she patted us all in turn. She turned to Little Bell and made a sign to bring the little girls forward. It was clear who was the boss in that family.

The children were both called Ching Mei, Golden Maiden. The seer who had been consulted when each was born had determined that on the days of their births metal had been missing from the elements. The five elements of China are metal, wood, water, fire, and earth. A child born on a day when one of the elements is missing must be given a name containing the name of that element. Gold is the most precious of the metals, so both little girls had been given the name Ching Mei. The elder was called Big Ching Mei and the younger Small Ching Mei.

Since the Old Boss had Ah-May's room, she and her family were installed in our garage. The lease of our house included a garage in the row at the back of the compound. For a short time our garage had housed a car, a dark green Essex in which, for a year or two in the heydays before 1937, we had all gone to school and office. Now the garage was empty, Father having sold the Essex as soon as the price of gasoline started rising. Later, many cars had to be abandoned and stood rotting in garages or in the open, cluttering the streets. The sale of our car was the best coup that Father, so innocent of the sharp practice commonplace in our city, ever executed. And the worst was what he did with the money—ten thousand Chinese dollars in brand new bright red one hundred dollar bills which he put into envelopes and fixed with tin tacks in back of the huge drawer of his wardrobe.

Young Ching had begged him not to. Young Ching had succeeded his father as compradore of Father's firm and had become a power in it. Only Father still called him Young Ching—to everyone else he was Mr. Ching—and only to Father did he speak simply and frankly. To everyone else he used a jovial, bumbling, back-slapping manner which concealed his shrewdness and allowed him to make the most offensive remarks to people he did not like without giving them the opportunity of taking offense. Father chuckled for years about an incident involving a son of the firm's owners—a lordly young Englishman who had deeply offended Young Ching by persistently, in a kind and condescending manner, speaking of the Chinese as "Chinks." This young man, it became known in Father's office, had been forced into a shotgun wedding. When he came to the Shanghai office on his next inspection trip, everyone studiously avoided the subject except Young Ching, who came in grinning his broadest grin, slapped the young man's back, and said in his most booming voice: "You very clever man, huh! You get marry you very quick catchee baby, huh!"

But about Father's ten thousand dollars Young Ching had been perturbed. "Please! You don't keep this money! After this money make wallpaper your room. You give me, I lend out for you, big interest, maybe ten percent per month. Please, you don't keep this money!"

But Father liked the feeling of those ten thousand new paper dollars behind the drawer that could be moved only with the utmost determination, and there they lay.

The morning after Ah-May's arrival, before it was fully light, Ah-May was there sweeping the halls and staircases, waiting for us to get up to start on our rooms.

"Oh, Ah-May!" we all said as we got up. "Isn't it wonderful to have Ah-May back!"

For the last year or two we hadn't been able to afford the salaries demanded by amahs. Dahsoo's Number One wife had been coming in daily to help with the housework and the clothes washing. We had all cooperated on weekends in giving the house a thorough cleaning. Now we not only had Ah-May back for herself, but also for all that horrible housework, plus Little Bell, who would help with the heavy work that had largely been skipped. It didn't matter that we couldn't afford them. We would pay them what we could, and we would all eat whatever and as much as we could afford to buy.

We were all a little late leaving for office that morning, talking to Ah-May, explaining the changes in the household, telling her of Jane's marriage, playing with the Ching Meis, who sat good as gold in the kitchen.

I was half an hour late when I rushed to catch my bus. It was more crowded than ever because of the later hour. I stood among the other strap-hangers, all of us so crushed together that it was impossible to lower one's upraised arm or to raise the other. There seemed to be some unusual commotion. The knot of passengers swayed to and fro as those near the windows craned to look out. Some exclaimed. Some tried to point. What was the matter? Had something happened?

At my stop I struggled to join the descending passengers being squeezed out of the bus like toothpaste from a tube. I dashed down Yuen Ming Yuen Road, looking neither right nor left. At the entrance of my building I was suddenly halted by two Japanese soldiers barring my way with bayoneted rifles. The cold steel, so often seen from afar glinting in the daylight, was shocking when seen from three inches away. I stopped dead, breath held. One sentry roared something at me. Ss si-sang bustled forward.

Last Moments of a World

He had been waiting for me just inside the doorway. He parleyed with the sentries, nodding vigorously. They let me pass.

"Ss si-sang, what's happened?"

"Very bad, very bad," he whispered. "Japanese take Shanghai."

"What ????"

"Yes, Japanese take Shanghai."

He looked at me in such a tragic manner that I patted his arm and whispered back: "At least it's not the Communists."

He began to nod in a relieved manner, then caught himself and glared, then smiled, then glared again. He didn't know what to make of that one.

In a way, the Japanese occupation didn't matter. By then we were so familiar with restraints and restrictions that it was just something else to learn how to handle. In a short while we became accustomed to the external manifestations of the occupation.

Patrols of three or four Japanese soldiers circulated constantly in the streets, rifles at the ready, bayonets poised. At first they inspired fear, but it was soon evident that these were not the veterans of the Nanking abominations. These were raw recruits, country boys, clopping about clumsily in their unaccustomed leather boots. They seemed to be taking part in a form of play-acting rather than war.

The barbed wire barricades were renovated and multiplied. They might suddenly be drawn across streets anywhere, blockading four or five routes for the passage of a Japanese VIP who selected his actual route at the last moment, while traffic piled up and pedestrians gathered in crowds, waiting interminably for the streets to be opened up again.

"Pass" became a watchword. Any movement the least unusual had to be authorized by a pass for which application had to be made days beforehand. A story circulated about a young man whose father died suddenly. His religion required that his father be buried within twenty-four hours, but to move the body he had to get a pass in a hurry. Trying to explain the matter, he said to the Japanese in charge, "If I don't bury my father by tonight, he cannot go to heaven." The Japanese replied furiously, "Japanese pass can go anywhere!"

Patrols and sentries who didn't know a single word of any language except Japanese all could say the word "Pass" in English.

"Pass!" they demanded, stopping any person or any vehicle that looked suspicious to them.

"Pass!" they demanded of us one day while we were walking along Avenue Joffre.

"Why pass?" we asked. We weren't doing anything unusual, just walking, a group of four or five of us going to visit a sick friend. Perhaps we had been talking too animatedly, walking too slowly—whatever, the patrol was suspicious.

"Pass!" the leader demanded again.

We shrugged. So sorry, no pass. Then we couldn't pass. We could go back the way we had come, but not forward. We retreated a little way, intending to cross to the other side of Avenue Joffre, but saw there was a patrol there too. We went into the Fronton building—jai-alai was one of the few public entertainments still permitted, because gambling gave the powers-that-were a lucrative income. What to do? We could go back home, but we wanted to see our friend. Someone had a bright idea. We got a copy of the day's program, a sheet of paper with an ornately printed heading, on which the day's events were printed on one side in English and on the other in Chinese. We went to the office and begged the use of some rubber stamps. We stamped the program in several places on the Chinese side, and signed it elaborately. Then we went out, crossed the street, and marched up to the patrol we hadn't met before.

"Pass!" the leader shouted.

"Hai!" we responded, the short, sharp Japanese affirmative, and presented him our program. It was highly acceptable. He almost saluted as he let us through.

Sentries were posted on top of the bridges, and we had to bow to them politely because they were representatives of the Emperor. Non-Japanese pedestrians who did not bow got slapped to teach them respect, but Japanese, especially Japanese women, who should already be imbued with respect, were more severely punished if they did not bow humbly enough. It was a common sight to see Japanese women doing penance by kneeling in the gutter before the sentry.

Trams crossing Garden Bridge had to stop at the top and their drivers had to call out to the sentry asking permission to cross— a long Japanese sentence that sounded very much like "Tsor naga nianga pee," which was a favorite and most obscene suggestion that Chinese made to people they despised. Very soon all the tram drivers were calling that out instead of the Japanese sentence. The sentry would respond by shouting "Yoroshi," an affirmative, thus apparently confirming that he would do as the tram drivers suggested, much to the amusement of passers-by. The sentries would sometimes smile, bewildered by the goodwill they seemed suddenly to have engendered.

The Japanese also installed sliding grilled gates on all the trams to prevent people from hopping on and off between stations and to prevent unauthorized articles from being carried onto trams. Other means of transport were so expensive that people took all sorts of things onto trams—they almost moved house by tram. The tram conductors had strict instructions to open the gates only for authorized reasons. Luke was on a tram one day when a loud quarrel broke out because the conductor was refusing entry to a Japanese who had a monkey perched on his shoulder. The clamor rose higher and higher until a scholarly old Chinese in the tram said to the conductor: "If the father is allowed to enter, why not the son?" The whole tram was laughing while the conductor bowed the man and his monkey in.

But these were only the everyday street aspects of the occupation, which were always tedious, sometimes dangerous, often so ludicrous that they afforded us all some badly needed entertainment. Other aspects were much more serious. Shanghai, with its enormous business network, its stocks of all sorts of primary and manufactured goods, was a rich prize. The Japanese were anxious to seize as much as they could as quickly as they could. Some assets clearly belonged to firms and nationals of the allied nations, and these were quickly seized. Japanese bankers took over the American and British banks, Japanese administrators moved into the American and British firms. The assets of Japan's Axis partners were untouched. Carlowitz & Co. continued its majestic course, its Prussian boss, disdaining the Japanese as he did the Nazis, conceding as little as possible to the Axis policies.

But Chinese firms presented another problem. The Japanese stance all along had been that they were helping the Chinese, defending them against communism, creating a coprosperity sphere. Their military might was being used only against those ungrateful Chinese elements who attacked them first. In accord with such a stance, the occupation forces could not seize outright the assets of Chinese who were ostensibly prepared to bow to the occupation. Excuses had to be found. And many Japanese were manufacturing and trading under Chinese names and licenses.

The confusion posed problems to the occupation forces, who were also divided among themselves, greedily snatching at the richest prizes for their own establishments. Various Japanese units were often delightedly seen to be at loggerheads in those firt days of the occupation. For Bill, it was a field day. He was in his element. We didn't see him at all for several days. He phoned once or twice to say he was very busy. Then, on the evening of the eighteenth, he came over. He came in furtively, reached to snap off the light that hung over our front door, walked into the parlor and made sure that the curtains were drawn over the windows. He was very tense.

"I'm going," he announced.

"Where to?"

"Kunming, if I can make it. Otherwise Chungking."

"What!!"

"Oh, it's not difficult if you know the right people. I'll make it."

"But why, Bill?"

He laughed sharply.

"Give me a drink. Anything. Some of that brandy you keep for toothache." Mother had a bottle of Napoleon brandy that she had kept for years. When we were children we had been given teaspoonfuls of it to swill around our mouths to deaden the pain of toothache.

Bill leaned back in an armchair in a pretense of ease, holding the glass in a convulsive grip, grinning tautly.

"What's up, Bill? Why are you so nervous? Come on, tell us!"

He told us. It was hard to understand, but it appeared that Bill and his friend Wong had sold to the Japanese navy a small warehouse full of copper ingots belonging to a Japanese businessman but stored in Wong's name, which the Japanese consular authorities had seized and sealed up.

"Wait a minute, Bill! Start all over! Say it again!"

It appeared that the Jap bastard who owned the ingots had paid Wong well to have them stored in one of Wong's warehouses.

The Jap bastard must have hijacked them or stolen them or smuggled them or something because he was so scared about it that he was prepared to trust Wong—of course, against all sorts of guarantees, Wong had been happy to chop all the papers that the Jap bastard wanted.

On the first day of the occupation, the Jap consular officials had descended on the warehouse and sealed it up. Wong didn't care —the ingots didn't belong to him—but the Jap bastard had nearly gone crazy rushing to the consulate to try and prove they were his. The consular authorities didn't care who owned them. They wanted that copper. The Jap bastard had even gone to Bill's house one night to beg for help.

"Please, please, sir! Yours faithfully. He actually said that— yours faithfully!"

In the meantime, Bill had been introduced to a buyer from the Jap navy. According to Bill, he had said to the buyer after lots of drinks:

"You want copper?"

"Hai!"

"Cash?"

"Cash."

"U.S. dollars?"

"U.S. dollars."

Bill roared with nervous laughter. "Can you imagine it! The Jap navy paying in U.S. dollars!"

So that morning Bill and Wong had gone to the warehouse and removed the Japanese consular seals from one of the doors to which Wong still had keys.

"I don't have to tell you how dangerous that was. But we didn't touch them until we saw the navy man's boat approaching. The warehouse is near the waterfront, and he came in a motorboat."

Bill laughed again. "The arrogant stupidity of those bastards! They thought their strips of paper were good enough to scare everybody off. They didn't even change the padlocks on the doors!"

The navy man had walked into the warehouse, taken one glance at the ingots, and ordered the sailors who had followed him in a big tugboat to start loading. Meanwhile, he and Bill and Wong had counted the piles of real, old, used, one-hundred-U.S.-dollar notes. As soon as the sailors had finished loading, the man jumped into his motorboat and roared off. It had all taken a little more than an hour.

"But why did he give you money? He could have just seized the stuff, couldn't he?"

"He paid us because the Japanese Navy can't seize stuff that the Japanese Consulate has already seized and sealed up! He knew damn well that the warehouse had been sealed by his own consular people. I wouldn't be surprised if he even knew how many ingots there were—he brought that tugboat and as many sailors as he needed to move the stuff quickly. What he really paid us for was to take the seals off for him. Of course he didn't pay us nearly what the stuff is worth in the circumstances, but what he did pay is not bad, not bad at all!"

"Oh, Bill!" Mother practically wailed. *"Must* you always be doing things like that!"

"I don't *must.*" Bill's grin was wolfish. "But I *wanted* to. And now I'm going."

He jumped up, pulling at his jacket, twitching with nerves.

"Goodbye! I'll write you a letter."

Before any of us could say a word, he was gone, slipping out of the darkened doorway, his right hand inside his jacket where his gun was.

22

❦❦❦

Flying Fortress

BILL'S LETTER, bearing ordinary Chinese postage stamps and postmarked Kunming, July 1943, was pushed into our letter box in December 1944. It was unsigned but we knew Bill's curly writing, and anyway the letter was typically Bill.

He was doing fine, he said, as an interpreter with the U.S. Fourteenth Air Force in Kunming. He was working very hard. The Kunming airfield was extremely busy. Flights roared in and out every three or four minutes and there were always planes cruising overhead waiting to land, including, Bill wrote, the B-29s, the huge new high-altitude bombers, the "Flying Fortresses."

Kunming handled almost all the air traffic in and out of China over the "Hump," the air route from Calcutta flown by the U.S. Air Transport Command, which for most of the war was China's only link with the outside world. The planes that flew the Hump traveled between Calcutta, Assam, Lashio in Burma, and Kunming—across the frozen Himalayas, over steaming jungles, through tropical monsoons and snowstorms, dodging the Japanese Air Force, carrying thousands of tons of cargo every month, mostly war materials but also newly printed Chinese dollars that H.H.

Kung was pouring into the economy, and all the American troops being sent to China.

Bill knew all the pilots of the Transport Command, wrote with sorrow of several who had died in the discharge of their acutely dangerous and difficult duties, whose bones lay forever in the wreckage of their planes in the high mountains or the impenetrable jungles. He wrote also with glee of his particular friend, a pilot also named Bill, who had ordered Madame Chiang Kai-shek's grand piano dumped out of his plane over the Himalayas. The piano had been included in the cargo, displacing a desperately needed army truck, by direct order from Chungking, and over the pilot's and his commander's strenuous objections. When the plane began to buck dangerously in the downdraft over the mountain peaks, pilot Bill had decided that it had to be lightened, and out went the piano.

Of course, Bill was still negotiating deals. He wrote that the Air Transport Command was building dug-hole latrines for workers at the airport, holes in the ground with cement step-plates and bamboo partitions. Each one was costing the Command something like US $10,000. The Command was obliged to pay in Chinese currency, which it was obliged to obtain from the Bank of China at the pegged rate of twenty Chinese dollars per U.S. dollar, when any G.I. in Kunming could get one thousand under the table from a black market peddler. Bill, of course, knew people at the Bank of China and he was doing something about getting a better exchange rate for the Air Transport Command's contractor.

By the time we received Bill's letter, anyone in Shanghai lucky enough to have U.S. dollars was getting three thousand or more Chinese dollars for each on the black market, and even the most law-abiding of citizens dealt on the black market if they could. It was simply stupid not to. Finance Minister H.H. Kung, responsible for the pegged rate, was the biggest profiteer of them all. He and his cohorts bought U.S. dollars for twenty Chinese dollars each, sold them again for three thousand, and bought gold bars with the profits. All the while he kept insisting that there was really no inflation: as long as the Chinese dollar was pegged at twenty, there was no inflation. Bill's friends at the Bank of China had perhaps found some way to siphon off a few of the Transport Command's U.S. dollars into their own pockets for a rate more favorable than twenty to one. If H.H. Kung had heard about it, he would no doubt have been pleased, as long as they didn't siphon off too many. The more guilty people around, the better —the fewer who could afford to speak up. The ideal would be for everybody who had any voice in Kuomintang circles to be at least a little guilty, and that ideal was very nearly achieved in those days.

Take care, Bill's letter ended. Keep well. Be happy.

We were trying to be, but it was getting harder every day. For one thing, we were always hungry. Our main diet consisted of porridge made of cracked wheat from Red Cross shipments, sweet potatoes, and pork fat rendered with an apple which we mashed into the potatoes or spread on bread. When bread was to be found, it had to be eaten quickly, because it turned green and began to smell bad a few hours after it was baked.

Now and then, however, we feasted on account of Luke's football. Football, always popular but now almost the only public entertainment, had become a craze, and Luke was one of the three most idolized players in the city. He got many advantages from it, such as never having to wait in the interminable queues in which people crushed against each other. People would recognize him and cede him their places—"Lukee? Ah! LUKEE!

Come, come!" and up the queue he would go until he was at the head of the line.

But for us Luke's most valuable asset as a footballer was that he was invited to play in "charity" matches for which rich people —the profiteers, the collaborators, those wishing to curry favor with the sponsors—bought up blocks of tickets at enormous prices. To augment the profits, and to give additional opportunity to favor-curriers, the ball, autographed by the winning team, would be auctioned off after the matches for fabulous sums. The players were not paid, of course—the sponsors said they respected their amateur status—but they were invited to dinner after the game. Buffet dinner, at which the tables were so loaded with good food that not an inch of tablecloth showed. The players ate their fill and then produced the bags they were expected to bring with them, filled them to bursting, and hurried off home. The only good food we ate in those days came from Luke's football, but we could never eat much of it—it was so rich and our stomachs had shrunk so small.

Sometimes when we had leftovers we gave a little to our next-door neighbors. A nice, simple, hardworking Japanese family had been quartered next door when our neighbors, holding British passports, had been sent to internment camp. The Japanese had carried out their commitments under their Axis partnership: allied nationals to internment camps and Jews to a ghetto of one square mile in the northeastern part of the city.

When the possibility of internment camp began to be talked about, Veronica, to our dismay, had suddenly married her English boyfriend, an out-of-work journalist. It was with sorrow that we saw Veronica go off with him to a tiny rented room. She had a job, walked to work every day, walked back at night, cooked dinner, did all the housework and washing, paid all the bills, while he did nothing but cerebrate. He was writing a book, he said, a history of current events. In fact, it was a scurrilous account of all the dirt he had managed to collect on foreign diplomats, bank managers, and other Shanghai ex-VIPs. Fortunately, it never saw the light. But Veronica was blind to all that. She was firmly under the impression that she was nurturing genius.

When he went to camp the Japanese would not take Veronica because she did not have a British passport. She took to sauntering around the camp and throwing parcels of precious food over the wall to her husband. We begged her to stop it. The people in the camps were eating better than most of those outside—toward the end of the war, better than their Japanese guards. They got Red Cross parcels every month, with solid stomach-filling foods as well as goodies like jam, and even cigarettes. Things from Red Cross parcels were the medium of exchange in the camps, of paying off debts, of bribing guards to close their eyes to clandestine radios. But what made Father really angry was that Veronica ran the risk of being taken to Bridge House if she had ever got caught throwing parcels over the wall.

Bridge House was the Japanese Secret Police headquarters. In 1937 it had been a new apartment building standing on the north side of Soochow Creek at the foot of one of the bridges. Now it was a place of terror—windows barred, doors heavily guarded by men from the elite Secret Police who looked far more dangerous than the sloppy peasant boys of our street patrols. People disappeared into Bridge House never to be seen again. Tales of torture were spun around it which, after the war, were known not to have been exaggerated.

A dear friend of ours had committed suicide to escape Bridge House. We were losing many friends, not only into internment camps and the ghetto, but also by death from disease contracted

Last Moments of a World

in the weakened state of semistarvation, and this one by suicide. He had worked at the Hongkong & Shanghai Bank and, desperate to feed his numerous family, had helped himself from the till. The Japanese auditors had discovered him. Threatened with Bridge House, he had climbed to the top of the clock tower in the Race Club building and thrown himself down. His wife and mother were afraid as well as heartbroken: would they now be dragged off to Bridge House? Not at all. The Japanese manager of the bank called on them to felicitate them: an honorable husband and son, who had honorably expiated his crime. The bank arranged and paid for his funeral, which the Japanese auditors and all the Japanese officers of the bank attended.

Like Veronica, I was walking almost all the way to and from my office. Buses had stopped running—there was no fuel for them. Trams were still running, but the service had been much curtailed and could take me no more than a third of the way. So I walked four miles each way, and then fought a desperate battle to get into or out of a tram.

To distract myself from the tedium, I had a game: trying to catch pickpockets red-handed. At the tram terminal there was a Chinese food shop, its shelves still holding a supply of sweet stuff. I stood every day and gazed at it, my mouth watering, imagining the taste of sugar, lovely, sweet, gooey, sticky, melting sugar. One day I had walked into the shop and recklessly spent twenty thousand dollars on twenty "li sing dong"—seeds of the lotus plant, round and big as marbles, preserved in a beautiful translucent crust of sugar. The shop attendant used his fingers to count them into a paper bag made of old newspaper. I put the bag into my coat pocket and struggled into the tram, wondering whether I would be magnanimous and share out my twenty li sing dong when I got home, or horribly selfish and eat them all myself before

I got there. I touched my pocket. The question had become academic: the little bag was gone. Somebody had picked my pocket. Almost in tears, I looked around me. Hopeless. All I could see, three inches from my eyes, was the cheek of the person crushed closest against me. Besides, the thief would not be on the tram. He must have picked my pocket at the tram terminal and then swiftly melted into the crowd.

After that, I watched for pickpockets, and one day I caught one —perhaps the same one, because it was at the same terminal. This time I had a pack of playing cards in my pocket. I was learning to play bridge, a fascinating occupation which cost nothing. In the melee at the door of the tram, in spite of the bumping and buffeting, I felt the twitch at my pocket. I pushed back. The cards were gone. Sauntering casually at the edge of the crowd was a filthy old man. I walked up and tapped him on the shoulder.

"Give me back what you took from my pocket."

"What! I took something from your pocket? Never! Never!"

"Give me back what you took from my pocket." I was calm, inexorable.

"I took nothing! You can search me!" He began to undo his vile clothing, shaking it to show me it hid nothing. I thought of the lice that were no doubt hopping from his garments onto mine and looked around for a policeman. One was standing a few yards away, his back turned. Policemen these days always had their backs turned. They stood on street corners, and if a person came from one direction to appeal to them, to say perhaps, "There's a dead body lying there," they shook their heads and said, "Sorry, that's not my beat. *That's* my beat," pointing in the other direction. Nevertheless, I called out to this policeman. He started to walk away. I turned back to my pickpocket.

"Stop that! It's no use pretending. I had a pack of cards in my pocket, and you took it. Give it back to me."

He stopped shaking out his clothes.

"What? What was it?"

"Cards. A pack of playing cards."

"Ohhhh." A disappointed grunt. "That's no use!" He turned to a small boy standing nearby. "Give them back to her."

Without a word the boy, who must have received the cards from the man a split second after he had lifted them from my pocket, took them from a hiding place in his clothing and handed them to me.

"Thank you," I said to him.

"Vior ka-che," he said politely. "Don't mention it."

"And don't steal from me again!" I shouted at the man.

"No, no!" He looked horrified at the thought.

I went back to the battle of the tram.

Because of that incident I reached home later than usual and met our new neighbor's two small sons coming back in the dusk from their compulsory military training class. They were shivering in cotton khaki uniforms, short pants, tennis shoes, thin socks, no coats.

"You're cold!" I said. "Haven't you got coats?"

We had all learned some Japanese. All offices these days had at least one Japanese staff member who gave a mandatory Japanese language lesson to the rest of the staff every day. That day our teacher had neglected his duties. Although we had all gathered for the lesson, he had spent the whole hour telling us in English that the Japanese didn't care at all about the American build-up in China. What if the Americans had marvelous guns! What if they had limitless ammunition! Japanese were Samurai! A fierce look around. Japanese had Samurai swords! When the Americans appeared the Samurai would leap out of hiding and each would slice off ten American heads with a single stroke of his Samurai sword. He gazed at us popeyed, then whirled around, arm extended, his pen the sword. "Haaaaah!" The throat-scraping Japanese battle yell.

"Ai-yah!" we said admiringly, stepping back out of the way.

He looked at us suspiciously but dismissed the class.

So now I understood what the two small boys said to me, standing proudly, trying to control their shivers. No coats. No money. The money for the coats had gone to the war effort.

"Oh!" I said. "Very good. Very Samurai."

They bowed politely, hands on their reddened little knees, and ran into our neighbor's house, now their home.

When I went into our home, Father was drawing the blackout curtains. He was very careful about that now. Some weeks earlier a small slit had shown and a Japanese patrol had marched into our house. Were we trying to signal American planes? Indeed not! We wouldn't dream of it. The curtain was a bit torn, that was all. Suspicious glares. Well, this time we would be forgiven, but the head of the house had to be taught a lesson. Father had to go to prison for the night. After a lot of parleying, they accepted the fact that Father was old and not well and allowed, as Ah-May suggested, that Little Bell could be punished in his stead.

Tonight, just as Father got the curtains well clipped together, the air raid siren sounded. We rushed up the stairs to the veranda at the top of the house which was intended for hanging out washing to dry and was a fine vantage point. Hardly anybody we knew took shelter when air raid warning sounded. Most people rushed to where they might see the planes—maybe they'd be American planes! Our neighbors' two small boys were on their veranda, across a couple of yards of space. We all peered up into the darkening skies. Nothing to be seen except a few emerging stars, but all of us clearly heard the drone of planes.

"Kamikaze!" the boys shouted. "Kamikaze!"

"What are they chattering about?" Father asked.

"Those Japanese suicide pilots. You know, they fly broken-down planes and dive into the American warships trying to sink them and killing themselves in the process."

"Kamikaze!" the boys shouted again, waving at me. Here was the vindication of their war effort.

I felt sorry not to agree, but I couldn't. The drone of the planes was too powerful, too serene, held too much authority, for kamikaze.

"I-ye," I said, shaking my head, smiling, hoping in my own joyous excitement to soften the blow for them. "B-29. Flying Fortress. American."

They looked at me reproachfully, the whites of their eyes glimmering in the dusk. They were hardly tall enough to see over the balustrade of their veranda.

"I-ye." They said it stubbornly. "Kamikaze. Nippon."

23

Civil War

THE SINO-JAPANESE WAR ended with Japan's surrender to the
United States of America in the Pacific.

The news arrived in Shanghai on a hot sticky evening in August
1945. The city's telephone system suddenly became wildly over-
loaded as everyone called everyone to tell the good news. The
streets flooded with people laughing, crying, shouting, dancing.
It's over! It's over!

The internment camps were opened to joyful reunions. The
Jews streamed out of the ghetto. Owners repossessed their premises and goods, checked anxiously for damages and losses, inquired
about processing claims. Managers and bankers moved back to
their august offices. People left town and people came back,
including Bill, healthy, cheerful, rich.

Everyone was very happy but everything was very confused.
The Japanese had yet to surrender. They had been ordered to
surrender to the Kuomintang, but the Kuomintang were not
there. There was a hiatus during which nobody quite knew what
was happening. In the city huge pictures of Chiang Kai-shek
appeared everywhere, garlanded with paper flowers, but outside

the city it was rumored that the Communists were gathering. There were one or two small strikes. At last the Kuomintang came, the Ninety-fourth Army, flown in on American planes. The Japanese surrendered formally and we began to see Japanese being paraded through the streets, hands tied behind their backs, ropes around their necks, faces painted with whitewash—the conquered on display by the pseudo-conquerors. It was as sickening a sight as any we had seen. I was on the street one day when a truck passed with ten or twelve Japanese soldiers in it in ragged uniforms, tied with rope, faces glaring white. The truck was being driven very slowly in first gear and on its running boards were Chinese soldiers with loudspeakers shouting insults at the captives. A crowd surrounded the truck, a mass of people, laughing, taunting, jumping up to hit at the captives with fists or sticks, to spit in their faces great clots of phlegm that they aaaarked triumphantly out of their throats. Suddenly two of the Japanese broke free of their bonds and, wild with fury, leaped over the tailboard of the truck into the midst of the crowd. I was twenty feet away on the sidewalk, but in an instant I was knocked over by the tidal wave of Chinese who fled the two unarmed Japanese, tumbling helter-skelter in their anxiety to get away.

Slowly some sort of order was restored to the city. Command posts were set up or taken over from the Japanese. Americans poured into the city, G.I.'s by the thousands and their officers, all of whom, we were told, had been temporarily promoted a grade or two, but without pay raises, because they had to be able to speak on equal terms with their Kuomintang counterparts. The Kuomintang admiral was a five-star admiral—one star for each ship, we joked.

American aid to China in the Sino-Japanese war had begun in the spring of 1942 with the establishment of the China-Burma-

India theater of operations. In Shanghai, with strict Japanese censorship, we hadn't known much about it. In fact, my Japanese teacher's fantasy about the samurai swords cutting off ten American heads at a single stroke had been a source of enlightenment: the Americans were near, they had wonderful armaments, the Japanese were worried and gloomy. In all those three years, news of what was really going on outside had come to us mostly from enthusiastic amateurs who had built clandestine radios. We had heard confused and contradictory stories, of which mainly the names stood out: Stilwell, the Burma campaign, Gauss, the Flying Tigers of General Chennault, P-40s, C-54s, B-29s, the Hump, Merrill's Marauders, Hurley, Wedemeyer. It was not until long after the war, after impartial and cool-headed histories and analyses of the war had reached us and we had read and studied them, that we were able to piece it all together.

General Joseph W. Stilwell had been the American commander of the China-Burma-India theater, a man with a distinguished military career and long experience in China, a soldier to whom compromise for the sake of political exigencies was distasteful. The Communists liked him and the Kuomintang hated him. He was assigned as chief of staff to Chiang Kai-shek, who was supreme commander of the China theater, but in China itself Chiang had his own chief of staff, General Ho Ying-chin. General Stilwell's purpose was to help the Chinese fight the Japanese. General Ho's was to support Chiang and protect the Kuomintang. As the Sino-Japanese war had been fought, these purposes proved incompatible.

For General Stilwell, it was essential to break the blockade of China by defeating the Japanese in Burma and opening up the Burma road. In 1942 he had proposed sending the Communist armies to fight the Japanese in Burma—the proposal of a fighting man who saw the most efficient way to his objective. To General Ho that was a most alarming and quite impossible proposal: the Communist armies would have to cross China with unpredictable results for the Kuomintang. Every decision, every order, had to be considered in terms of the political advantages or dangers to the Kuomintang. For two years General Stilwell bargained with General Ho, haggled every step of the way, parlayed every ounce of American aid into reluctant concessions.

At last, in 1944, the Burma road had been opened by a combination of American, British, and Chinese troops. The Chinese soldiers had been those who had earlier fled into Burma, whom General Stilwell had salvaged, fed decently, clothed, trained, equipped, and built up into the crack Sixth Army, which after the war became one of Chiang Kai-shek's mainstays.

But with the opening of the Burma Road, General Stilwell and Clarence Gauss, the American ambassador to Chungking, had come to the despairing conclusion that no amount of American aid would drive the Japanese out of China as long as the Chinese government with which they were dealing, the Kuomintang, remained what it was: rotten with corruption. In September 1944 a mission arrived from Washington with plenipotentiary powers to revise American/Chinese relationships. Its leader was Patrick Hurley. Chiang Kai-shek was forced by his desperate need of American supplies to agree that General Stilwell be appointed commander-in-chief of all Chinese armies. But General Stilwell's first command, a blunt memorandum regarding reorganization of the Chinese military, shocked, insulted, and infuriated Chiang in every fiber of his being. He demanded the removal of General Stilwell.

General Stilwell was replaced by General Wedemeyer. Ambassador Gauss resigned and was succeeded by Patrick Hurley.

The conduct of the war went on as before, but Hurley was instructed to do something about China's internal politics, to somehow bring about reconciliation between the Kuomintang and the Communists. Mr. Hurley, it appeared from what we read, was not the person for that mission. He had not consulted Ambassador Gauss' files crammed with information on the recent history of China. After months in Chungking he still referred to Chiang Kai-shek as "Mr. Shek," and his pronunciation of Mao Tse-tung's name sounded something like "Moose Dung." Nevertheless, Hurley assumed he knew how to handle the situation and confidently embarked on an early version of shuttle diplomacy. In the fall of 1944 he flew between Chungking and Yenan with proposals for a coalition. First to Yenan with Chiang Kai-shek's cynical offer of lackey status for the Communists within the Kuomintang government. Then, when that was flatly rejected, back to Chungking with a lavish proposal of his own invention which Chungking dismissed as the height of unreality. His stock dwindled to the vanishing point. Invective between Chungking and Yenan rose to epic proportions and negotiations collapsed.

Within two days of the end of the Sino-Japanese war, civil war was again brewing, the Kuomintang and the Communists speeding troops headlong to disarm Japanese garrisons, to take possession of the great areas of China that had been under Japanese control. The Communist armies were in better position for this scramble, but in their giant C-54s the U.S. Air Force flew Kuomintang armies to strategic positions, and U.S. Marines landed in north China.

In the fall of 1945 a last effort was made for a coalition government. Under American guarantees of safety, Mao Tse-tung flew to Chungking and the last desperate bargaining began between the two whom the Editor had called the Titans. Between them stood twenty years of struggle, of death and bloodshed, and the bitter memory of betrayal.

The bargaining failed. Chiang Kai-shek stood adamant on his own sole supremacy in China. Wrote *Time* staff correspondent Theodore White: "He had America on his side. Hurley supported Chiang and Wedemeyer was ready to implement any policy approved by Hurley, however grave the consequences. Chiang's hand was strengthened as the negotiations (with Mao Tse-tung) rounded out their fourth week, by the news that American marines were being assigned to the occupation of northern China to help him. The Americans had already helped him secure the Yangtze Valley; now, with their finest combat troops moving to take northern China for him too, he could see no reason why he should make concessions to the Communists."*

And so, in that fall of 1945, Mao Tse-tung went back to Yenan and civil war began to engulf China, while in Shanghai, all unknowing, we were so full of joy and hope. Still hungry, still threadbare, but full of joy and hope.

---

*With Annalee Jacoby, on page 288 of *Thunder out of China*, published by William Sloane Associates in August 1946. On page 322 of the same book, the prophetic words: ". . . for our tortuous diplomacy has already earned the bitterness and enmity of the Chinese Communist Party; it will be a long time before they return to the friendliness of 1944."

24

***

Go–Going–Gone

WHEN FATHER DIED toward the end of 1948 the joy and hope had withered. The Japanese time was more than three years in the past, yet things in Shanghai were worse, not better. Worse than the worst we remembered.

The Kuomintang was on us like a scourge. They had taken over the city and all its services; the Customs, the Municipality, Bridge House, and everything was grist to their mills. Business at Bridge House had flourished. Anyone who was accused by anyone of collaboration with the Japanese was immediately rushed off to Bridge House. Nobody discussed innocence or guilt. There was only one question: how many gold bars? Only one investigation: the capacity of the accused or his family to pay for his release. City government churned out new rules and regulations by the hundred, each one costing the public money, each one lining the pocket of some official. Businesses, shops, restaurants, bars, nightclubs, all had to get new licenses. A whole new breed of license brokers sprang up. All motor vehicles had to be repainted according to their function: blue for private cars, green for company cars, yellow for taxis, etc. The new director of the Vehicle License

Bureau owned a paint factory. The pension funds of those who had toiled long years on tiny salaries for the foreign-controlled Customs and Municipality vanished overnight. If anybody had been keeping statistics, the suicide curve would have shot up as the older ones with no savings, who had always looked forward to their pension, killed themselves and often their families with them.

And more and more Kuomintang were coming to the city. As the country flamed with civil war, as the Communists won Manchuria and the whole of the north and west of China, as battalion after battalion of Kuomintang troops deserted to the Communists, as the People's Liberation Army began its sweep southward down the Yangtze River, as Chiang Kai-shek himself fled to Formosa, the rats had started a mass desertion of the sinking ship. Many of the rats were with us now, in our city, some scuttling straightaway for Formosa, some pausing in their flight to see what scraps they could pick up.

And with them had come the new flood of refugees fleeing the fighting. A million refugees lived on the sidewalks of our city, snowed on, rained on, broiled by the sun, sleeping on the filthy concrete, begging, dying. The sorrow of the universe sat on the streets of our city. There were families still, trying to survive together. I saw a father with utmost tenderness carry his scarecrow son, a tiny burden, across the sidewalk and hold him over the gutter to relieve himself. What came from under the soiled rags was a thin stream of brownish liquid, then blood. The child seemed to shrink, to collapse on himself. His eyes rolled up into his head. With a little sigh he died in his father's arms. The mother, watching, cried out. The father made no sound, just stared at his son.

I saw a little girl who reminded me of the one who had pulled

Veronica's curls on Peking Road so long ago. She had found a small bundle of dollar notes that somebody had torn up and flung onto a heap of garbage. The child was crouched on the sidewalk, intent on piecing them together. She looked up as I passed.

"Look what I found!" Eyes shining, joyous. "Money!"

"I'll change with you," I said. "You give me that and I'll give you this." I held out a note of two thousand Chinese dollars. She looked dubious. "This one's better," I assured her, "truly, it's better. See, it's much bigger and it's a prettier color, and it's not torn." She considered. Finally she decided I wasn't fooling her. She took the two thousand dollars, thanked me gravely, and sped off with her prize.

The biggest difference since the end of the war was that there was much more money—billions and billions more of it, all in clean paper notes which bought less every day. Prices rose from hour to hour if one paid in paper money. If one had silver money, real silver dollars and cents, prices might vary. "Big Head" dollars were more valuable than "Small Head" dollars. The Big Head was Yuan Shih-kai, first president of the Republic of China after the overthrow of the Manchu emperors. The Small Head was Sun Yat-sen. In Yuan Shih-kai's time more silver had been put into the dollars than in Sun Yat-sen's. The value of the dollars varied not only with the size of the head etched on them, but also with the fluctuations in the price of silver. And each silver dollar was worth a million or more paper dollars. Shopping had become a matter of higher mathematics.

The factories were paying their workers in the goods they manufactured instead of money: shirts, underwear, sweaters, pots, pans, kettles, medicines, Tiger Balm, cosmetics. When the workers needed cash to buy rice with, their relatives went out onto the streets to sell part of this remuneration. They set up counters on the sidewalks—a plank on bricks, an old camp-bed—and laid out whatever was to be sold. As soon as something was sold, the relatives ran as fast as they could to the nearest rice shop and plunked down the money quickly before the price of rice went up.

Between the sidewalk dwellers and the makeshift sidewalk shops, there was hardly room to walk on the streets. It was an endless, weary, push-pull-stumble. Around the bakery shops it was worst. Beggars congregated around those, waiting for the unwary who came out with a loaf of bread held loosely in their hands. The beggars snatched it, and ate it standing there a foot from their victim. What could one do? One walked away empty-handed.

The police? They weren't in evidence. If one caught a thief and phoned the police station, the questions came:

"You've caught a thief?"

"Yes!"

"And you want us to come and arrest him?"

"Yes, of course!"

"Are you prepared to pay cash for the costs of arresting him?"

"What? What costs?"

"Well, we'd have to send two policemen and that would cost so-much. And are you prepared to pay cash for his board and lodging in jail?"

"*What!*"

"If you're not prepared to pay, why don't you just beat him up yourself and let him go?"

If one was prepared to pay something, two policemen arrived in due course, collected payment, took the thief around the corner, beat him, and let him go. Thieves were not good potential for squeeze: they carried nothing on them and were usually paupers. It was no use arresting them.

But good potential squeeze-payers got arrested. Our cousin got into an altercation with a pedicab coolie, was arrested and marched off to the police station by four policemen, together with the coolie to give evidence against him. At the station our cousin and the desk sergeant recognized each other: our cousin was a jockey and the desk sergeant's previous occupation had been pickpocket at the racetrack. They banged each other's backs and called each other "old friend." The sergeant said he wanted to be scrupulously fair since such a dear old friend was involved: he would send the coolie to the hospital to have his injuries assessed. The altercation had been a shouting match only, but our cousin thought it politic to agree. While waiting for the result, he had dinner sent in for all the policemen on duty at the time, which gave the sergeant so much face that he announced that the medical report, which was not in evidence, showed the coolie's injuries to be not serious. The fine would be a small one: would four million dollars be OK for his dear old friend? That was between one and two U.S. dollars. The dinner had cost the equivalent of eighty cents. Our cousin thought himself lucky. That would be very fair, he said, and handed over some "pa-ko-dairs," which were a kind of local travelers' check that banks would furnish on request because obviously it was impossible to carry around enough cash to buy anything of any value. A bottle of Coca-Cola cost 250,000 Chinese dollars, and even that was a big pile of money. Train travelers were restricted to carrying not more than forty pounds of money on the trains. The desk sergeant accepted the pa-ko-dairs and declared eternal friendship. As our cousin left the police station, the pedicab coolie was being beaten up in the courtyard by some policemen. They had given him 500,000 dollars for his part in the farce, and he had had the cheek to demand a million.

The fire department was a farce too. When an alarm was

received, the firemen would phone the owners or occupants of buildings surrounding the one on fire to ask how much they would pay to avoid water damage from the fire hoses. The Fire Brigade's biggest success had been with the Commercial Press, which had hundreds of tons of paper stored in its warehouse when the building opposite caught fire. Water would have ruined their paper, so they had been happy to pay several gold bars to encourage the firemen to put out the fire and leave their paper alone.

The reactions of those who fell victim to these farces ranged from fury to philosophy, but philosophy was wiser and more humane. These were all small people, pinched inexorably in a choice between corruption and starvation. Their official monthly salaries could pay no more than two or three days' living for their families. If they were injured in the course of their duties, nobody paid for hospitalization, and there were no free hospitals or clinics. If their injuries prevented them from working, they were dismissed, given "passes" to retire from the front like the wounded soldiers of the Japanese time. So most people paid up and shrugged it off. And, anyway, that was "small squeeze." "Big squeeze" lay elsewhere.

The biggest visible squeeze was the Import/Export License Bureau that all firms had to satisfy before they could obtain licenses to carry on their business. New companies had sprung up, all owned by relatives of Kuomintang officials, whose sole business was to obtain licenses for their clients. That cost a lot, so our company was trying to satisfy the License Bureau on our own. The Bureau's standard tactic was to demand a document that they thought the applicant did not have—a letter from the manufacturer in America or Europe stating this-or-that, such-and-such, thus-and-so. On Ss si-sang's advice, our company had blank letterheads from most of the manufacturers we represented. Where we lacked them, Ss si-sang's relative's printing company printed fac-similes for us. I was the one who forged the signatures. I had a talent for it. I forged particularly well the signature of Mr. R. Meiklejohn, who was export manager of the tire factory. We were doing quite well with the License Bureau on our own. We could produce any letter or document that the License Bureau wanted.

"Ss si-sang," I said one day. "The company had better think about how to protect me. I don't want to go to Bridge House if the Bureau finds out that the documents are forged and that I'm the forger."

"No, no, no," he said consolingly. "We pay few gold bars, you come out right away."

"Well, how about putting those gold bars away in the safe so you'll be sure to have them handy? I don't want to spend even one night in Bridge House."

"No, no, no! You no worry! Everything OK."

Ss si-sang was now the manager of our company. Before the Japanese time the foreign owners had turned it over to him on paper. Now they came once or twice a year from their homes in America to check on the profits and to arrange for the money to be clandestinely channeled out of China. Ss si-sang was well paid for his services.

I switched to Chinese.

"Ss si-sang, you know that the whole thing is very dishonest. Even though our business is perfectly legitimate, still my conscience hurts me."

"No, no, no! Your conscience shouldn't hurt you. You're only doing what your employers order."

"But all this rubbish about licenses! They might as well just ask frankly for gold bars."

"Well," he said forgivingly, "they have to put up some sort of face. And they may have to run soon. If the Communists catch them—chop, chop."

I began to feel very annoyed with Ss si-sang, his few-gold-bars cure-all, his complacency toward the crooks in the License Bureau.

"Poor fellows!" I said. "H.H. Kung got away with eight hundred tons of gold bars, and they can't have more than just a couple of tons among them. But they have time yet. The Communists aren't coming *here!* Haven't you heard about it? The Kuomintang generals are going to defend Shanghai to the death!"

Some smart generals had got away from Nanking well before the Communists' advance and had swooped upon Shanghai eager for their last chance at big money. One had set up his artillery behind a row of new houses in the outskirts of the city and had commanded the proprietor to move his houses so as not to obstruct the guns. It had cost the proprietor several hundred gold bars to persuade the general to move his artillery to a spot some distance in front of the houses. Another was going to build a new Great Wall of China around Shanghai—all patriots would no doubt wish to contribute large sums to it.

"Have you contributed to the Wall yet?" I asked Ss s-sang.

He nodded glumly.

"Why so sad? Aren't you a patriot?"

"You laugh at me," he said reproachfully, and then suddenly burst out. "But I am eating bitterness! My eldest son has turned Communist! My favorite son! He's taken his wife and children —my grandchildren!—and moved them all out of my house into a small poor house he's rented. I went to see him. I, his father, went to plead with him to come home. Not only did he refuse, but he asked me not to go to his house again! You see what the Communists are? They turn children against parents, sons against fathers!"

"I'm sorry, Ss si-sang, but . . ." He was not listening. His grief was welling.

"He said it would be better for me if I did not see him anymore. He said that all my life I have been compradore of a foreign firm. Since the Japanese time the firm has been in my name. I must have made lots of money. I must be on the Communist records. He doesn't want to know anything about me, where I keep my money, what I do, so when the Communists come he won't have to report about me. You see what the Communists are!" His voice broke. "My own son would report to them against me!"

"But that's why he doesn't want to know anything about you. That's why he moved out. He loves you. He doesn't want to be forced to do anything against you!"

"But if he were not Communist he wouldn't have to do anything against me! He'd still be at home! I'd have my grandchildren around me and my favorite son beside me!"

"But . . ." It was hopeless. I looked at him; tears were streaming down his face. I said gently, "But you have other sons and grandchildren, don't you?"

"In America! I've never even seen them! Just before the Japanese time I sent my two younger sons to America. You remember all the Chinese universities moved their campuses up-country? I didn't want my sons to go up-country. I was afraid they would be forced into the army. So I managed to send them to America to study. Ai-yah! How much money it cost me to get them passports! And they are ungrateful! Unfilial! When I asked them to come back, they wouldn't come! When they finished their studies they both got jobs in America, and they both got married there. I've never even seen their children, my grandchildren! My wife and I are alone! Three sons and five grandchildren, and we're alone in our old age!"

"You're not old, Ss si-sang!" He was only about fifty-five.

He shook his head, the heavy tears pouring from his eyes.
"I'm too old."

Too old to try and understand his children, too old to face the
changes that understanding might entail. Old enough to be enti-
tled to grief instead of understanding, to take refuge in grief.

"I'll go to Formosa if I have to."

I patted his sleeve. There was nothing else to do or say.

Go. Go. The Communists are coming. We'll have to go. No!
I'm not going. My business is here. How can I leave it? But there
won't be business any more! You won't be allowed to do business.
We'll all have to go. But where? We were born here! Its our
home! How can we go? Where can we go?

The arguments raged all around us every day.

"You understand, Doo-bebe," Bill said to me seriously. "We'll
all have to leave. I'm going myself soon, and you all should leave
just as soon as you can."

"If we stay on, Bill, what would happen?"

"I suppose you'd be allowed to stay on, but how could you live?
You wouldn't be able to earn a living as before. The foreign
companies will be closed down, and the Chinese companies will
be nationalized. There won't be any foreign trade for a long while.
You won't be able to get a job using any of the skills you have.
And what else could you do? You couldn't go to work on the land.
You might get work in a factory, but you wouldn't earn any more
than a factory worker. You'd have to live like one—work twelve
or fourteen hours a day, eat rice and cabbage, never change
clothes because you'd have no clothes to change into, sleep in a
dirty dormitory with a hundred other women. Would you rather
do that than leave and go to another country?"

I said yes, of course, I understand. But we're scared of leaving.
Who wouldn't be? Leave everything we know? Everyone we
know? Just go off into the blue?

"I know it's frightening," Bill said. "But think of it this way: the city is not the same city that we knew. That city, that Shanghai, is already gone. So the sooner you leave, the better. Company employees will probably be paid termination benefits, several months' salary at least. Use the money to travel and get settled elsewhere. Those who hang on will eat up their money and in the long run they'll be worse off. Better leave as soon as you can."

I thought of the Editor. "When the time comes, I will be prepared to move out of my houses and my courtyards. . . ." Where was he now? We too would move out of our houses and our courtyards. Where would we go? What would we do?

"Yes, Bill," I said. "We'll go. As soon as Father is better."

When the war had ended and Father's firm had opened up again, he had gone back to clean up the horribly scrambled accounts. He had worked for nearly two years. When everything was clear, the firm had held a lunch in his honor at which some graceful speeches had been made and he had been given a gold watch and a small pension. His speech of thanks, practiced for days beforehand, was the one and only public statement of his life. He had been so happy about it all. None of us had the heart to mention that the reward fell far short of the service, that the Englishman whose place Father had filled for so long would have had far more.

After that, still smiling every now and then and saying, "By Joj, that was nice, wasn't it," Father had begun to fade. He kept more and more to his armchair, and then to his bed. The doctor said there was nothing really wrong with him—just the machine winding down.

Bill left a month or two after our talk. Then the Old Boss left. His house a ruin, hunting a remote dream, there was nothing to keep him. He got on a boat for Macao.

Then Luke had gone. He worked for an oil company which

offered him a transfer to Hongkong. He and Yvonne had decided to get married immediately and take up the offer.

Jane and her husband had gone, with little Danielle and Christophe, war babies, born during the Japanese time by the light of candles in lice-ridden hospitals empty of equipment. Christophe, in spite of his mother's near starvation when she was carrying him, had been born an enormous baby, over ten pounds in weight. When he was being born the Japanese doctor had decided that Jane, swollen with bites from the lice in her hospital bed, needed chloroform. It was Jane herself, who fortunately remembered the Chinese word for it, who had told the jittery little Chinese nurse's aide to bring the mask. It all seemed such a very short time ago, and yet there was Christophe, a fat toddler in his father's arms, waving a chubby fist at us from the deck of the ship that would carry them to France.

And now Veronica was going, in her arms tiny straw-blonde Shirley, to Manila, where her husband had a most important job, so he said.

Only Mother and I were left to wave goodbye. We turned away as the ship slid from the wharf, pulled by chuffing tugs into the brown waters of the Whangpoo. Each time we waved goodbye we were sadder. We went home to Father, who was lying quietly in bed. He stirred as we entered.

"They've gone?" A whisper.

"Uh-huh." We nodded. A tear slid slowly onto his pillow. We busied ourselves with something and were silent. Ah-May stood in the doorway, as silent as we were, tears in her eyes. After a while Dahsoo came up and stood there too, head bowed.

For several weeks Father had hardly eaten. On the way home Mother and I had paid half a million dollars for a cream puff to tempt his appetite. That evening he ate a little of the cream, whispered "that's good," and closed his eyes. Mother and I sat by him, talking softly. After a while he opened his eyes, looking anxious.

"Am I poor?"

"Of course not, Father! You've got your pension, remember? And that ten thousand dollars?"

"Ah!" The anxiety faded. His eyes closed again.

It was time for dinner. As we tiptoed from the room Father said, quite loud, "I've closed my book."

So many times, all our lives, we'd heard him talk about closing his books. But this time, he said "book."

"Was it balanced?" Mother asked.

He nodded, smiled, eyes closed. He was lying a little on his right side, resting quietly, slipping in and out of sleep.

We went down to dinner. When we came upstairs again he had not moved. He looked exactly the same, the little smile still on his lips.

"I wonder if he's too warm," Mother said, and put her hand on his forehead.

He had gone too.

25

The Liberators

WHEN MOTHER AND I left the cemetery after Father's funeral,
we refused the rides that were offered us because we didn't feel
like having to talk to people. We started to walk home, but after
a few blocks Mother became very tired and I called a pedicab.
While I bargained with the coolie, a crowd of street boys gathered. They had become a feature of the city, wandering the streets
in groups, picking up a livelihood by watching parked cars, shining
shoes, thieving. They could be very annoying. Exasperated elders
called them "pi-sair!"—urchin! bad boy! But they were generally
harmless and often amusing with their quick-witted tricks.

But the pi-sairs who crowded around us now were not amusing,
and suddenly, catching sparks from each other, they began to
mean us harm.

"Foreigners! They're talking Chinese but they're foreigners!
Get out, foreigners! Get out! Tsor-lor! Tsor-lor!"

The cry rose to a raucous screaming and the kids pushed nearer,
jostling us, pulling hideous grimaces. Mother and I tried to ignore
them but the pedicab coolie, intimidated, started shouting too
that these foreigners might as well kill him immediately as pay

him the price I had proposed, which he had been about to accept with pleasure. He rode away. Mother and I were left in the midst of the growing crowd of shrieking, jeering pi-sairs, now joined by several grown-ups.

"Tsor-lor! Tsor-lor!" rose all around us. I remembered wryly how we had been so shocked the first time a coolie had said that to Veronica.

Our situation had begun to look serious when a pedicab coolie rode his vehicle strongly into the crowd, scattering those nearest.

"Get in." He waved at us. "Never mind, you pay what you like when we get there. Get in!"

As Mother stepped in, one of the bigger boys, screaming out of a hate-filled face, leaped forward and punched me on the shoulder. I managed to keep my balance and to sit down in the cab as though nothing had happened. The coolie rode off quickly.

"Are you hurt?" Mother was anguished—it was impossible for such a thing to happen!

"No. It's nothing. Calm down, Mother."

It was quite possible for such a thing to happen! I waited for the seething to subside.

The coolie was talking to us over his shoulder.

"Don't pay attention to those pi-sairs! They've no parents to teach them any better. And everything's mixed up. Kuomintang. Gungtsetang. Foreigners. Chinese. Good. Bad. Everything's mixed up!"

Indeed it's all mixed up! Its a muddle!

"There's nobody to give orders any more," the coolie said. "All those big city guys with money, they've run away. Only small guys are left at the top. And them!! They're scared to sit in case the Communists arrive and say 'why aren't you standing?' and they're scared to stand in case the Communists say 'why aren't you

sitting?' " He laughed. "They don't even dare fart in case the
Communists smell it when they come! And in the meantime, the
city is in a mess!"

It's falling apart. Traffic jamming for blocks while traffic cops
gossip on street corners. Garbage everywhere on the streets. Broken down trams and buses settling where they fall like monu-
ments to chaos.

"Lots of foreigners have gone away already," said our coolie.
"It's getting too dirty for them. Are you going?"

"Yes," said Mother suddenly. "We're going. It's time to go,
isn't it?"

Yes! It's time to go! Not because the city is in chaos, but
because its not our city anymore! The pi-sairs aren't our pi-sairs
any more! We don't have to feel sorry about it all anymore! We
can just go away and leave it behind. It's time to go! High time!

I laughed as I paid off the coolie.

"You're not afraid of the Communists, are you?"

"Me! I fart any time I like. We're people after all, aren't we?"

"Yes. We're all people. And you should be a happy person.
Thank you."

"Thank *you!*" He grinned and rode away.

The next day I made the round of shipping companies. They
all had lists of would-be passengers. I put our names down, but
we were very low on every list and no company could give definite
news of future sailings. "There's a blockade, you know?"

I knew. The five-star Chinese admiral, now on Formosa, was
directing a naval blockade of the mainland. It was not very effective, but ships carrying full loads of passengers were particularly
vulnerable and no company was scheduling sailings ahead.

"I don't know when we can leave," I told Mother. "It doesn't
look very hopeful. If we can't leave before the Communists come,

we may have to wait a long time. And the money! It's going to cost a fortune and I don't know how we'll scrape up the cash."

"But we'll leave eventually," Mother said, "and I think it's only fair to tell the servants to give them the best possible chance of making plans."

When we told Dahsoo he said not a word, just bowed his head sadly.

"We'll give you as much money as we can, Dahsoo. At least a year's salary. Perhaps you can find another job? Or perhaps you can go back to your country? You can leave whenever you like. There are only Doo-bebe and me to cook for now, and Ah-May or Little Bell can manage."

Dahsoo smiled wryly.

"I don't have to wait for the People's Liberation Army. I've already been liberated. Liberated out of my job. And you, Tah-tah, and Doo-bebe, you're being liberated out of your home."

He sighed, a theatrical, long-drawn Dahsoo sigh. But the hairs growing out of his wart trembled and his hands trembled as he got out his fiddle. He's old, I thought, my heart hurting, he's old. Mother and I closed the kitchen door behind us before the first screech from the fiddle sounded.

Dahsoo left two weeks later. One of his sons-in-law had a noodle shop and had long wanted him to handle the cooking. "Cook noodles!" I was horrified at the thought of our famous turtle stew cook cooking noodles for coolies. "You!" He was comforted, he even smiled a little when he left, but we were not. We wept to see him go. "I would never have dreamt that I would cry for him," Mother said, sniffing. "I used to get so *mad* at him!"

When we told Ah-May she said, "I'll die if you go."

"Ah-May! Don't be ridiculous!"

"When are you going?"

"We don't know yet. Perhaps not for a long time."

"But you'll go?"

"We have to. There's no help for it."

"Then I'll die," she said flatly, smiling.

We didn't argue with her anymore at that moment because a horrible cacophony broke out. We rushed to the windows. Beside our house the road curved inward for a short distance, making a sort of niche. In that niche now stood twenty or thirty young men working away energetically on drums, cymbals, and trumpets. Facing them stood their conductor furiously waving a baton. None of the musicians was keeping time to it. None of them was playing quite the same tune. It was excruciating.

"The only good thing about Dahsoo leaving was that we got rid of his fiddle!" I shouted at Mother. "And now this!"

"What?" she shouted back, covering her ears. Ah-May was laughing. I marched out of the house and up to the conductor. He stopped waving his baton and the band trailed off raggedly, except for one trumpeter who went on blowing with his eyes closed and had to be shaken before he stopped.

"Good evening," I said to the conductor. "Who are you?"

"We're from the Evening Star High School," he said proudly. "Our band is practicing to welcome the People's Liberation Army."

"Oh. Well, d'you think you could practice somewhere else?"

"Why?"

"You're so noisy."

"Noisy?" He stared uncomprehendingly. A band making noise was a delightful thing, always had been. People always crowded around to listen and applaud. If the band were marching crowds followed, children darting delightedly between the marchers. And I didn't like it? Incomprehensible. He repeated, loudly and slowly as to an idiot:

"We're practicing to greet the People's Liberation Army."

"Yes, I know, but could you go a little further down the street? To the other end perhaps? Or why not your own school?"

"This place is fine. We've decided to practice here every night. We must be worthy to welcome the People's Liberation Army."

He turned back and lifted his baton. The band blared forth again. A crowd had already gathered, shuffling happily in anticipation of free entertainment. I gave up.

For the next three months, between 8:30 and 9:30 every evening, the band practiced. We kept the windows tightly closed and stuffed cotton in our ears, which made the noise fainter but no less awful.

"Well," Mother said, "it's just one more thing! And it's so heavenly when they stop!"

But when the People's Liberation Army actually came, the band wasn't there to welcome them. They came quietly, in the night, without fanfare. We woke one morning in April 1949, and they were there. Soldiers clad neatly in blue-gray uniforms sitting quietly on the curbs in long lines. Not threatening, molesting no one, not even standing. Just sitting quietly, their rifles across their knees, ignoring the masses of people who milled around gaping at them. Here and there someone came forward and offered a soldier something—a bowl of tea, a sweet cake. He gravely refused, shaking his head, saying nothing. They stayed all day. In the evening they marched off, quiet, orderly, to the camps their commanders had arranged for them.

The city buzzed.

"They're here! Did you see them?"

"They look very clean and neat, don't they?"

"And so disciplined!"

"They won't accept a thing—did you notice? Not a thing!"

"They've got orders. They're not to take a thing from the

people, not a drink of water, not a needle and thread—nothing
for free. If they take anything, they'll pay for it."

"What! Chinese soldiers pay for things!"

"These are Communists, remember, not Kuomintang!"

The stories multiplied, as people sighed with relief. It's true!
They're leaving people alone! Yes, I heard some people have
disappeared, but rich people, crooks. Not ordinary honest people.
They're not doing anything to ordinary people!

And, you know, they're fair. And smart. Did you hear what
happened at one of the small Bank of China branches? Well, I
heard the office boy refused to make tea for the manager—he was
liberated, he said, he was just as good as the manager. There was
a row about it, of course, and a Communist officer came. He said
sure, the office boy was as good as the manager, and he let the
office boy sit at the manager's desk. The office boy was all smiles,
sitting behind the desk in the big chair. Then the officer said,
"Well, now, start work." The office boy said, "What?" and the
Communist said, "If you sit in the manager's chair you'll have to
do his work, won't you? And if you don't know how, then the
manager will have to do it, won't he, since he does know how, and
you'll have to do the work that *you* know how to do, won't you?"
Isn't that a marvelous story!

What Mother and I thought was really marvelous was that our
band disbanded. Little Bell reported that they had been refused
permission to play for the People's Liberation Army. "Too noisy,"
the Communists had said. "Too boisterous."

"I'm beginning to like the Communists!" I said to Mother.

In the blessed quiet of the first evening after the disbandment,
our doorbell rang. Little Bell opened the door to a country boy
in a blue-gray uniform. His face was almost absolutely round, with
red red cheeks and solemn black eyes. He came into the dining

room, where Mother and I were sitting with our after-dinner tea, bowed, cleared his throat, shuffled his feet, and stood very straight. He began to speak in the Kang-poh dialect, which we understood perfectly because Dahsoo was a Kang-poh man, though an exceptional one. Kang-poh—"river north"—people were generally laughed at, ridiculed for their naiveté.

We listened to the little speech in the strong country accent. The fresh-faced soldier boy had learned it by heart, complete with illustrative gestures. He was a representative of the People's Liberation Army. He was assigned to explain the intention of the Army to the people living on our street. If we were honest people, we had nothing to fear. If we were prepared to cooperate (right fist gently clasped into palm of left hand), we had nothing to fear. But if we were not honest, and not prepared to cooperate (fists struck together sharply, back to back) it would be very bad for us. He fell silent and looked at us gravely.

"We are honest people," I said, as gravely, "and we are prepared to cooperate with honest people."

He burst into a wide smile.

"You understood me!"

"Yes, you're from Kang-poh, aren't you?"

He shook his head. "Not Kang-poh. Now its called Poh-kang —"north river." The People's Liberation Army changed the name, so people won't laugh at us any more."

"That's fine, but we wouldn't laugh at you anyway. Our cook, whom we had for many years and whom we liked very much, was from Poh-kang too."

It made a bond between us. We smiled cordially at each other as he went off to our next door neighbor.

The street cleaners went back to work, and gradually the layers of filth and scum were scraped off the sidewalks. Garbage trucks trundled about once again. The river was dredged, the drains unclogged, and the foul puddles seeped away. Traffic cops resumed their duties. Even the refugees began to disappear— where to, nobody quite knew. Into camps? Back to their country? Wherever, it proved that something could be done about them.

Sentries of the People's Liberation Army were posted at intervals in the streets. They were armed, but their guns were slung loosely on their backs and were not bayoneted. They did not demand passes or obstruct people. They simply stood at ease and watched. But one mild look from a sentry's eye was enough to set a traffic cop to directing traffic with snap and vigor, to make a street sweeper wield his broom industriously, to send a group of pi-sairs scuttling around the corner.

I was passing one day when there was a loud crash on the street. Two pedicabs had collided. They were unwieldy vehicles at best and a patch of oil could send them skidding. Nobody had been hurt in the collision. The only casualty was a large pane of window glass that the occupant of one of the pedicabs had been delivering. It lay in shards all over the street. The glass man began wailing. The coolies began yelling at each other, shaking fists. The sentry walked over. At once they all lowered their voices and turned to him, appealing, explaining. The sentry listened to everybody and nobody. He contemplated the scene for a few moments, looked around, and beckoned to me. Astonished, I stood still, and he came to me, followed by the litigants and the usual crowd that had gathered.

"Tah-tah," he said politely. "You will pay for the glass."

"What!"

"The broken glass. You pay for it."

"But I had nothing to do with it!"

"I know. But the glass was broken through nobody's fault; it was an accident. And those involved are all very poor. But you can afford to pay for it."

He smiled mildly.

"How much is it?" I asked.

The glass man named a very reasonable figure, probably the true cost of the glass. In the circumstances I would have expected him to try for four or five times the cost. Surprised, I laughed. Everybody except the sentry started laughing, nodding their heads, approving, delighted. I counted out the money and handed it to the sentry. He was unsurprised. He gave it to the glass man, indicated that the coolies should get the broken glass off the road and into the gutter, and went back to his post.

It's wonderful! everybody was saying. The most pleased of all were people who had court cases pending, some of them for several years. District court decisions had gone to the Court of Appeals, thence to the Supreme Court, back again to the Shanghai police force, which claimed that it had to have an order from the district court to execute the Supreme Court's decision. Back again, then, to the district court.

A friend of ours who owned a house had finally, after nearly three years, arrived at the point where everything had been set for the police to execute the Supreme Court's decision that the tenant who illegally occupied his house should be evicted. But when he arrived at the house with the police the order could not be executed because the tenant had changed: the original illegal tenant had sublet to another, collecting key money from him, and the second had sublet to a third, in turn collecting key money.

Despairingly, our friend had prepared to start the process all over again. Court cases had traditionally been a question of pay, pay, pay—pay the lawyers, pay the court officials, pay the "ke-men-ti," the guardian of the door. He especially had to be paid;

otherwise one couldn't even get into the court. But now the Communists issued a decree: all pending court cases would be cleared up within a brief time limit, and to expedite the matter no lawyers were to be allowed. Plaintiffs and defendants would plead their own cases before a Communist judge, in plain Chinese with no fancy speeches and no documents. No appeals. And the door of the courthouse remained open, with only one soldier of the People's Liberation Army standing beside it.

Two weeks later our friend's case was settled: the third tenant had to surrender the house, but since, when he had paid key money to the second tenant, he had been unaware that the whole deal was illegal, he could retain one room in the house for six months to give him time to find other lodgings.

Our friend phoned me in the office to invite me to lunch to celebrate the occasion, but I could not accept. I was due for an interview with the Communists. Ss si-sang had vanished on one of the last ships to Formosa just before the Communists arrived. The accountant of our company had been left in charge, but I knew far more than he did about the actual working of the company, and I had been summoned to an interview.

It took place in a large office building which held several Communist headquarters units. It had been one of the most modern buildings in Shanghai, with chrome chairs scattered in the lobby around an artificial garden made out of plastic, the new material which had not long before reached Shanghai. All that was gone now. The big space was bare except for a small table in a corner on which reposed some lowly rattan-covered thermos flasks of hot water for tea. On the fourth floor I entered a waiting room and a few minutes later was shown into an office where two men sat, one behind a desk with a single file on it, the other beside the desk. I sat on a wooden chair before it.

The interview was conducted in Mandarin by the man behind the desk, translated into English by the other. Questions were asked, to which I replied. Yes, our company was owned by foreigners. Yes, Ss si-sang had been their surrogate since just before the Japanese time. I had last seen the foreigners about a year ago when they made one of their regular visits. No, I did not know anything about the financial transactions between them and Ss si-sang. No, I did not really know where Ss si-sang was, but he had told me he would go to Formosa.

The questioning went on and on, detailed, intricate. The man behind the desk registered no reaction whatever to my answers. He was neither polite nor rude, warm nor cold, simply impassive as a statue. I began to feel disconcerted. His control was not human. A kind of power emanated from it, which gradually became almost tangible in the severe, bare room. It's dangerous, I thought. It's dangerous. I tried to make myself impervious. I thought before answering, answered carefully, as clearly as I could.

Suddenly I saw the direction in which the questions were leading and my heart lurched. The forgeries! The forgeries that I'd forgotten about because they were so logical at the time, a necessary measure of defense against being driven to the wall by the rapacity of the Import/Export License Bureau. But the Bureau had been set up to regulate the use of scarce foreign exchange and, if it had functioned honestly, might have done so. Could I be accused of helping to misuse China's fast-vanishing foreign exchange? My heart pounded. Sometimes I had forged signatures for Ss si-sang on papers that I myself had not prepared. I thought of Ss si-sang's "You no worry! We pay few gold bars, you come out right away." Here there would be no paying of gold bars, no coming out right away.

The man's eyes flicked at me, and I thought for a terrified moment that my face must have given something away, then realized with relief that it was because I had not answered his last question. My silence had evoked what my willingness to speak had not: a tiny response.

Then, as suddenly, I was furious. The blood in my veins ran amok, sending heat in waves through my body. Fragments of pictures flashed through my mind—Luke and Yvonne, the wind whipping her pretty black hair, standing on the deck of the ship that carried them away. Christophe's chubby fist. Veronica, laughing Veronica, gazing across the widening gap between ship and shore, not laughing. And Mother and me, waving, waving, always waving goodbye. The hell with it, I thought. We've suffered too, you stone-face image! Enough, now. Enough! I'm not going to be frightened on top of everything else!

I said into the silence, my voice surprising me by its calm:

"I've thought of something that may interest you. Our company had, of course, to deal with the Import/Export License Bureau. We couldn't afford to go through one of the new companies that were getting licenses for clients. So we dealt with the Bureau ourselves. The Bureau always waited to see what documents we had, and then asked for documents we didn't have. So we manufactured the documents they asked for. We forged the documents. I forged the signatures."

The translator translated. The man heard him through, impassive as ever. Then he looked at the file on his desk, riffled through it, shut it with a snap.

That was all. He had no more questions. I looked him in the eye.

"Thank you," I said in English, as coldly as I could.

Perhaps the faintest ghost of a smile touched his eyes.

"Thank you," he said in Mandarin.

I collected my things, rose, and unhurriedly left the room, trying to hide the trembling of my knees.

What a man! With men like that, no wonder all China was Communist now! My heart was still beating heavily. I was still frightened, no matter how hard I tried not to be. And I had a clear conscience! With a guilty conscience I'd be ready to try swimming to Formosa!

I wasn't in the clear yet, I knew. Anything could happen. For weeks I worried, saying nothing to anyone, losing weight, not sleeping, seeing new significance even in the mild gaze of the sentries.

It was the mildness of total discipline, and the discipline of the soldiers came from the total commitment of those who commanded them. And total commitment is power, unmalleable, inflexible, frightening in its independence.

26

⚊⚊⚊

Tickets to Heaven

TWO MONTHS LATER our accountant called us together. The company was to be closed up and its assets, whatever remained, turned over to the Communists. That was only to be expected since it was a foreign company and had been found guilty of several crimes. But Ss si-sang was deemed the main criminal. The rest of us were to be paid a month's salary for each year of service, up to a maximum of twelve months.

The relief was so exquisite that it was some hours before I appreciated the fact that I was going to get a year's salary. A year's salary!

"We've got the money!" I said to Mother. "Now we'll have to find a way to travel!"

But months passed before we did. One ship, the *President Jackson,* came and went again crammed with passengers, but not Mother and me. No more ships would come, the President Line people told me. Their huge office was already reduced to a small space with only four or five desks in it. Soon they would close. I made the round of the other shipping companies. Many were already closed. The rest: sorry, nothing.

We waited. I still went every day to help our accountant with the last details of closing up the office. It was sad and dull, but it was something to do in those dreary months.

Then one day our jockey cousin telephoned. Jardine Matheson had arranged to operate a series of sailings of their coastal freight boats from Tientsin to Hongkong and would take passengers. I rushed to Jardine Matheson carrying a valise full of money. Success! I paid over piles of money and got in return two slim little booklets—passage from Tientsin to Hongkong on the S/S *Fanling*, which would sail in three or four months time.

I rushed to the Exit Visa Office. The man I dealt with there was trying to be as imperturbable as my interviewer, but he was a different class of person. He succeeded only in being cold and rather rude, but he accepted applications for our Exit Visas. It would take about two months to obtain them. First our names had to be published in the newspapers for three weeks, to give anyone who had a claim against us the opportunity to make it. If there was no claim, the visas would be processed and issued in due course.

I rushed home and collapsed onto the sofa, too excited to be exhausted.

"Mother! We're going! We'll have to go by train up north to Tientsin and come back south by sea to Hongkong. It'll take about ten days or more, I suppose, but in three or four months time we'll be in Hongkong! Quick, quick—we must start packing!"

And then I saw Ah-May's face. She had come quietly into the room. It was as though my heart split in two, one half still bubbling with excitement and relief, the other quiet and sad.

That night I called out to Ah-May to come up to my room. She came in smiling, not widely and gigglingly as usual, but smiling.

She was pregnant again and it had begun to show. Her short jacket stuck out in front and she moved a little clumsily.

"Ah-May, you know that we really have to go. There's no help for it. My office is closed down and there's no money coming in. We have the money I got from my office as compensation, and we have to use that for traveling. Otherwise, if we stay here, we'll just eat it up and then there'll be nothing. We have to go somewhere else, where I'll find a job and we'll make a new home. We simply can't stay here any more."

"Yes, Doo-bebe. I know. You have to go."

"You'll be all right, Ah-May. We'll give you as much money as we can before we go. And you'll go back to Zose with Little Bell and the Ching Meis. You can farm again now. There's peace in China now."

"Yes, Doo-bebe."

"And this new child, it'll be a son, I'm sure. You'll have a son, and maybe another later."

We looked at each other. I willed her not to be sad—at least not sad for long. She had to be sad for now, and so did I, so did Mother. But I willed her over the sad time, willed her to the Zose farm, to the rich fields golden with tall rice, to the flowing irrigation waters, to the little Ching Meis playing on the hard-packed earth before the farm house, to the new son who would be gurgling in a hammock slung between two trees.

"Yes, Doo-bebe."

She looked down at her swelling stomach and rubbed it gently with both hands.

"It's a son!" I said.

She smiled a little. "You'll be going about April?"

"Yes."

"I'll be dead before then."

"Ah-May!" I banged my fists on the bed. "Don't talk rubbish! Why should you die? Are you sick? Are you feeling bad? Do you have pain?"

"No. I feel fine."

"Then why do you keep saying you'll die?"

"I don't know. But I think so. I think when you go I'll die." I gazed at her, exasperated. She smiled and patted me. I had the impression she wanted to console me.

We began to pack. A three-story five-bedroom house that had been lived in for fifteen years by six or seven people. There were millions of things in it, all of which Mother and I had to go through, sort out, throw away, give away, try to sell, pack to take with us. We decided to take the absolute minimum: just some clothes, the good crockery and cutlery, some crystal and silver that Mother had had for wedding presents, and my three pieces of carved Chinese furniture—a chest, a small cabinet, an opium table. There was no use transporting the rest of our furniture. It was worn by a lifetime's wear and tear. We had bounced on the sofa when we were toddlers, made sticky fingermarks on the dining room table, teetered back and forth on the chairs. The sewing machine, a Singer which still worked perfectly although its cabinet was shaky, had been Father's gift to Mother when Luke was born.

"What shall we do with Father's wardrobe?" Mother gazed longingly at the monstrosity.

"Leave it behind," I said firmly.

"But Father loved it."

"We'll sell it to a second-hand dealer on Peking Road." Mother sighed.

"We'll go to the cemetery," I said consolingly, "and take a photograph of Father's grave."

When we got there we found that the cemetery was being used for gun emplacements. Antiaircraft guns mounted on huge-wheeled carriages stood between and over the graves, pointing menacingly at the sky. Soldiers were on duty at each gun. They paid no attention to us, so I went forward with my camera toward Father's grave. Instantly a soldier barred my path. When I didn't move, he said angrily, "Chi!—Go!"

I retreated toward an officer standing nearby, who regarded me sternly.

"I want to take a photograph of my Father's grave," I said. "My Mother and I will be leaving soon, and we will never see it again. So I want a photograph of it."

He considered. I held the camera out to him.

"Here. You take the photograph if you don't trust me."

He took the camera and walked over to the grave I indicated. The rear half of an antiaircraft gun showed behind it. He peered through the viewer, handed the camera back to me, and gave orders to the gun crew.

"Move that gun."

They hopped to do his bidding. When the gun was some distance away, he turned back to me.

"Take your photograph."

I did so.

"Thank you," I said to him. His stern expression had not changed throughout, and it still did not change. He ordered the soldiers to move the gun back to its position. Mother and I left.

"That was awfully nice of him!" she said.

I agreed, though I didn't think that he had intended to be *nice.* He had been—well, a good communist? A good Chinese communist? I had made a reasonable request with the best kind of Chinese reason for making it—it was my Father's grave. He had granted it. If it hadn't been reasonable he wouldn't have granted it, and his manner would have been exactly the same.

When we got home we began again on the packing. We had finished the bedrooms and were starting on the trunks and valises piled in the boxroom. Mother called Ah-May to help move them.

As she reached up for a suitcase, Ah-May fell full length on the floor. She didn't collapse and sink down. She simply keeled over, her body fully extended as it had been to reach for the suitcase, and thudded heavily to the floor, unconscious.

We sent Little Bell scurrying for the ambulance from the nearby hospital, with cash to pay in advance. We couldn't move Ah-May. Her body was stiff and heavy as a stone. The ambulance men carried her out on a stretcher and we followed immediately. In the hospital she was put to bed in a large ward with twenty or thirty beds in it. We waited beside her until the doctor came and explained to him what had happened.

"She's pregnant?"

"Yes."

"This is the husband?"

"Yes."

He would have to make a thorough examination and would telephone us. The next morning he phoned and asked us to come immediately and to bring Little Bell with us.

Ah-May was not pregnant. She had a growth in the womb which would immediately have to be excised if she were to live. Little Bell should at once sign the papers authorizing the operation.

But Little Bell wouldn't.

"Open her with a knife! Ai-yah! Ai-yah!"

"Sign, Little Bell. People have operations every day, all the time. It's a proper medical procedure. The doctor knows how to do it."

"But I can't write."

"Well, make your thumb mark."

"But what would she say? She might be very angry with me! She wouldn't want to be opened with a knife! No, no, I dare not!"

We argued, the doctor scolded, but it was no use. Without Ah-May to tell him what to do, he would do nothing. At last I asked the doctor:

"Is she conscious?"

"Barely."

"Come with me," I said to Little Bell, and went into the ward. Ah-May lay on her side, her protruding stomach looking loose and flabby. She was pale as death, breathing in light gasps. She seemed to be held together by the frailest of threads.

I knelt beside the bed so that my face was close to Ah-May's. "Ah-May."

She gave no sign. I called her again and again, softly, insistently. At last her eyes half opened. Her lips moved. On a light exhaling breath, the whisper "Doo-bebe."

"Ah-May. Listen. Are you listening?"

A tiny nod.

"Ah-May, the doctor says you must have an operation. You *must* have it. But Little Bell must sign first, and he won't sign, he won't make his mark. Tell him to do so."

I beckoned him to the bedside. He leaned forward, regarding her fearfully. Her half-open eyes moved to him. With a tremendous effort she said one word: "Stupid!" and sank back into her pillows.

My heart bounded. Ah-May would get well! Ah-May was still Ah-May, her spirit was still there! I pushed Little Bell back into the corridor. A nurse hurried forward with the paper and an ink pad. Without a word, in a daze, he made his mark.

Ah-May got well. From the day after the operation she began to improve by leaps and bounds. Her face filled out, her hair got glossy, her eyes shone. She giggled. She bloomed again, the way she had bloomed when she came to us, a little girl, after she got over her first fear. She reproached me, laughing:

"You see, Doo-bebe! You said it was a son. It wasn't."

"You see, Ah-May! You said you would die. You didn't."

We were happy. Mother and I were still going away, the sadness was still there but overlaid now with happiness. Ah-May hadn't died, Ah-May was well again.

Before she left the hospital, the doctor sent for us.

"I'm letting her go now, but as soon as she is strong enough, within the next two months at the latest, she must return for a hysterectomy. I didn't do it at once because she was too weak. But it must be done very soon."

When we told Ah-May she was indignant.

"What! I'm perfectly well now. It wasn't *me* who was sick—it was the baby, or whatever it was. As soon as they took it out I got well again. I'm not going back to the hospital! What *for?*"

"For another operation, Ah-May."

"But there's nothing more to operate!"

"There is, Ah-May. You have a kind of sickness."

"What sickness? I've never been sick until the baby made me sick!"

"It's a sickness that doesn't make you sick like a cold or a fever. You don't feel it. But you have it. You have to have another operation."

"Oh Doo-bebe! Look at me! How can I be sick? No, no, I'm not going back to the hospital again!"

For the time being we contented ourselves with mentioning the matter every day or two. The doctor had said two months. There was time yet, we thought, to force Ah-May back to the hospital.

We went on packing. There was so much to do. So many things

that we were giving away to be delivered, so many people coming to see the things we were trying to sell, so much simply to be discarded, thrown away, bits and pieces of our life in the trash can.

I went to the Exit Visa Office several times. At last one fine day I got our visas. No claims had been made against us, and the visas had been issued. After a search through a big pile of them, the man handed me ours. Pieces of thickish paper folded in the middle to make four pages, printed in Chinese and sealed with a four-inch-square stamp in red ink. On the inside pages were our photographs and details of our passports, our names written in English. Mine was No. 3029, Mother's 3030.

Pieces of paper, precious as gold. The importance of "papers" had suddenly dawned on the people of Shanghai. They had become the subject of feverish activity, sometimes of lamentation because many people had no papers at all, had never been registered anywhere, had never felt the need to document their existence. I had a passport only by grace of Father's thoughtfulness and persistence. Father had gone to record my birth when I was a year old, and the Consul had wanted to write me down as illegitimate because Father and Mother had not been married in a civil ceremony at the consulate—only the religious ceremony in church had been important. Father had refused to have me on the records as illegitimate, so I had lived until the age of sixteen with no official existence. Then Father had insisted that the Consul recognize my baptism certificate, and I had been inscribed in the records in my own name and given a passport, which Father had insisted I renew regularly. How thankful I was!

When we were told the date of our sailing, I went to the railway station early in the morning with more piles of money to buy our train tickets to Tientsin well in advance. The girl who was selling the tickets counted the money stolidly—several million. It took her an hour. The queue behind me lengthened and went around the corner. Finally she handed me the tickets, first-class sleepers Shanghai-Tientsin. The slim bits of cardboard seemed like tickets to heaven.

27

Death of Ah-May

WHEN I GOT HOME nobody was there but the Ching Meis, sitting
on the last step of the staircase, looking frightened.

"Doo-bebe, your mother said to tell you to go to the hospital
as soon as you came home. M-Ma is sick again."

My heart plummeted, sucking my breath into the void it left.
The children began to cry. I held them to me.

"Big Ching Mei, can you tell me what happened to your
mother?"

"She fell down!" The words came out in a long wail.

"Come. I'll take you back to the garage."

I left the two little girls sitting on their mother's bed, looking
woebegone. A neighbor said she would feed them. The hospital
was very close, and I almost ran there.

Ah-May lay in the same ward, conscious, bewildered.

"Doo-bebe, I don't know what happened! My foot wouldn't
work. It was stiff for some days, and today suddenly it wouldn't
work. It tripped on the other foot, and I fell down."

Her foot?

"Well, Ah-May, whatever it is, you had to come back to the

hospital anyway for that other operation, and the doctor can cure your foot at the same time."

"Oh, I'm not going to stay here! I wouldn't have come, but when I fell down I hit my head and didn't know anything for a while, and your mother brought me here. But I won't stay."

"Oh, Ah-May! Please don't be so stubborn! You must stay and have your foot treated and have that other operation."

"But Doo-bebe . . ."

"I know, Ah-May! You're not sick. You're perfectly well. But if the doctor told me I had to have an operation, I'd have it no matter how well I felt. And if he told Mother, she'd have it. And you have to have it, no matter how well you feel."

Mother came into the ward, Little Bell following her like a lost dog. She looked ghastly.

"Ah-May, the nurse is going to give you an injection and you'll go to sleep soon. Little Bell will stay with you until you sleep. Doo-bebe and I will come back tomorrow."

She put her hand gently on Ah-May's forehead, smiling a smile that frightened me. Then she took my arm and led me from the room.

"Don't bother her anymore about the operation. The doctor says it's no use. She's going to die."

We walked out silently. My throat had constricted so painfully that I couldn't speak. The hospital boomed and hummed around us, every bed filled, nurses hurrying to and fro, wheelchairs, stretchers, bins of bloody unnamables, the choking smells of chloroform and disinfectant. The noises—tapping footsteps, creaking wheels, banging doors, voices, cries. Relatives everywhere, coming, going, squatting on the floor around patients, talking, crying, wailing.

When we were on the street Mother told me what the doctor

had said. Ah-May was a congenital syphilitic. Her blood tests had turned it up. There were thousands of patients, tens of thousands of blood tests, only a few doctors. Ah-May's blood tests had been taken routinely and the doctor hadn't got around to seeing the results until two or three days ago. But even if he had seen them on the first day, it would have made no difference. In her the disease was taking the form of paralysis. From the feet up. The hysterectomy would be useless. Let her die as peacefully as possible.

Oh, Ah-May!

The next morning I said to Mother: "She hates the hospital. She can as well die at home."

"Yes," said Mother. "We'll bring her home."

But we didn't. She ran away from the hospital. That afternoon, while Mother and I were working in the box-room, she came stumbling up the stairs.

"I ran away. When they weren't looking, I ran away. I'm not going back. If you want somebody to go to the hospital, you can send Little Bell."

She looked defiantly at Mother.

We walked her back to the garage home. Her legs were dragging. She lay back on the bed with a sigh and closed her eyes. In just that day or two her cheeks seemed to have fallen in. I covered her and patted her shoulder.

"Doo-bebe, what's the matter with me? I want to walk properly but my legs won't work!"

I said nothing, just patted her. After a time, she said softly, wonderingly:

"It's true then, what I thought. I'm going to die?"

"Yes," I said.

Ah-May sank rapidly. The paralysis rose swiftly—her ankles,

her calves, her knees, the whole lower half of her body. She could no longer move herself in bed and had to be turned from side to side. Her mind wandered, going back into the past. She seemed to think sometimes that she and I were children again together and spoke to me, giggling slurred words that I could not understand. Once she said loudly, "Quick, quick, quick, Doo-bebe," and laughed. Once she said in a clear whisper: "It was right, Doo-bebe. Little Bell is a good man. But he's so *stupid!*" It was as though we were continuing a conversation. Sometimes she looked at the Ching Meis in a puzzled way as though wondering how they came there. Sometimes she held them to her breast, patting them frantically. Sometimes she spoke slowly and sadly of the son she never had. And at last she didn't speak anymore— just lay there, weeping slow tears.

Our doctor came to see her and gave her placebos because Little Bell begged him to give her medicine. In an access of courage or desperation, Little Bell, on his own, sent for a Chinese practitioner who shook his head but put gold needles into Ah-May's joints. When neither foreign nor Chinese doctor did any good, Little Bell sent for the witch woman. By then Ah-May was off and on in coma. The witch burned incense, swallowed raw rice, walked around the room calling loudly for Ah-May's spirit to return to her body.

When she had first become ill, Ah-May had said to Mother: "I want to belong to your Heavenly Spirit, the same one that you and Doo-bebe belong to. They say that your Heavenly Spirit makes the dead meet again in a beautiful place." So the priest had come to baptize and anoint her, and a nun came every day to pray by her bedside.

They came and went all day, the foreign doctor, the Chinese doctor, the nun, the witch woman, the neighbors wandering in and out, exclaiming, lamenting. Little Bell sat by the bed silent, in a daze. Big Ching Mei solemnly cared for Small Ching Mei, hushing her when she cried, leading her away when she plucked at her mother's sleeve saying "M-Ma? M-Ma?" in a puzzled way. Ah-May lay quiet, unknowing, tears sliding slowly from her eyes.

A week before we left, she died.

28

The Last Moments

LITTLE BELL AND the Ching Meis had been to the hospital for blood tests, and they were clear. We gave Little Bell Ah-May's money and told him what to do, as Ah-May would have done: take the Ching Meis and go back to your parents' farm. Buy seed with the money, buy a buffalo, a cow—don't keep the money. If you want to marry again, be sure to choose a woman who will be kind to the Ching Meis.

To everything he said "yes, yes," not taking it in. Big Ching Mei listened carefully, nodded sagely, and repeated it all to her father. He said "yes, yes," and she clucked her tongue and said, "I will tell him again later."

"If he wants to marry again one day, Big Ching Mei," I told her, "you'd better choose your new mother yourself."

"Yes," she said seriously, "I think it would be better."

They went.

And now it is time for us to go. It is ten o'clock in the morning of the thirteenth of April 1950. Our suitcases are ready. The trunks and nailed-up cases have gone ahead. Our footsteps echo as we walk through the house. It seemed that we would never be finished with sorting and packing, but now the house is empty, resounding. The front door clicks behind us. The pedicab is waiting. Mother and I step in and start for Shanghai North Station. For the last time we are passing through the city that was ours.

How ugly it is. Nobody has ever thought of making it beautiful —just of making it functional for generating money. No statues, no fountains, no squares. There used to be those strips of garden on the Bund along the river front, but they are long since gone, overcome by refugees, by garbage, by the fumes of traffic. The only beautiful statues were the lions outside the Hongkong and Shanghai Bank which the Japanese removed to be melted down for cannon. Imperial Chemical Industries has two statues in the façade of its building, but they are hideous—huge, tortured, bulging-muscled Atlases pretending to carry the building on their shoulders. The only thing that might be called a fountain is the square stone balustrade around the well on Bubbling Well Road, which might once have really bubbled. Now it's mostly oozy black mud.

I have never really noticed how unlovely the city is. When we were children we were delighted with a tram ride across Garden Bridge, the driver tap-tapping his foot on the pedal to make the bell clang merrily, the view from the top of the bridge so far-flung to our childish eyes. Big Park must have been pleasant too, but I never really looked at it—I was always so busy peering around fearfully for Barstud Red Face.

Some of the builders tried for adornment—the Cathay Hotel has a squat gilded tower, the Palace Hotel its Victorian arches, the Park Hotel a greenish roof. From the Park Hotel one looks over the Race Course—it was beautiful that night of the Torchlight Tattoo on the King's birthday when we were children—it was all dark and we saw only the flickering torches moving in intricate patterns—the dusty tracks were hidden in the dark, and the dozens of shacks in the middle that used to serve as club houses for the tennis and cricket clubs. The cluttered Race Course is the only open space in the city, and the only really green spot in the whole Race Course was the smooth green velvet of the hallowed all-British lawn bowls club.

An ugly, unlovely, graceless city.

But it has no time for beauty, has it? No need of beauty. It's so vivid, so clamorous, so vigorous and relentless and cruel. But even in its cruelty, the city's pulse is always quick with life.

"It's the last time," says Mother.

"It's the first time," I reply, my own pulse quickening. "It's the first time we're going away forever."